THE CY YOUNG CATCHER

SPIRIT OF SPORT

A Series of Books Focusing on Sport in Modern Society

Sponsored by James C. '74 and Debra Parchman Swaim,
Nancy and T. Edgar Paup '74, and Joseph Wm. and Nancy Foran

THE CY YOUNG CATCHER

Charlie O'Brien &
Doug Wedge

TEXAS A&M UNIVERSITY PRESS
College Station

This paper meets the requirements of ANSI/NISO Z39.48-1992 (Permanence of Paper).
Binding materials have been chosen for durability.

♾ ♻

Library of Congress Cataloging-in-Publication Data

O'Brien, Charlie, 1960– author.
    The Cy Young catcher / Charlie O'Brien and Doug Wedge. — First edition.
        pages cm — (Spirit of sport)
    Includes bibliographical references and index.
    ISBN 978-1-62349-292-2 (cloth : alk. paper) —
    ISBN 978-1-62349-293-9 (e-book)
    1. Pitchers (Baseball)—United States—Biography. 2. O'Brien, Charlie, 1960–
3. Catchers (Baseball)—United States—Biography. 4. Cy Young Award.
I. Wedge, Doug, author. II. Title. III. Series: Spirit of sport.
    GV865.A1O25 2015
    796.357092'273—dc23
    [B]

                    2014047924

To the original Charlie O'Brien:
Charles Raymond O'Brien (1935–2012)

CONTENTS

A gallery of photographs follows page 94.

THE CY YOUNG CATCHER

INTRODUCTION

Charlie was an unbelievable catcher. Top notch. One of the best receivers I've ever seen. He knew how to call a game, and Charlie would never get crossed up—he was that good. You know, if he called for a slider and they threw a fastball, he would catch it easy. Ninety-nine point ninety-nine percent of catchers can't do that. But, Charlie was just way ahead of most catchers in the intellect part of the game, of calling a game, of knowing hitters' weaknesses. I can't say enough about Charlie's defensive capabilities.

—*Bobby Cox*

Some catchers play their entire careers and never catch a pitcher who's won a Cy Young Award, a guy who's been recognized as the best pitcher in his league. I spent fifteen seasons behind the plate in the Major Leagues, and I caught thirteen Cy Young Award winners: Pete Vuckovich, David Cone, Frank Viola, Dwight Gooden, Bret Saberhagen, John Smoltz, Steve Bedrosian, Greg Maddux, Tom Glavine, Pat Hentgen, Roger Clemens, Chris Carpenter, and Jack McDowell. At one point, I had a four-year streak where I caught one of that year's winners: Maddux in '94 and '95, Pat Hentgen in '96, and Roger Clemens in '97. And, I caught these guys in different situations. When I was in Atlanta, we were World Series champions. In New York, we finished dead last. We were so bad that one writer wrote a book about us and called us the worst team that money could buy. Sometimes, I worked with great managers. Guys like Bobby Cox. Dallas Green. Cito Gaston. Guys who treated their players like professionals. Guys who created a pleasant environment so everybody worked hard and put the team ahead of themselves. I also worked for managers who hollered and screamed, talked behind your back, talked shit about you in the papers. Sometimes, I caught pitchers at their peak. Guys like Maddux who were pitching as well as anybody has ever pitched. And, I worked with some talented guys who just hadn't pulled it all together yet. Hadn't figured out how to get hitters out consistently at the big league level. On the other side of that coin, some pitchers faced the end of their playing days. Their stuff wasn't as good as it once was.

Baseball has a phrase "personal catcher." It's where a pitcher prefers working with the same catcher each start instead of a random rotation of guys behind the plate. I guess I was doing something these pitchers liked because I caught Dwight Gooden nearly every start for three seasons, fifty-something games. Same thing with Maddux and Hentgen: when Greg won the Cy in '95 and Pat won it in '96, I was behind the plate most times they were on the mound, twenty-seven times with Greg, and twenty-six with Pat. The compliment was that they wanted me back there.

I had some amazing experiences. I played with four guys—Maddux, Glavine, Clemens, and Don Sutton—who won three hundred games. Three of these dudes are in the Baseball Hall of Fame. When Sutton was inducted into the Hall, he thanked me during his speech. Said that I made him feel like his veteran experience counted for something. I caught a couple of World Series games. Hit a home run off David Wells during the playoffs that broke open a tie game. Caught Roger Clemens's first game back at Fenway after he left Boston. Caught David Cone when he tied the National League record for most strikeouts in a game. Worked with Dan Plesac when he closed three straight games against the Twins in the Metrodome, one of the loudest places in the world. I played for the Brewers then. Milwaukee and Minnesota had a big rivalry. The fans were so into the games that they created this roar. Sounded like a jet taking off. Plesac was standing right in front of me, and I knew he was talking because his mouth was moving, but I couldn't hear a word he was saying—the crowd was that loud. Had some really cool moments playing in 800 Major League games and having the best seat in the house, behind home plate where you see everything. The batter digging in and waiting for the pitch. The second baseman turning a double play. Base runners trying to advance. The umpire over your shoulder and judging whether a pitch is a ball or a strike. You're the one dealing with the umpire and figuring out what he wants, what his strike zone is. All of the action is in front of you and no other player. It's cool as hell, and I miss it. I didn't realize what a privilege it was until I retired, and I went back to Atlanta for a game. I was way up from the field. So far removed. Most folks think it's great because they're in a box with air conditioning and food and drinks in a little refrigerator. All I could think was this sucks. You can't see the pitch selection. You can't see how the pitcher is working hitters. It's nothing like seeing the game from behind the plate. The game moves so much quicker on the field than it does from the stands. After seeing it from the angle that I saw it from for all those years, it's kind of boring to be up in the stands.

To play Major League Baseball, you have to be a freak. A ton of guys would love to spend a minute in a big league uniform. Take the field and step on that grass and scoop up a grounder or throw a pitch. Very few make it. The reason why is because the guys in the big leagues can do things that normal people can't. You swing a bat better. You run bases faster. You throw a ball with more control or more movement. It's abnormal. And, how you do it, a lot of it, you can't explain.

This is the thing about the guys I caught who won the Cy Young: they had different personalities, but when they crossed the line, they were the same kind of pitcher. Every one of them was a competitor. It meant something to each of them to step on the mound and do his best. Help their team win. Every one of them was stubborn, and they never beat themselves. They made smart, quality pitches, especially when the game was on the line. That was the main difference between these cats and the .500 pitcher who wins one game and loses the next. A lot of guys have great arms, great stuff. But, the .500 pitchers just can't get over the hump. They don't have that same single-mindedness, intensity, and drive to compete like hell like the Cy Young guys have. With these thirteen guys, if the game were on the line, it didn't matter who was hitting; he wasn't beating the pitcher. Good pitching will always beat good hitting, no matter how strong the lineup. But, the .500 pitchers, they're going to make a mistake. They'll hang a breaking ball. They'll give in and throw a pitch that the hitter wants to hit. The Cy Young winners didn't do that. The pitcher threw what *he* wanted to throw, not what the batter wanted to see. You'd have to hit some bastard pitches down and away or on the inside of the plate to beat him. It's a simple concept: make quality pitches and don't throw bad ones. It sounds easy, but not everybody does it.

These thirteen guys understood this. They could focus and make the pitch when they needed to. They're just wired differently. In the big moment, they'd shine and find a way to win. It's funny, but I think part of that drive is a fear of failure. Because these guys were so successful, it was like they were pushed that much more to continue to excel. It's high stress. It's competition at the highest level, and you can't fail. If you do, you do everything in your power to straighten it up so that, next time, you produce a better result. It's like all thirteen of them, they're the same guy with their stubbornness. Their confidence. Their focus. With their mental makeup, it was like they had removable heads that you could plop it on a different body, and you've got the same guy be it Gooden, Cone, Maddux, Glavine, or whoever.

Personality-wise, they're thirteen different dudes. Greg Maddux and Roger Clemens: different ends of the spectrum. Maddux is an intellectual. We'd sit in the locker room and talk about how he pitched to certain hitters. He'd remember how he got guys out, and he asked me question after question about how I worked with other pitchers, why we threw so-and-so a changeup in that situation because he never got him out with a changeup—that kind of thing. He'd also play video games and clown around. Shake your hand all weak like he was a girl and lisp, "Hey, Badass, how are you?" With Clemens, though, hanging out with him was like hanging out with John Wayne. Bigger than life. He didn't mess around. Clemens carried himself as a man's man, the go-to guy you could always rely on to take care of things.

Even though the guys had different personalities in the clubhouse, different lifestyles, and come from different parts of the country, once they put that foot on the rubber, they'd all do whatever it took to win a game. And, they're all winners. Most of these guys were on teams that won a World Series. Saberhagen won with Kansas City early in his career. Gooden with the Mets. Viola won with Minnesota. So did Bedrosian. Cone, Gooden, and Clemens won with the Yankees. Maddux, Glavine, and Smoltz were champions with the Braves. Hentgen with the Blue Jays. Carpenter with the Cardinals. Guys this good make a big difference on the pitching staff and on your club. Part of it is things that you can read in a box score. Low ERAs. Pitch a lot of innings. Rack up a bunch of strikeouts. But, these guys bring some intangibles you can't put a price on. You watch them on the mound, how they compete, and they're just different. A class apart. The bottom line is they help you win, and that's the whole goal. And, they set great examples for the rest of the team. They're on time to meetings. They challenge guys to improve. They hone their craft, focusing on the details, like working on their pick-off move, making it faster, more accurate. The rest of the guys on the team or the young kids in spring training see this, how devoted these guys are. How much time they spend to be the best. It rubs off. Maybe not immediately, but it sends the message of if you want to be one of the best pitchers in the league, follow my example.

I'm convinced that you can't teach this. I'd love it if I could go to guys and coach them to pick up the three or four things they need to have the makeup of a competitor like Bret Saberhagen or Roger Clemens, but you can't learn this. If you could teach it, a lot more of these guys would be out there playing the game. You're born with it. It's a gift from God. You refine it and develop it, but these guys, the masters I played with, they're different. The freaks of all freaks.

Speaking of a unique fraternity, catchers are a special breed. No other position gets the shit beat out of them like a catcher. It's hard to describe what it's like to someone who'll never get hit with a ball moving ninety miles per hour, never feel what it's like. You may think, "Well, that's no big deal. They have all that protective gear. They probably don't feel much." Are you shitting me? Some cotton padding as a chest protector will absorb a Dwight Gooden fastball? Come on. Foul tips, getting hit with baseballs off your hands, off your knees, off your shoulders. Balls smashing into your mask, and you wind up seeing stars and waking up the next day wanting to vomit. Getting hit in the front of your throwing shoulder—your arm goes numb. Only the guys who do it, who squat behind the plate for a couple of hours, understand.

To get a taste of it, let somebody get a baseball bat and take a swing at you. Hit you in the arm or shoulder. Swinging a bat won't reach ninety miles an hour, but that's probably close to what it feels like. Or, maybe put your hand on a kitchen counter and let somebody slam a hammer on one of your fingers. Think about it: How'd you feel if your buddy threw a baseball as hard as he could and hit you in the thigh? Your buddy can't throw ninety, probably not even seventy-five. But, catchers get pelted like this all the time, and nobody thinks anything of it. My wife Traci could tell you about the bruises all over my body, the different colors.

It's funny: if a shortstop or an umpire gets hit with a ball, the game stops. Everybody is concerned about the player. Is he okay? Is he hurt?

Not when a catcher's hit. Everybody expects it. Nobody even notices it.

Catchers play through pain. They have to keep going. Sometimes, after the season, I'd have X rays, and doctors would tell me, "You have some broken toes."

I was like, "No shit. They hurt."

I always told trainers not to come onto the field and check on me unless I asked for them. When I played with the White Sox, our trainer, Herm Schneider, a real good dude and one of my favorite trainers, smiled when I said that.

"Somebody else told me that," he said.

"Who?"

"Fisk."

Makes sense. Great catcher. And, like I was saying, it takes a different kind of cat to take the beating and still be able to play well. It's a combination of physical ability and toughness. And, it's a fine line you're walking because it's pretty damn close to being stupid.

Like when I was in Triple A in 1987. I tore the ligament in my catching thumb. I literally had no ligament attached to one side of my thumb. Couldn't hold it up. But, the trainer taped it up and put kind of a splint, hard cast thing on it so the thumb would stand up and wouldn't bend back. Hurt like hell catching a ball, but

I played another twenty-seven games like that, hoping the Brewers would call me up when they expanded the roster late in the season.

Later in my career, I broke my thumb. It was bent sideways. Real sharp pain. I could feel it throb. If it has its own heartbeat and throbs away, you know it's broken.

Herm Schneider came out and popped it back into place.

He asked, "Are you okay?"

"Yeah."

"Can you throw?"

I threw. "It hurts," I said. "But, I can keep playing."

And I did.

Catchers get the fire beat out of them, but you don't get days off. You don't come out of the game. Hell, I hated for guys to see me hurt. Even if the pain were horrible, like how my stomach churns now thinking about a sledgehammer coming down on one of my fingers, I'd keep a straight face. Press on and act like I didn't feel a thing. And, that's the mind-set of a catcher. You're different from everybody else. Not many people in the world can do that. It's kind of neat in some respects. And, like I said, it also shows your stupidity. But, would I do it again? Play a month without a ligament in my catching thumb, just hoping the Brewers decided to call up a third catcher at the end of the season? Keep playing with a broken thumb? Yeah, I'd probably do the same thing. Just for the opportunity. Just that chance. It's the kid in you. It's what you do. You love the game.

It's physical. You have plays at the plate. Base runners running you down, knocking you over. That happened to me one time in Baltimore. Big guy who played college ball at Baylor plowed into me, and I really felt it. After that play, I was ready. I'd run into guys and knock *them* down instead of the other way around. Use my glove to punch them in the chin. I wasn't going to get smoked like that again. No way.

I tried to learn as much as I could to improve myself as a catcher. Part of it was as a minor leaguer and listening to the A's minor league catching instructor, Bob Didier. He caught Phil Niekro, the knuckleball pitcher with the Braves, a few seasons. Bob was a real hard-ass. Gruff. But, he did a great job of teaching. He made things simple. Baseball can be a complicated game, and you don't want to clutter guys' minds with lots of details. Guys need to be able to react quickly and not have to think through a lot of steps and processes. Bob was great about breaking things down and showing you finer points so they were easy to apply. He taught me about positioning my hand, making my thumb and forefinger form a *V*. What this does is keep your hand up and relaxes it. By relaxing it, you don't have to move it as much to catch the ball. This is important because if the umpire thinks you're moving, he thinks the pitcher missed his target. That makes him more inclined to call the pitch a ball. Bob also taught me about cheating with your feet. If you keep your left foot in front of your right, it helps your turn when you throw. Makes your throw to the bases quicker. Watch Yadier Molina playing today, and he does this better than anybody. Fires that ball. Bob also helped me with blocking balls. He taught me to practice using tennis balls. You use the same technique blocking and catching a tennis ball as you do a baseball, but you do it with a lot less pain involved. Bob's philosophy was that you get beat up enough during a game—you don't need to get beat up practicing. And, he makes a good point. Human nature shies away from pain. Nobody likes to get hurt. You want to avoid it. To avoid it, you'll cheat, cut corners. So, during practice, you can work on your technique and make sure you're blocking correctly without worrying about hurting if all that's going to hit you is a tennis ball or a softball.

Another way I worked on the game was by watching good catchers. Like Carlton Fisk. I'd go up to bat when Fisk was catching, and I listened to him talk to the umpire. If the umpire called good pitches, didn't miss balls and strikes, you didn't hear a word from Fisk. He was quiet. But, if the pitcher threw strikes, and the umpire called them balls, Fisk chirped. "Damn, Bob. You're a way better umpire than that. You got to bear down." He did it in a way that wouldn't offend them, but push them to do better. They have a job to do—do it right. And, the cool thing was, nobody knew that he was battling the umpire. He didn't do anything to show the umpire up. Kept his mask on. Never turned around and confronted the umpire. Never threw his hands up like he was exasperated. Never did anything to get the crowd involved. All of this meant that Fisk had respect. Umpires listened to him when he talked because he knew the right time and way to do it.

Good catchers share all of this. I guess that's why I call us a fraternity. A couple of years ago, I talked with Johnny Bench. We started going on about catching, and we were saying the same things. That nobody notices when a catcher gets hit with a ball: he's just expected to take his lumps and keep rolling. And, I guess it's knowing what catchers go through that makes me appreciate what guys like Bench, Fisk, and Bob Boone did before me, and what guys like Buster Posey and Molina are doing now. And, it's not just me. It's a mutual respect that catchers have for other catchers and how they go about doing their work.

With the Cy Young winners, with all pitchers I played with, really, I did a few things as a catcher that seemed to help them.

I tried to call a smart ball game. I loved calling games and being involved in 125–30 decisions of the right pitch selection and not screwing that up. I'd rather do that than go up to hit four times a game.

To decide which pitches to call, my job was to find out what a pitcher liked to do. Unlike a lot of catchers, I took the time to figure out what a pitcher liked and didn't like to throw. I adapted the way I called a game around that, based on that pitcher's strengths and weaknesses. Some catchers just call the same pitches, set up the same game after game, and it doesn't matter who's on the mound. I didn't. I understood the pitchers I worked with. Knew which pitches they had the most confidence in, because that's the pitch they're going to want to throw when the game is on the line. In those situations, I wanted to sign for the pitch they wanted to throw so we'd be in sync. That way, they'd be like, "Hey, we're on the same page. We're thinking alike." I don't want them getting frustrated with me, waiting for me to go through a few signs. We need to click. To get to this point, you just have to work with your pitchers, so I caught guys whenever I could. If they wanted to do some extra bullpen work, I was there. A lot of guys hated catching bullpen sessions. They were hard work, sure, and sometimes you get the shit beat out of you, but that's where you build trust with your pitcher. You're helping them as they're trying to fine tune. You learn more about them. And, their confidence in you grows because you're spending so much time with them. They start looking for you. They'd say, "Hey, where's O'B? I'll get him to catch me. He won't bitch and moan about it."

Part of why I worked so closely with pitchers was so I could also understand the things they didn't do well. I wanted to know this so I wouldn't ask a guy to throw a pitch he couldn't make. This sounds simple, but like I said, a lot of catchers call pitches without really knowing the pitcher's strengths and weaknesses. A catcher's number one job is to adapt to who's pitching. If they don't throw a good forkball, don't ask them to throw a forkball. If they don't like throwing a curveball in certain counts, don't ask them to. It's very basic, but, for some reason, some guys ignore this concept. The catcher is either sticking to the scouting report too closely or he's thinking about what kind of pitch he wouldn't want to face if he were the hitter. Again, the critical thing to think about is the guy on the mound. What does he do best? It doesn't matter if the scouting report says a hitter can't hit a slider if your pitcher can't throw a slider. Don't ask your pitcher to do things he's not good at. It's a lot like what a good manager will do: put your guys in positions where they will succeed. Play to their strengths. Bobby Cox understood this better than anybody. For me, this message really clicked when I was playing college ball at Wichita State. Our best pitcher was Don Heinkel. He still holds the record for the most wins in college baseball (fifty-one). I caught him for three years. He went on to play a couple of seasons in the big leagues. He didn't throw very hard, nothing over ninety miles per hour, not what you would call big league stuff. But he threw four pitches well. Had great control. It didn't make sense to ask him to smoke a fastball past a guy because he didn't have the ability to do it. But, because his control was so accurate that he could place the ball wherever you set the target, it made sense to ask him to pitch on the outside part of the plate and make a hitter chase a pitch. I picked up on this, and we had a lot of success. Now, we might have a situation where we had a five or six run lead, and I had more room to experiment. Ask him to throw a heater or a breaking ball that he usually didn't throw.

Another thing that I focused on was throwing off the hitter's timing. I first noticed this in high school when I was playing with a guy named Mike Vickers. He had a decent fastball and a big slow curveball. I couldn't figure out why guys couldn't hit him. Then I realized that hitters didn't like being slowed down and then sped up. It threw off their timing to wait for the curve and then speed up for the fastball. So, I started calling for the slow curve followed by an inside fastball. We had great results.

With pitch selection, one of my goals was to develop a pitcher-catcher relationship where the pitcher didn't have to think. I wanted them to have enough faith in me to block out pitch selection and just focus on making their pitch. Sometimes, this worked out well. Guys like Tom Glavine, Frank Viola, and Roger Clemens trusted me and the pitches I was calling, and they went on autopilot. All they had to do was throw. Concentrate on executing their pitches. Sometimes, though, it didn't matter how much homework I did; I couldn't figure out which direction a pitcher wanted to go. Like with Chris Bosio. I caught Chris quite a bit when we played together in Milwaukee. One time, I put down two or three signs. He shook me off each time. Finally, I put down a five and set up. He stepped off the mound and looked at me kind of funny. Then he called me out there.

"What's a five?" he asked.

"Five is I don't know what in the hell you're going to throw, but I could give a shit. Just throw it."

Bosio howled. We had a few games like that where, after I called for a couple of pitches and he shook me off both times, I just put down a five. I was like, "Dude, your stuff's not that good. I can catch it without knowing what's coming." I would catch anything he or anybody else threw. Take that back: John Smoltz shook me off a bunch. He threw some wicked stuff, a lot of balls in the dirt. I couldn't put a five down for him. His stuff would embarrass me if I put a five down because he was so tough to catch, even when you knew what was coming.

Another part of my job was to challenge pitchers, to push them to make them better. The specifics varied depending on the situation, but when I'd go out to the mound, I'd say, "Okay, here's what we're going to do." And then I'd go in to what I called the three-step rule. Ball or strike, we're going to throw this pitch, that pitch, and this next pitch. If you gave guys a direction, you'd get better pitches, better results. The model gave them focus. It's kind of like you're sitting in a room and you're trying to figure out how to get to the door. I was like here's the goal: let's get to the door (let's get an out). Here's how we're going to get there: first step (first pitch). Second step (second pitch). Third step (third pitch). Each pitch gets us closer to the goal.

I didn't go out to the mound a lot. When I did, I usually wasn't very nice. I wasn't saying, "Hey, man, how are you doing today?" all touchy-feely. I was coming out there to chew on your ass. Some guys, I figured out that they were fragile and I couldn't get on them too much or they'd turn to shit. Like Sid Fernandez. When he was in a rocky spot, I couldn't jump on him. I just had to let him go. Or, I'd say, "Look. This is the biggest situation in the game. If we get out of this, we'll win. I promise. If you make this pitch and get a ground ball or a strikeout, then we'll win." Build their confidence. I started doing this at Wichita State. Kept doing it in the minors and later on in the big leagues. It worked well for a long time and with a lot of different guys.

Good catchers figure out how to adjust when a pitcher doesn't have his best stuff. I was good at figuring out what a pitcher's best pitches were on a given day. If a pitcher threw four pitches, some days he's going to have only two of them that are really good. Take these and work with them. The strange thing is that you have to figure this out during a game. From warm-ups, you can't tell how a guy is going to pitch. I used to think that you could gauge how a guy was going to play based on how the ball was moving, how he was hitting his spots during warm-ups, but that's not the case. Practice is practice. Game situations, when the adrenaline is pumping, that's a different deal. Your intensity picks up. With some guys, it picks up only a notch. Other guys, it picks up four or five notches. And, when the game is on the line, some dudes throw harder. Some don't. Some guys can come up with shit that they hadn't had all game. Their breaking balls become nastier. Like one time when I was in Toronto catching Woody Williams. Good pitcher. Great slider and curveball. But, one game we were in a jam, and to get out of it, I called for a knuckleball. He *never* threw a knuckleball during a game. That was the only one I ever called for him. He threw it, though, and it was amazing. Moved all over the place. One of the best knuckleballs I've ever seen. But, it's like that for the Cy Young winners: they come up with stuff to get out of a jam.

Catchers are kind of like psychologists or psychiatrists or whatever you want to call it. They have to figure out when to prod a pitcher or when to pat him on the ass. If a guy had nothing, I couldn't go out to the mound and say, "Gah, man, you got shit tonight. What am I going to do with this?" Instead, you've got to convince him it's good and build him up. Then bullshit your way through it by doing something different from the norm. Sometimes, I might go the exact opposite of what we ordinarily did. If I was catching a great changeup pitcher but his changeup wasn't working, I might call for more fastballs. You have to strike a balance, though. Can't give up on pitches. Keep asking the pitcher to throw what he usually throws well. Ask him to throw it in situations where there's a little more room for error, like when the pitcher's ahead in the count, so if he misses, it's no big deal. Or, keep it down in the zone and see if you get a swing on it. Maybe that pitch doesn't show up until later in the game, but once the pitcher's found it, you have a great weapon to use. This keeps the hitters honest, too. If you quit throwing one of your good pitches, the hitter thinks, "Well, he's not throwing this pitch today. I don't have to worry about that one." He concentrates on looking for other pitches. The more you let hitters eliminate pitches or locations, the more you're narrowing down the pitcher. Don't give hitters that advantage. You need to keep the seed planted that, "Hey, this guy's a slider pitcher. I need to be thinking about a slider," instead of letting the hitter know that the slider's not on today, so the pitcher won't be throwing it.

Improvising when a guy doesn't have his best stuff is part of baseball. If a starting pitcher averages thirty starts in a year, he'll have fifteen games where he's throwing well. All you've got to do is not get in the guy's way. But then you'll have ten games where the pitcher's stuff is average and another five starts where the guy's stuff is shitty. That's just how it is—doesn't matter who's pitching. And, I miss those starts where I convinced a guy we could make it through the game when he didn't have his best stuff. I don't miss the hitting. The clubhouse. I miss the pitcher-catcher relationship and figuring out a way to get through a game by calling the right pitches. Of doing the little things so the pitcher was comfortable. I didn't need a whole lot of recognition or articles written about me or being on an all-star team or winning a Gold Glove. I think that stuff meant something to my mom, but I didn't care about that. All I needed was, after the game, when he's icing down his shoulder, the pitcher saying, "Thanks for getting me through that." The normal player, the coaches, they wouldn't know the things I did to help the pitcher. But the pitcher did, and it created a special pitcher-catcher bond that I miss.

Catchers need to know umpires' personalities, too. I chewed on umpires' asses if they missed calls. But, like knowing who you're working with on the mound, you have to know who you're working with behind you. Some guys, you can get on them. Ninety percent of them are good. You can point out a mistake, and they'll say, "Ah, you're right. I missed that one." That way, they're tuned in, and they don't miss the next one. Other guys, you can't talk to. Either way, you need tact. What I tried to do was establish a conversation with them at the beginning of games. Hopefully build some rapport so that, later in the game, if he misses a pitch, he's more receptive to hearing your complaint. Like what I was saying about Fisk, I didn't bitch just to bitch. If it was a bad pitch, I didn't say anything. I complained only when umpires missed calls. Sometimes, when they missed a call, I'd say something like, "Damn, Bob. You're better than this. You usually don't miss that." Get on guys in a way that was kind of fun and that didn't piss them off. Do it so that maybe then they laughed about it, but later on, they thought, "Damn, I can't believe that guy said that to me." Some catchers, they don't say a word to umpires. Fisk: he chewed on them. Bench: same thing. Bob Boone: not so much. Pretty quiet when I went up to hit. I guess I could get away with it because I had a reputation for knowing what I was doing behind the plate. And, I didn't show umpires up. When I was talking to him, I faced the pitcher. With the mask covering my face, nobody could tell that I was getting on the guy's ass.

Catchers and umpires have to figure out a way to work together. While catchers can't step on umpires' toes while they're fighting for their pitchers, umpires don't want to piss off catchers. If they do, they'll get the fire beat out of them. A few umpires were shitty to me, so I was shitty right back. Wouldn't block balls for them. Let the umpire take the abuse or get out of the way of them real quick. After a while, one umpire said, "Uncle. What do we have to do to figure this out?"

"All right. Now we're talking."

And, the two of you start fresh and make it work.

I don't know how many pitchers told me I was the best catcher they ever threw to. A lot. That meant something to me. That was my goal. And, it's something I worked on my whole career, trying to find that missing piece that would make a guy that much better. What's that one thing that makes him better as a pitcher or feel comfortable where I could call a pitch that I hadn't called all game, and he could throw it, and we could get great results? Like one time, I was catching Tim

Belcher with the Angels. He didn't throw sliders, but in a 3-2 count, I called for a slider. He threw it and punched the guy out.

We were walking back to the dugout, inning over, out of a big situation, and he asked, "Why did you call that?"

"I just felt like you were going to throw me a good one."

And, that's a lot of it. Understanding that this pitch is going to work in this situation. How do you figure it out? I don't know. Part of it was a gift. Part of it is knowing the game, knowing what the hitters like, what the pitchers do and don't do well, and figuring out the right way to handle the situation. That's something you pick up by studying the game over time.

One time early in my career, I was with Milwaukee. We were playing in Cleveland. The team decided to send me down to Triple A. I was walking across the bridge back to the hotel, over the little waterway that ran by Cleveland's old stadium, and Steve Carlton was walking the other way. He was pitching for the Indians then, toward the end of his career.

I said hello.

He stopped and asked me how I was doing.

I said, "They're sending me down. I'm going back to Triple A."

"You'll be back," he said. "You're too good a catcher. I like the way you catch."

Hearing that from a Hall of Fame guy like Carlton was great. He didn't have to take the time to say that. Gives you confidence. Reinforces that you're doing things the right way. Calling the right pitches. Working the hitters. Framing pitches. Blocking balls. And, when all that comes together and you get the guys you're catching to believe in what you're doing, they'll do anything in the world for you. Pitchers may think, "I may not usually throw a knuckleball, but hell, if this guy thinks it'll get guys out, I'll throw it." It's one of the things that makes baseball such a fun sport. A lot of players and coaches hate being around pitchers because they can have a different kind of personality. But, I spent a bunch of time with them. I tried to get to know them, understand them. I had to figure out what made them work and get them to think that I knew what in the hell I was in doing. Make them believe that I was going to help them get through a game when they couldn't figure it out.

How do you do it? You make them feel comfortable. Like I said, some of it is telling them their stuff is better than it really is. I've done that a lot of times and then, after the game, told the guy, "Damn. I can't believe you got guys out with that shit."

They look at you kind of funny. "I thought you told me it was good."

"I had to say that. What else could I say out there?"

Some guys you could tell this to. Some guys you couldn't. Some guys, you couldn't tell them their stuff was good when it wasn't. I remember one guy telling me, "Dude. Save the bullshit. My stuff sucks today."

I said, "No shit. But, I've got to do something with it."

"Well, what are you going to do?"

"This is what we're going to do," and I went on with my three-step rule.

CHAPTER 1

PETE VUCKOVICH

I hung it up in spring of '87 after two unsuccessful shoulder surgeries. I did get to watch Charlie develop as a young Brewer and can tell you he became an extremely good defensive catcher. Even got him a gig with a boat company, and he got traded immediately!

—*Pete Vuckovich*

[*Note: In spring training 1987, Charlie caught Pete Vuckovich. Vuckovich won the American League Cy Young Award in 1982 while playing with the Milwaukee Brewers team that reached the World Series, going 18-6 with a 3.34 earned run average and throwing nine complete games.*[1] *Toward the end of this season when he enjoyed his greatest success, Vuckovich tore his rotator cuff.*[2] *After the injury, he never regained his elite form, and he retired at the end of spring training in 1986.*[3] *His retirement was short-lived as, in July 1986, Vuckovich signed a contract to pitch for the Brewers' Triple A club in Vancouver. He played well, and the Brewers called Vuckovich up to complete the season with Milwaukee. His return to the Major Leagues earned him an invitation to spring training in 1987.*

As Vuckovich was departing the Brewers at the end of spring training in 1986, Charlie was joining them. After Charlie made the Oakland A's roster as the backup catcher, the A's traded him, along with Mike Fulmer, Pete Kendrick, and Steve Kiefer, to Milwaukee for Moose Haas on March 30, 1986.[4] *With the A's, Charlie had enjoyed a taste of the big leagues, appearing in sixteen games in 1985 and earning his first hit, a double off the Detroit Tigers' Frank Tanana. Yet, joining Milwaukee, Charlie was placed in the unenviable position of being the number two catching prospect in the organization behind the first overall draft pick from 1985, B. J. Surhoff. Facing limited playing time at Triple A behind Surhoff, Charlie accepted an assignment to Double A El Paso and the chance to play every day. While it was difficult to go from the Major Leagues to Double A, being two steps backward, the decision paid off as Charlie played solidly for El Paso, clubbing fifteen home runs and hitting .324. As a result, he was invited to the Brewers' spring training in 1987 where he worked with Vuckovich.*

Despite the progress Vuckovich displayed at the end of 1986, he continued to battle injuries. After pitching eight innings and going 0-2 with a 12.38 ERA in spring training games, Vuckovich retired on April 1, 1987.[5] For his eleven year career, he won ninety-three games, lost sixty-nine, had a 3.66 earned run average, and struck out 882.[6]]

When I was a young kid and new to the big leagues, Pete Vuckovich pulled me aside and worked with me. He was a veteran. Had been around the game and achieved a lot of success. I was the opposite. I hadn't been in the big leagues very long. The season before, I'd been called up to the A's, but I didn't play much at all. At one point, I went forty-six days without getting into a game. Before that, I had made my way up in the minors, but I wasn't well-known or anything. Still, Vuke made it a point to get to know me. He wanted to know how I approached catching. How I called a game. And, he took the time to teach me some things. He talked about how he liked to set up hitters. How he didn't like to throw inside on certain counts. Your margin of error shrinks when you pitch inside—if you miss your target, the ball winds up in the middle of the plate, and it's perfect for hitters to crush it. That he didn't like to throw too many sliders because he hurt when he threw them.

One time, he asked, "Do I need to let you know when I'm changing speeds?"

I said, "You can, but it doesn't matter. I'll catch whatever you throw."

He laughed. Some guys would've been pissed off by what I said. It was true, though. I may not make it look as pretty as I could if I knew what was coming, but I'd sure as hell catch the ball. I had good hands. Vuke was a different kind of cat, though. A funny guy who liked to jab and mess with everybody. So, I could flip him some shit, and he was fine with it. Part of the give and take. Like one time, he gave up a home run. He looked at me and said, "Man, what were you thinking back there?" Like the dinger was all on me because of the pitch I called. Another time, he got on to me, saying I was giving away signs: "Everybody can see your fingers. They're dragging the ground."

Guys like Vuckovich are a good example of veteran players mentoring the younger ones. When you're new to the big leagues, it makes sense for a young player to keep his mouth shut, ears open, watch, and learn. And, at the beginning of my career, I was lucky to work with some great pitchers who were willing to spend time with me, let me ask them a million questions, and give me a chance to get in their brain and figure out what they did that made them so successful. Tommy John. Don Sutton. Sutton especially. He was very patient with me. Took a lot of time to explain things to me. Working with him was like going to a pitching clinic and learning from a genius. Sutton had pitch selection down to a science. His success was based on throwing off hitters' timing by speeding them up and then slowing them down. When I played with him, it was toward the end of his career. He threw four pitches. Didn't throw any of them very hard. None of them was ninety miles per hour, but he threw them all for strikes. He changed speeds, worked the count. Changed the placement of the ball so that the hitter had to adjust his eye level with each pitch. Sutton would throw a fastball away, then a curve. Follow that with a fastball inside, then a slider. Then he might come back inside with another fastball. Then a changeup. It was fast and slow, in and out. With slightly above average stuff, he stifled hitters, and it was all because he kept them from getting comfortable. Kept them guessing, mixing his pitch selection and speeds, and moving the ball around so they never knew what was coming. He had pitching down to a tee. And, he was so cool. Under control at all times. Business-like even. Reminds me a lot of Tom Glavine when I caught him a few years later. And, Don's mechanics were smooth. He knew exactly how many pitches he would throw during a warm-up. Made sure that his foot landed in the same spot all the time. Seeing his great results without throwing the ball all that hard brought home the importance of location, getting the ball to the right spot, and changing speeds. Watching him, I was like, "Damn. He's forty-something years old. He's not throwing very hard, but he's still getting guys out at the big league level. It's pretty cool how he's doing it." What I learned from Don about throwing off hitters' timing—I used those lessons throughout my career.

Don was good to me. I caught him in spring training. He liked to pitch a few games in the minor league camp where there's less focus on pitch counts, and he had more freedom to work on the things he knew he needed to have ready for the season. We clicked, and after the game, he was nice. Thanked me for helping him get through the game. I appreciated that, especially coming from a guy like him who'd been around baseball for a long time and was on the verge of winning 300 games. But, more than that, Don went to bat for me. He went back to the big league camp and said good things about me to our manager, Jackie Moore. I'm convinced that Don's vouching for me helped me get to the big leagues sooner.

As I said, I tried to learn whatever I could from Don. I'd sit next to him on the bus. After games, he'd have a big bag of popcorn and some chardonnay, and I'd listen to him talk about pitching, explaining it like, number one, I know what I do. Number two: I have an idea of how to get guys out, and number three: I think

I know what the hitter wants to do. Let's put all three of those together and try to make it hard for him to do it. What Don meant was, start with an idea, and watch and build on that idea. Don't get stuck on it. You've got to adjust. But, his whole philosophy was that pitching is starting with what you do naturally, trying to make it hard for the hitter to do what he does naturally, and then somewhere along the way, fine-tuning this to get the guy out.

Tommy John was a great guy to work with too. He did a lot of the same things that Sutton was doing. Changing speeds. Changing locations. Not really throwing all that hard, but getting guys out. Threw a real slow hook. A sinking fastball that ran away from right-handed guys. And, he threw a pretty good changeup. Because I was new to the league when I caught him, TJ took charge. He'd say, "All right. This is what we're going to do. The first time around, we're gonna start everybody off with a curveball. No matter what the situation is: first pitch is a hook." That's what we did most games I caught him. For some reason, nobody ever swung at that first pitch hook. Nobody ever figured that pattern out.

I also learned some good baseball and life lessons from TJ. He kept things in perspective. His demeanor was to have fun while you're playing. If he gave up a bomb, he'd say, "Dang. I can't believe a guy can hit a ball that far." Instead of getting pissed off about it, he made a joke to keep an even keel. The game can be intense, but he was real good about stepping back and not getting wound up in the moment. Make fun of what just happened. Humor gets you to lighten up. Relax. Forget about a bad play or a bad pitch. And move on. Sometimes, you just need to take a breath and shake things off. If you get a good laugh in, that calms everybody down.

I worked with Vuke at the end of his career. He was trying to make a comeback, but his arm wasn't what it once was. At one point, he threw real hard, but he had developed arm problems. Had to transition to being a different kind of pitcher. It hurt him to pitch. In the spring training games when I caught him, he got smoked. He threw a batting practice-type fastball. Had a good slider. Solid changeup. His stuff was average really, but he was a pitcher, not a thrower. What I mean by that is that he didn't rare back and blast the ball past hitters. Instead, he had good control and a great feel for pitching. He knew when it was time to paint the outside corner and nibble at the hitter. Make him reach for a pitch. Kind of like what I was saying earlier about Don Sutton, Vuke kept hitters off balance by changing speeds. He would throw a fast pitch followed by a slower one to throw off their timing. The word that comes to mind is guile. He didn't have overpowering stuff, but he could set up hitters to get some outs. He wasn't going to strike out a ton of guys, but he could put the team in a position where we'd win some close games four to three or five to four.

When he pitched, he was goofier than hell on the mound. He talked to himself, to the batter, to different people. He just talked. He horsed around with his face, his hair. His hands fluttered and twitched a lot. He'd take his hat off, then plop it back on and take it off again two or three times before he threw the ball. I never saw a pitcher as manic on the mound. I think some people saw these antics as a way to distract hitters or get in their heads, but I don't think so. I just think he was quirky. His fidgeting—that was part of how he handled his nervous energy out there. He marched to his own drummer. Fit in perfectly with the '82 club that went to the World Series. He had a great team playing behind him that played hard and had fun, and that describes Vuckovich. He liked a cold beer and a good time, and he liked to play baseball. He was willing to do whatever it took to win.

Even though his arm wasn't what it once was, he competed like hell. If he had to chunk the rosin bag at a guy to win, he'd do it. Mean son of a bitch. Didn't take shit off anybody. He looked intimidating. He was a big guy. Probably six four and two hundred fifty or sixty pounds. Fu manchu moustache. And, he pitched aggressively. He wouldn't hesitate to throw inside and knock a dude down on his ass and then laugh when he got back up and dusted himself off. He'd do that if a hitter took a big hack at him. If a guy swung so hard that he grunted or fell down or if he got pissed off because he fouled a pitch off, and he's like, "Man, I should've killed that one," that fired Vuke up. His reaction was kind of like, "Okay, dude. You think you should've smoked that ball. I'll show you." He was intense, a very competitive cat.

Vuke would do anything to get guys out. Even though it hurt him to throw sliders, he'd do it when he was behind in the count. That's usually a fastball count, so that's what the hitter is looking for. Vuke knew that, so he'd try to throw the hitter off by giving him something unexpected. A different look. He never gave in. Never threw a fastball down the middle of the plate. Never gave hitters the pitch they wanted to see. Instead, he pitched to the corners. Kept the ball away from hitters. Because he had good control, he placed the ball where it was tough to hit. Another thing he did to get an edge was to slop a spitball in there on occasion. When I was with Oakland, Billy Martin had been the manager, and he made all of his pitchers throw spitters. That's where I learned to catch them. With a spitball, the ball spins like a forkball. Comes at you like a fastball, and then it just drops. Dives at the end. You throw a spitball by getting your pointer finger wet and keeping your thumb, which is holding the bottom of the ball, dry. Grip the ball without touching a seam, and the ball almost squirts out of the pitcher's hand. Creates a tumbling effect. Some of Vuckovich's pitches had the same kind of rotation. Vuke sweated like hell, though, so maybe some of the hat on, hat off stuff got his hands a little moist and made the ball a little slippery. Gave it some extra movement. When I first came up, I saw quite a few spitballs. Don't see them so much anymore.

At the end of spring training, Vuckovich retired. I hated to see him leave. I was pulling for him. One time he asked me what I thought he should do, and I told him to keep going. But, his shoulder was bothering him, and he was dealing with several injuries. I think he had cysts of some kind. He just reached the point where he couldn't do what he normally did and get people out like he used to. That's usually a sign that it's time to move on. No one wants to go out there and get hammered. But when you don't throw as hard as you used to, you lose velocity. Just can't get that fastball past guys anymore. The loss of velocity affects your breaking balls too. Without the same speed behind them, they don't move as much. They start straightening out and aren't as effective as they used to be. It's too bad I didn't get a chance to play with him when he was healthy. He stayed around the team, though, doing radio and TV work. He liked to stop by the clubhouse and talk baseball. You could tell that he loved and missed the game. And, he was a good guy. He may have given me grief about this or that, but he looked out for me, too. Landed an advertising deal for me—I was going to promote truck bed camper covers for a company based around Milwaukee. But, with our luck, I was traded to New York soon after we agreed to everything.

CHAPTER 2

DAVID CONE

You know, it was like there was almost no movement of his glove when he caught a ball, which is, when you think about it, I'm throwing a ball ninety-two miles per hour and it hits his glove and his hands are so soft that he can have almost no perceptible movement when he catches the ball. That's just a tremendous talent that Charlie had, and we all knew it, but it was hard to put a number to like a batting average or a defensive average. But, Charlie had it as good as anybody.

—*David Cone*

[Note: In his second game with the New York Mets after being traded from the Milwaukee Brewers, Charlie caught David Cone in a 10-6 victory over the San Francisco Giants on September 2, 1990. Cone had not yet won the Cy Young Award (winning it four years later with the Kansas City Royals), but when Charlie played with him, Cone had already established himself as one of the game's best pitchers. In 1988, Cone led the league in winning percentage (.870) with a gaudy 20-3 win-loss record, and 1990 marked the first of three consecutive seasons when Cone led the league in strikeouts.[1]

Despite his success, Cone was also known for letting his emotions overwhelm him. In a game against the Atlanta Braves, Mets second baseman Gregg Jefferies fielded a ground ball. He tossed it to Cone who was running toward first base to tap the bag for the out. Slightly off balance, Cone tried to brush the base as he moved past it, but umpire Charlie Williams called the base runner safe. Stung by the call, Cone confronted Williams while play continued. As Cone argued, two Braves base runners scored. Cone was so distracted that he didn't hear his teammates pleading with him to throw them the ball as the base runners advanced.[2]

In addition, off-the-field controversy swirled around Cone. In October 1991, he was accused of rape (ultimately, no charges were brought).[3] During spring training the following season, a woman alleged that she was gang-raped at Cone's residence the prior year.[4] A story also surfaced that Cone allegedly exposed himself to a woman in the Shea

Stadium bullpen.[5] Meanwhile, newspapers regularly commented on his negotiations with the Mets for a long-term contract extension.[6]

Within this context, Charlie caught Cone in four games in 1990 (three wins and one loss), thirteen games in 1991 (seven wins and four losses), and two games in 1992 (one win and one loss) before the Mets traded Cone to the Toronto Blue Jays.[7] Charlie and Cone experienced great success, culminating with Cone tying the National League record for most strikeouts in a game when, on October 6, 1991, he struck out nineteen Philadelphia Phillies.

Cone played seventeen seasons in the Major Leagues, pitching for the Kansas City Royals, New York Mets, Toronto Blue Jays, New York Yankees, and Boston Red Sox. He retired in 2003 with 194 wins, 126 losses, a 3.46 ERA, and 2,668 strikeouts.[8]]

Being traded from Milwaukee to New York was a culture shock. I went from a last place team to a pennant race. Instead of one or two reporters covering the team, we had twenty. And, the Mets were wild. The airplane trips between the teams were two different worlds. In Milwaukee, the plane rides were quiet. We just flew. Minded our own business. But, New York plane rides were out of control. Music blaring. Guys drinking and hollering and playing cards. Fighting. Raising all sorts of hell. I just stayed up front and read my hunting magazine and stayed out of all that.

Our plane rides were a good example of what kind of team we were. On the Mets, we had guys who liked to party. Chase women. Stay out all night. Personalities where guys liked to burn the candle at both ends. New York is a hell of a place to be if you're drawn to that sort of thing because the candle is always burning in New York. They were good guys, talented guys, but they were wild. That was totally different from the Brewers where you had Robin Yount and Paul Molitor, guys who weren't flashy but who busted their ass all of the time. Did things the right way on and off the field. Robin Yount never jogged to first base, never took a day off. Went full speed every day and played the game the way it is supposed to be played. Even though he was a Hall of Fame player, he treated everybody the same. Didn't think he was better than anybody. Just a down-to-earth good dude. If there's someone I want to hold up to my kids and have them model, it's Robin Yount. But, with the Mets, you had Darryl Strawberry as the best player. When I played with him, he was a miserable teammate. It was all about Darryl Strawberry, not the team. He took some time off during that last month of the season, complaining that his back was sore. Guys knew that it was because he was going to be a free agent, and he was pissed that the Mets weren't negotiating with him more. He wasn't coming back to New York, so it was kind of like, "You're not going to sign me; well, I'll show you." His time with the team ended very badly. If his bat had been in the lineup every day, he would've been the difference. Made us a winner. But, we lost some close 1-0 or 3-2 games and finished in second behind Pittsburgh. With Strawberry, we were a better club than the Pirates, no doubt, and I wasn't used to this me-first approach. I heard that Strawberry changed later in his career when he played with the Yankees. Became a good teammate. I hope so. When I played with him, I thought he was a piece of shit.

David Cone fit right in with the team's wild personality. He was kind of like a latter-day version of Joe Namath, going out and enjoying the city and women and having a good time. While the game was going on, he was attentive, but as soon as it was over, he was ready to move on to something else. He liked to live on the edge, liked the limelight. New York was the perfect place for his personality—smart, witty, quick, and competitive as hell. He would've been perfect for the '86 team that won the World Series, wild and brash. And, he handled the spotlight well. When I played with him, all sorts of crazy stories floated around about him. As I mentioned earlier, rape charges. Exposing himself to somebody in the bullpen. A lot of that stuff was bullshit, really, stuff for the papers. And, I don't want to get into the he said/she said of it. I wasn't there to see firsthand any of the stories. But, my two cents is these stories usually make a big splash with accusations. Stir everybody up. Sell a lot of papers. They're on the sports talk shows; maybe ESPN picks it up. Then, when the truth comes out or the whole story is presented, that doesn't get anywhere near the same attention. It winds up buried in the middle of the section instead of being on the front page—if it gets mentioned at all—which doesn't seem right to me. But, I didn't see Coney distracted by any of the media stuff. Guys are there to play baseball, so that's what they do. You take the field, and you do what you do since you were a kid. Maybe the stories stressed him off the field, but I didn't see it affect his game or change how he was in the clubhouse.

Even though he was from Kansas City, not too far from where I grew up and still live, Coney reminded me of a California surfer dude. Somebody who was just kind of out there. Sometimes, I'd go out to the mound to talk to him, and it was like the guy was somewhere else. Look at you like you're not even there. Or, he'd scan the stadium. Check out the crowd. Look at a plane flying overhead. Kind of like he didn't want me out there and couldn't wait for me to leave.

Don't get me wrong. Coney was a great guy. Well-liked in the clubhouse. Everybody appreciated how he got his bonin' done. He was out there every fifth day to take the ball and play hard and keep his team close and in the game. Some games, maybe he didn't get a whole lot of sleep the night before, but it didn't affect him.

When he was on the mound, you had a good chance of winning. You knew that because of the nasty shit he threw and also because winning and doing his best meant something to him. After I retired, I was watching the MLB Network's profile of the '95 American League playoff series between the Yankees and Seattle. Coney was with the Yankees then, and they lost the last game of the playoff. Even though he pitched a hell of a game, Coney said he just went back into the clubhouse and cried like a baby. I could see that. Real emotional guy. I could see him feeling like he let his teammates down because he left a pitch over the plate or gave up a hit. Some cats, they may be like, "Oh, well. I did the best I could." Not him. He was such a competitor. Hated to lose. Guys loved that—that's the kind of guy they want on the mound.

And, he was a cool dude. Kept the clubhouse loose. One thing he did to crack guys up was to get girls to show him their boobs. Didn't matter where we were, home or away, but during batting practice, he could get a girl to flash us. Guys would hang around him just to see how long it took him to get one to do it. Usually didn't take long. Girls might be screaming to get his attention. Coney would dangle a baseball at them and then act like he was taking off his shirt. Like Clark Kent ripping off his suit and becoming Superman. Nine times out of ten, the girl would follow his lead and lift her top. Then Coney would throw her a ball. Guys in the bullpen, we lost it. In Shea Stadium, a female security guard worked on the second level, right above the bullpen. Coney would warm up, and when he was finished, she'd come to the rail, show him her chest, and then he'd flip her a ball. Automatic. *Every* time he warmed up in the bullpen.

When I think about the talented pitchers I worked with, Coney's at the top of the list. He threw six quality pitches. Most pitchers have two or three. They want to simplify things and master a couple of pitches. Not Coney. He wanted to throw six or seven pitches well. And he did. His fastball was overpowering, topping out in the mid-90s. He threw hard. Had great arm speed. He also threw a two-seam fastball that ran a bunch on his arm side and moved in toward right-handed hitters.

Mainly, Coney was a breaking ball pitcher. His curveball, slider, and forkball were filthy. When he threw his slider, he could make it move like a whiffle ball. Instead of a curveball that drops from the twelve on a clock to the six, the slider moves to the side, across the plate and away from the head of the bat. He threw the pitch hard—in the mid-80s, I'd guess—and the ball moved so fast and quick. Most guys don't have the arm speed that Cone had to make the ball break as much and as quickly. It's funny, but I've heard Cone attribute his nasty breaking stuff to playing whiffle ball in the backyard with his brothers as a kid. The tricks he learned there to make the ball dip and move while he was copying the different deliveries of guys like Luis Tiant, he applied in the big leagues. Putting spin on the ball. Throwing a sidearm curve or slider. Using different grips. His slider grip was a little unusual in that he'd place his index finger on the seams. That created some spin, but he also included a lot of wrist action, cocking and snapping his wrist when he released. He kind of cupped the ball middelivery and bent his wrist forward, trying to generate a lot of wrist action to create that movement. As far as something that a pitching coach would teach, this isn't it. They'd see these things and probably think, "Arm injuries. Too much strain on your shoulder or elbow." You can't argue with the results, though. By far, he threw the best breaking balls of anybody I ever caught. They were so good that he'd pitch backwards. What I mean is that where a pitcher normally throws his fastball in the count, that's when Coney would throw his breaking pitches. Most guys get ahead in the count with their fastball, then go after a guy with breaking pitches. Not Cone. He started off with breaking balls and put hitters away with his fastball.

On top of already throwing six quality pitches, Coney adjusted his arm angles. It was like he could invent stuff out there by throwing one pitch over the top and the same pitch at a three-quarters delivery or sidearm. Changing the arm angle changed the arc of his pitches and made the ball do different things. So, really, it was like he had eighteen or twenty options out there, depending on if he threw overhand, three-quarters, or sidearm. I think he got a kick out of throwing side-arm especially. When he threw his breaking ball from the south, he called it his "Laredo." He liked to improvise with the different deliveries. Sometimes, after I signaled for a pitch and we agreed that he'd throw whatever, Coney would think, "I'll throw this one three-quarters." Hell, sometimes middelivery he decided to change arm angles. I had to adapt and be able to catch whatever he was throwing on the fly. The crazy thing was how astute he was at picking up pitches and knowing how to throw all of them for strikes at different arm angles. I never caught anyone who changed arm angles so drastically or as often as Coney. Most guys just stay in the same arm slot over and over again so they know where their pitches are going.

Having all these options complicated things for him. He wanted to throw all of his pitches, so he could have a hard time deciding which pitch to throw. All this talent made him so much fun to catch. You could ask him to do so many things. I just tried to figure out what he was throwing well on a given day and go with him. Create a good flow so he didn't shake me off. If his arm was hurting and throwing a certain pitch made him hurt more, that made things a little easier—he just wouldn't throw that one that day. Coney worked through a similar process too. During warm-ups, he'd run through his repertoire. See what was working well for him that day. Decide if his fastball was exceptionally good or if his curveball was breaking really well. Shape pitch selection around that rather than being in a defensive mode and pitching around hitters' strengths or to their weaknesses. He'd challenge guys and see if they could beat him and what he was throwing best that day.

Because Coney was a breaking ball pitcher, he usually had high pitch counts since breaking balls are more difficult to control than fastballs. That can make them harder to throw for strikes. Instead of just throwing a fastball down and away that the hitter rolls over and hits a grounder to short giving you one out with one pitch, breaking ball pitchers may throw a first pitch fastball for a strike followed by a few pitches that miss the strike zone. Hitters may foul off a few balls because they're tough to get a good hack at. So, you're looking at six or seven pitches to a hitter. Take that by the number of hitters faced in a game, and you'll have high pitch counts. Coney is a good example of this. In some of the games I played with him, he threw a ton of pitches. He was young, so he pulled off throwing so many pitches just fine. But, if I could change one thing about our experience, I would've called more fastballs. At that stage of his career, his fastball was so good that he could've gotten some guys out on a first pitch outside fastball. Could've saved some wear and tear on his arm instead of what we normally did: a slider-curve-change-forkball pitch selection. Like one game against St. Louis. We lost 7-3. Coney pitched seven innings. Threw 138 pitches. That's a lot of pitches. But, that's where Coney was as a young gunslinger pitcher. Fast-forward ten years to when he pitched his perfect game and he had lost some arm speed and velocity: he threw only eighty-eight pitches to get twenty-seven hitters out. Over time, he became a different kind of pitcher.

When I caught Coney, though, I don't know that I could've convinced him to throw more fastballs. Coney loved throwing breaking balls. Like I said, I called a game based on the pitcher's strengths. What he likes to throw. I adapted to the guy on the mound. I didn't have a blueprint for pitch selection that I used no matter who was pitching. And, I wasn't one of those guys who insisted, "Hey, you've got to do things my way." The bottom line is that Coney was a breaking ball pitcher who threw some nasty shit. So, those were the pitches I called. And, with his breaking balls, Coney made hitters look bad. He could tie the hitter up in knots. Have him fall down on his ass swinging. It's funny: just a called strike or a strikeout bored him. That wasn't enough. He needed the challenge of piling up a ton of strikeouts *and* making good hitters look shitty. Hitters would strike out, and they'd walk back to the dugout, shaking their heads, amazed at the stuff he threw. Like one of the first games I caught him was against the Pirates. Good team. He just shut down their top guys. Bobby Bonilla went 0-3 with three strikeouts. Bonds went 0-4. Sid Bream went 0-4 with a strikeout. Later on, as he got older and lost some arm strength and had to rely more on finesse and off-speed stuff, I think Coney was fine getting outs with less pitches, but when I played with him, he wanted to make hitters look ridiculous. Didn't care how many pitches it took him to do it.

Nearly every time I went out to catch him, I thought he could throw a no-hitter. Toward the end of '91, he almost threw one. We played St. Louis in Shea, and he went seven innings without giving up a hit before a dude hit a double to lead off the eighth. He sailed through the game. Incredible breaking pitches. He was pretty let down after that game because his stuff was so good.

He followed that up a couple of weeks later by tying the National League record for most strikeouts in a game. That was one of the most dominating performances I ever saw. We were playing the Phillies on the last game of the season, a getaway day that some guys, including the umpires, just go through the motions to get in and out because they're ready to wind up a road trip and head home. Neither team was going anywhere. I think we finished in last or next-to-last place. The Phillies played a lot of guys from their Triple A club that day. Coney was very attentive, though. So was the home plate umpire, Ed Rapuano. I'd been in situations earlier in my career when I'd go out toward the end of a tie game to warm up the pitcher and, on a getaway day, the umpire might say, "I can tell you right now, this game isn't going into extra innings." Or, if the umpire was hungry, you could be damn sure that the game was ending sooner rather than later so he could go get his bite to eat. Things that most people wouldn't believe. For a while, umpires had *way* too much control over games, but Ed did a nice job that day of calling a consistent and fair strike zone. And, Coney was locked in. His slider was hard and ugly. Sharp fastball. He just mowed guys down. I don't know how many guys he punched out three times. Some of his dominance had to do with who he was facing—a lot of guys from Triple A and not an everyday big league lineup. With that lineup and as sharp as his stuff was, it was the perfect setting for him to have a big game. And, he was impressive. Dale Murphy was the last guy up for the Phillies. Murph hadn't caught up with Coney's fastball the entire game. He had struck out before on fastballs, so, for his last time up with two strikes and two outs in the bottom of the ninth, I called for a heater. Coney shook me off. He didn't shake me off much during that game, but he did then. He wanted to throw a slider, so that's what he threw. That's the only thing that Murph could catch up to. He tapped a groundball to short to end the game. If Cone had thrown that fastball, he would've punched out twenty dudes, I promise. His fastball was that overpowering. But, that kind of goes back to what I was saying earlier: he didn't want to just strike somebody out—he wanted to make them look bad. He did that most with his breaking pitches.

Later, I found out that earlier that day, Coney heard the police were going to arrest him on rape charges. He never said a word about that stuff to me. I had no idea. He really maintained his composure. I couldn't tell that he was distracted by anything. During the game, he concentrated on the hitter and on throwing his pitches. That game, he held it together well. Other times, if he threw some bad pitches or got a bad call, he could get pissed off and let it rattle him. This was one of the areas where I tried to help him. If he threw a good pitch and the umpire called it a ball, I'd say to the umpire, "Come on, let's get locked in. We got a lot of baseball left to play. You can't miss shit like that." Coney liked that I was defending him. On the mound, he couldn't show up the umpire. Couldn't say anything. Really couldn't even look at the guy the wrong way. Doing this would only hurt him. Catchers can, though. Because of the mask, we can get away with saying things throughout the game. Nobody can tell we're saying anything to the umpire. So, I'd tell him, "I'm chewin' on his ass right now. We don't need both of us doing it. I'll take care of it." If an umpire was going to be pissed at anybody, I wanted him to be mad at me, not the pitcher. And, I didn't want Coney losing his cool because of some bad calls. He just needed to keep a straight face and keep moving. Losing your temper can only hurt you. Make you lose focus. Lose your focus, and you can get beat around pretty quick.

I'd try to help him in other ways, too. I'd suggest how we should face certain hitters or adjustments he should make in his motion. Usually, I'd point out that he shouldn't drop down to a three-quarters or sidearm delivery as much or that he should cut back on his breaking balls. That's because his arm speed was just a little slower than usual. With slower arm speed, the ball isn't thrown as hard. Doesn't come to the plate as fast and doesn't break or move as much. So, in those situations, I'd say lean on his fastball more. Keep his breaking balls off of the middle of the plate. And, Coney was pretty good about taking my advice. My job was to make him better. He knew that. And, he liked my defense. Knew I could block the ball well. That gave him the confidence to throw his breaking pitches when some of them would wind up in the dirt. With me behind the plate, the pitches would stay there and not get behind me. He liked my arm, too. Knew I could throw out base runners. Our first game together, I threw out Kevin Mitchell trying to steal third base. It's the same deal as handling umpires: my defense meant he had less to worry about. He could focus on pitching.

As far as dealing with Coney, we had some games when I needed to go out to the mound and say something to break the ice. Maybe something smart-ass to ease the tension. If we had base runners on and it was a critical situation, that wasn't a time to pick him apart and tell him how he could improve. Coney didn't have the temperament to take that. Instead, I'd say something like, "How's your love life?" Something completely unrelated to baseball. Get him to ease up. That seemed to work for him.

Sometimes, I needed to pull his attention back into the game. I could reel him back in by how I signed for pitches with my fingers or how I pounded the glove or set the glove as a target. Subtle things, but something just different enough to capture his attention. A few times, I had to go out to the mound and say, "Hey. Get your head out of the stands. I see you looking at that blonde over there. Pay attention to the game. Make your pitches."

Coney also respected that I was honest. If the pitching coach or the manager came out to the mound and asked Coney how he was feeling, he'd say, "Man, I'm fine. I'm great," even if he was dragging. Sometimes, the coaches asked me how he was doing, and I told them the truth, even if it wasn't what Coney wanted to hear. I'd tell them if his stuff was getting a little short. That his fastball was losing velocity or that his breaking balls weren't moving as much as they were earlier in the game. His fastball might be more elevated. His breaking balls wouldn't drop down and away—they'd hang more and stay around the middle of the plate. It made sense that he'd get tired because he threw so many pitches. If he was done, I'd say, "He's done." Most times, these conversations took place in front of Coney, but sometimes it'd be when the pitching coach or manager was walking off the mound, and I'd tell him, "Keep him on a short leash." Plus, late in the game, I thought it was fine for Coney to hand the ball over to somebody else because, in New York, we had a good closer, John Franco. That made pitching change decisions a lot easier when you've got a Hall of Fame-type guy ready to come in and wrap up a game.

Despite having a guy like Coney on the roster, the Mets teams I played on were shitty. In '90, we were in second place. But, in '91 we were below .500. In '92, I think we were in last or next-to-last place. Look at the roster, and you'd expect the team to do better. We had some good lineups with guys like Kevin McReynolds and Howard Johnson. Our starting rotation was one of the better ones in baseball with Coney, Dwight Gooden, Frank Viola, and Sid Fernandez. But, one of our problems was injuries. Gooden had health problems. Fernandez got hurt. Cone missed a few starts here and there. Later on, the Mets signed Bret

Saberhagen, and he had long stretches when he was hurt. Those core guys never played together day in and day out. That was the difference between the Mets and the Braves staff that I later played with where, consistently, the team trotted out Maddux, Glavine, Smoltz, and Avery. Injuries to our starting pitching killed the Mets in the early nineties. And, our everyday players were hurt too. I remember in '92, we were hanging around, only a couple of games out of first place, when we lost our two best hitters on the same day. Literally, when X rays showed that Howard Johnson broke his hand and the trainer told this to our manager, Jeff Torborg, Torborg looked up and saw Bobby Bonilla make a diving catch where he wound up breaking or bruising his ribs, putting him on the shelf for a while. A couple of days after that, our second baseman, Willie Randolph, wound up breaking his hand, too. Good teams usually stay pretty healthy. And, injuries are kind of a flukey deal. They just happen, even if you emphasize conditioning and stretching and taking care of yourself.

We had some other problems too. For some reason, all the talent on the team didn't gel. Wasn't good chemistry. Part of it was that, at times, we didn't have a strong manager who kept the team in check. Kind of like what I was saying earlier about Darryl Strawberry. A good manager would've gotten in his face and said, "No. You're playing today. We need you in the lineup. You make us better." But, we had some managers who didn't want to challenge the big-name guys. They were more hands-off and just let it go and gave a guy a day off. Along those same lines, we didn't have real strong leadership in the clubhouse, any enforcers who'd push other players if they weren't giving one hundred percent. Frank Viola said that, when he played on the Twins team that won the World Series, you could count on Kent Hrbek and Kirby Puckett to embarrass the shit out of somebody if they didn't play hard all the time. They'd call guys out and get them back in line. With the Mets, we just didn't have that same kind of leadership. A few years before, when the Mets won the World Series, they had a real veteran presence with guys like Keith Hernandez and Gary Carter who played that role. But, by the time I was there, those guys were gone. Nobody stepped in to fill their shoes.

We also had some young guys who were placed on a pedestal. Gregg Jefferies came in, and he was supposed to be this young phenomenon who'd turn the team around. He kind of received special treatment. That didn't sit well with some of the veterans. It was just a tough, tense atmosphere. A lot of egos. A lot of chiefs, but nobody really stepping up and saying, "Hey, guys. Let's get our shit together. Let's play the game the right way. Cut the bullshit."

The secret to team chemistry? I wish I knew it. It's incredible when you have all twenty-five guys working together, all having the same goal. That's what it was like when I played in Atlanta. But, in New York, we didn't have it. We had the talent. But, we didn't have the chemistry, that's for sure.

To top it off, it seemed like we always had some drama. The gang rape story. The exposure deal. Guys throwing firecrackers at people. Guys squirting bleach at reporters. Hell, one time, I was in a situation where I played peacemaker between Vince Coleman, one of our outfielders, and our manager, Jeff Torborg. Vince was mad because of a play at the plate. I can't remember if Vince was arguing balls and strikes with the umpire, he was called out trying to score, or what. Vince had a temper, though, and he was starting to lose it with the umpire. So, Jeff went out to home plate. He was trying to keep Vince from being suspended. Stepped between Vince and the umpire. Separated them, then he bent down to pick up a bat, and he kind of pushed Vince when he was doing it. Vince took that as Jeff showing him up, and Vince snapped.

"Don't you touch me, man! Don't touch me! I'll kick your ass!"

Jeff was like, "Hey. Wait a minute. That's enough of this stuff out here in the open. We'll talk later inside."

Somehow, Jeff herded Vince back to the dugout. But Vince was fired up. Wanted Torborg to take it back to the clubhouse so they could settle it.

It was ridiculous, but Jeff followed Vince to the clubhouse. To maintain the team's respect, he had to. He couldn't let a guy run over him like that and back down.

I didn't think any of this was a good idea, so I followed them. They were going back and forth at it pretty good and getting close to throwing punches. I wasn't worried about Jeff, though. He's a former catcher. Like I said, catchers are a different kind of tough than other positions. Plus, Jeff worked out a bunch. Was a stout dude. I wasn't betting against the old catcher. Old catchers will beat the piss out of you.

Anyway, I didn't want anything to happen that either of them would regret. So, I stepped in between Jeff and Vince. Kind of defused things. I told Jeff, "I'll handle it. Go back to the dugout."

Vince kept on screaming and carrying on. I just kind of picked him up and got him to the training room.

"Sit down," I said. And, I waited for his fit to blow over. Kind of like you do with kids when they're riled up.

Years later, Jeff thanked me. He said that, walking to the fight, he looked back and saw me following him. He appreciated that.

He said, "I was surprised you were there behind me. The club and I weren't treating you right. You weren't getting to play much. Out of anybody on the team, you were in the best position to want me to get my ass kicked. But, you were behind me. That night, I told Susie [Jeff's wife] how much that helped me. How much I appreciated it."

Credit goes to both of them for putting this episode behind them. Jeff suspended Vince for a couple of games—the whole thing he was trying to avoid when he ran out to home plate to calm Vince down when he lost his composure with the umpire. When the suspension was over, Jeff sat Vince down and told him, look, what happened isn't something either of us is going to forget, but put it behind us. It's over. Jeff didn't have any more animosity on his end, and he was ready to put Vince back in the lineup whenever he was ready to play.

When the Mets fired Jeff, Vince came into Jeff's office and thanked him. Said something like, "You were truthful with me and treated me like a man, and I appreciate it."

With all of this drama, part of me asks, "How come? Was it because of all the media coverage? They just picked up on everything?" I don't think so. I don't think stuff like this happened on every other big league club. It was just something about the guys on the Mets. A lot of them were drawn to partying and being in bad situations. We got into shit, and it seemed like it happened all of the time. It was the damnedest thing. I never saw anything else like it on any other club I ever played with. It was like a black cloud hanging over us that we just couldn't shake.

Coney loved pitching. Loved giving all he could to put his team in the best position to win. He could be absolutely dominating, like how he struck out nineteen dudes in a game. He was fun to watch, throwing some absolutely nasty shit and making smart-ass comments from the mound depending on who he was facing. If a guy swung really weak, you could count on Coney to say, "Come on. Swing the bat, Sally." Or, "Nice hack." Sometimes, when I was hitting and facing a guy I knew or I had played with before, I'd say stuff to them. They'd throw me a first pitch slider, and I'd be like, "Come on, dude. What are you scared of? Throw a fastball." They'd laugh. Then they'd throw you another slider because they know you're not a very good breaking ball hitter. They know you can hit a fastball. It's like anything else: they don't want you to get a hit off them. Some guys, during a game, they're so intense that they really don't say anything. Not Cone. He could play well and harass people and have a good time while he played.

Before a game, though, Coney was pretty solitary, in his own little world. Some guys like to blast metal music or whatever to pump themselves up. Some guys like to visualize the hitters they're getting ready to face. Others are rigid about sticking to a routine of throwing *X* number of warm-up pitches at such-and-such time before every game. Coney wanted quiet time. I figured that out and pretty much left him alone. Didn't force myself on him. Let him work through whatever he needed to. I left him alone during the game too. Didn't talk much to him on the bench between innings.

Coney's stuff was so good that I don't see how he won only 194 games for his career. I say that knowing that 194 wins in the big leagues is a hell of an accomplishment. His stuff was way better than 194 wins. I think part of it was that he played for some mediocre teams. Like I said, when I played with him in New York, we weren't very good. You can look at his ERA for those years with the Mets and see that it's in the 3.00s. Pretty salty. That tells you he was getting the job done on the mound. He kept us in most games, but we didn't score many runs. With his filthy stuff, we had a chance to win every time he took the mound.

CHAPTER 3

FRANK VIOLA

When I tried coming back from my elbow surgery with the Blue Jays, Charlie was catching. They had a young catcher there at the same time by the name of Sandy Martinez. The Blue Jays were going young. They knew that the kid [Sandy] had a good bat, and they wanted him to learn. So, they figured a veteran pitcher would teach a young catcher, and it was the opposite. I was coming back, and I wasn't sure of myself. I needed Charlie. The one time he caught me, I threw six innings, gave up a solo home run, and I got my win. The other five games I started, all Sandy, I got my tits ripped. I really needed help. And, I went up to Cito Gaston, who was managing at the time, and I said, "Cito, I understand what you're trying to do, but I need help myself." Basically, the next thing I know, I'm given my release papers because they decided to go another way. And, as I left the clubhouse, the last person I talked to in a Major League uniform was Charlie. He had his locker at the end, and I went up to him and said, "Honestly, Charlie, do I have anything left?" And, he said, "Yeah. You've got a lot left. It's up to you. Don't give up." The problem was, at that time, I had three young kids. And, somebody actually hit me where it hurt and told me I couldn't do it anymore. Instead of saying, "You know what? Screw you, I can do it," I decided to walk away. But, those words will always be in the back of my mind, Charlie saying, "You can do it if you want to." Knowing what kind of defensive specialist he was, that means a lot. He invented that damned stupid hockey mask too.

—*Frank Viola*

[*Note: Charlie first caught Frank Viola during the 1990 and 1991 seasons with the New York Mets. Traded to the Mets while they were in the midst of a pennant race, Charlie played nearly every day in September 1990 for a club packed with talent: Darryl Strawberry was one of the best hitters in the league, and Howard Johnson (twenty-three home runs and ninety runs batted in), Kevin McReynolds (twenty-four home runs and eighty-two runs batted in), and Dave Magadan (.328 batting average) rounded out the lineup.*[1] *Despite the loaded roster, the team finished in second place behind Pittsburgh in the National League Eastern Division. Viola was one of the main reasons why the club stayed in contention, winning twenty games and posting a 2.67 earned run average, numbers similar to his 1988 form when he won the Cy Young Award with the Minnesota Twins.*

After the 1990 season, Strawberry departed New York as a free agent. Losing his bat and suffering some injuries left the Mets stumbling to a 77-84 record and a fifth place finish. Viola's individual record in '91 mirrored the team's: he started the season strong and was 11-5 at the All-Star break. During the second half of the season, he struggled, earning only two wins and losing ten games.[2] *Viola became increasingly frustrated, stating that he knew the season would be bad because the Mets had so many players playing out of position defensively, that he did not enjoy coming to the park anymore, and that he played "the worst half of baseball in my life."*[3] *He left the Mets at the end of '91, signing as a free agent with Boston.*

Charlie caught Viola in five games in 1990 (one win and three losses, two of which were one-run games) and six games in 1991 (two no decisions and four losses). Five years later, Charlie and Viola reunited while with the Toronto Blue Jays, Viola's last stop in his Major League career. Charlie caught him in two games before Viola was released in June 1996. One of those games was Viola's last win, a 6-2 victory over the Kansas City Royals on May 18, 1996, when Viola threw six innings and scattered five hits, walked two, struck out four, and gave up one run.[4]

For his career, Viola had a record of 176 wins, 150 losses, a 3.73 earned run average, and 1,844 strikeouts. He played for fifteen seasons.]

Baseball can be cruel. If things aren't going your way, it can eat you alive. The game involves a lot of failure. If you get a hit three times out of ten, you're a Hall of Famer, so even superstars fail more times than they succeed. One day, you can play well. Help your team win. The next, you can fail and be in the doghouse. It's a humbling game. Hard to excel at day after day with all of its ups and downs. Of all games, baseball is the one that's most like life with the good times and the bad, and trying to figure out how to deal with the bad times. Because you'll go through streaks when it doesn't matter how good of a pitch you throw, the batter waffles it. You'll have slumps when things won't go your way. You start doubting your ability to perform. The New York media makes slumps even worse and can create a snowball effect with all of the negative talk in the papers and sports shows about how shitty you're playing. You can't overstate how the New York media picks apart everything down to the smallest detail with the pregame shows, the postgame shows, analyzing and second guessing every move. It can become all-consuming. I know it ate up Jeff Torborg, one of my managers with the Mets and one of the smartest and most likeable guys in baseball. Add a bad reaction from the fans, and it's a lot to handle mentally and keep negative thoughts from taking over.

The best guys deal with failure by developing short memories. They figure out why they played badly, and then they forget about it. It sounds hard to believe. It's true, though. What I did was to see the positives. While I was hitting, I may have gotten an out, but I considered it a good at-bat if I hit the ball hard. For pitchers, I'd try to put it in perspective: they may have had a bad inning, but they also threw six good ones. My advice: figure out what didn't work. Make some adjustments, and go back out there. Learn from it, and move on. If your own fans pile on and boo you, tune them out. I sang to myself so I heard that instead of the boos.

I caught Frankie while he was in a slump. For the last half of '91, he was 2-10, which is pretty bad no matter how you put it, especially for someone as good as he was. Sometimes, he'd be doing his job and pitching well enough to keep the team in the game. If the offense wasn't doing its part and scoring runs, he'd chirp about how guys needed to step up and get some hits. He was a typical New Yorker, an opinionated guy who'd let you know what he was thinking when he was irritated.

Frankie's main complaint, though, was our defense. Or, more accurately, lack of defense. At times, he'd get so frustrated about how shitty we played on the field that it distracted him on the mound. We had three or four guys playing out of position. Defensive liabilities. Howard Johnson was a great bat, but he didn't really have a place on the field defensively. Gregg Jefferies played second base, but he struggled there. Dave Magadan was more of a first baseman, but we had him at third. For some reason, the ball has a way of finding guys who don't field well. We just weren't a very good defensive club. But, the Mets' philosophy valued offense more than defense. The front office put bats in the lineup and didn't really think about where they fit on the field. Their thinking was that Gooden, Fernandez, and Cone were strikeout pitchers, so they'd get outs that way, and the offense would support them by scoring a bunch of runs. This whole approach made things tough for Frankie. He wasn't a big strikeout guy. He relied on his defense to make plays and get outs, so our weak defense really hurt him. Frankie came from the Twins who were solid fundamentally. With the Mets, he was at the other end of that spectrum, and guys booting balls in the field drove him crazy. I get it. I also understand why a general manager might want certain guys' bats in the lineup, but you can't ignore your defense. A good defense improves your pitching. A bad defense makes your pitching worse. What would have been an out becomes a guy on base when you don't execute in the field. Or, a single becomes a double and you have a runner in scoring position because a ball wasn't fielded cleanly. Defensive mistakes put your pitcher in a bind. Instead of getting twenty-seven outs, which is hard enough, a bad defense makes your pitcher or pitching staff get thirty or thirty-one outs because of all the errors. It's very discouraging. Can lead to clubhouse dissension. Pitchers disenchanted with front office moves where good defensive players were traded away for offensive-minded ones, and intentionally putting players out of position on the field just to get their bats in the lineup.

Making things worse, the team was losing and not playing well. I think all of this weighed on Frankie. Plus, he had a small tumor in his left pointer finger. He didn't think it'd impact how he pitched, so he'd just keep quiet about it, finish the year, and then have it removed. But, this small growth affected him. His changeup lost its edge. He wasn't throwing as many strikes. He wasn't in sync. And, maybe he didn't like where he was. Maybe he was tired of the team. Tired of New York, even though it was home for him. Maybe he was trying too hard. I know all of the media pressure had to be a lot to deal with. He was pitching so badly that one of the radio shows had a "Frank Viola Suicide Watch." They positioned somebody at Shea Stadium every day, and they'd call in to the station and report that, yes, they saw Frankie drive in to the park that day, that he made it one more day. I know it had to be difficult for him, pitching poorly after achieving so much success and being one of the top pitchers in the game. Sometimes, a player needs a fresh start. A change of scenery. I think it was good for Frankie to move on and sign a free agency deal with Boston.

Put aside that rough last half of '91, and Frankie was a fine pitcher. He threw three pitches: fastball, changeup, and curveball. His changeup was outstanding. One of the better ones in the league when he played in Minnesota and then when he came over to New York, if not the best. He used a circle change grip. You grip the ball by making a circle on the side of the ball with your thumb and pointer finger, kind of like making a big "OK" sign. By sliding the pointer finger off the center of the ball and moving it to the side, you reduce velocity. Johnny Podres, the old Brooklyn Dodgers pitcher, taught Frankie the pitch when he was coming up in the Twins system. He experimented with a bunch of different grips. The first time he threw the circle change, he barely threw it thirty feet. Practically threw the ball straight into the dirt. The grip just felt funky. But, he worked on it. Refined it. After a couple of years, he was comfortable enough to throw it in games. Once he did, he had great results. The pitch was deceptive because he used the same arm speed as when he threw his fastball. He fooled hitters into thinking he had thrown a fastball, but the pitch traveled ten miles per hour slower. It just stopped. And, his changeup was difficult to pick up because it didn't spin differently than his fastball. What also made the pitch so good was that it had some movement to it, turning over, sinking, and moving away from right-handed hitters. Guys would pull off the pitch and hit the ball off the end of the bat. That meant a lot of ground outs. It was a pitch saver he could throw in any fastball count (1-0, 2-1, or 3-1) to fool hitters. No doubt, the changeup was his bread and butter. When he was pitching well, hitters had a tough time hitting the ball hard off him. And, Frankie had confidence in that pitch. One time, when he was with Minnesota, he struck out the side in ten pitches, all of them changeups. At one point, he was throwing the pitch so well that he could've told batters what was coming, and I doubt they would've been able to hit it. Hell of a pitch.

On top of that, his curve had a good twelve to six drop. Later, when he was with Toronto, he threw a slider instead of a curveball, but his changeup is what made him so effective. If he had these pitches working for him, it was going to be a short game because he threw them extremely well. Plus, he was athletic. Most lefties are a little clumsy. Don't field their position well or cover first base well. Not Frankie. He was agile. Held base runners on well. Had a good slide step to first to pick off base runners if they crept out too far for their lead. His delivery home was good with a quick leg kick. Because he took less time with his delivery, I had more time to throw the ball to a base. I liked this. I liked trying to throw out base runners. I grew up admiring Johnny Bench and his arm strength. With a guy like Viola with a quick delivery on the mound, I had a better chance of throwing out a guy trying to steal second base.

Frankie didn't immediately trust his catcher. But, before games he pitched when I caught him, I went over to his locker. Explained what I thought we should do. How we should handle certain guys. I guess Frankie bought in that I knew what I was doing because he didn't shake me off much. And, it didn't take me long to pick up on things I could do to make him more comfortable. Some catchers might set up kind of high and create an upright target. That guides the pitcher so that he throws more up and in the zone. That's not what Frankie liked. He wanted a nice low target, so that's what I gave him. He wanted me to be as still as I could during his delivery. If I had to move, he wanted it to be subtle. That was fine—I had no problem doing that. And, I played to his strengths. Like I said, wicked changeup pitcher, so I called lots of fastballs and changeups. Asked him to move the ball in and off the plate. If we were facing somebody who was a good low fastball hitter,

I still called for low fastballs and challenged the hitter. Frankie threw a good low fastball, and just because the hitter may hit this pitch well, that doesn't mean that you run away from the pitcher's strengths. Frankie liked to challenge guys and see if they could beat him and his best pitch.

One time, I heard him say that he pitched best when his catcher thought for him. I agree. If I was calling the pitches he wanted to throw and was good at throwing, he could go into cruise control. Not think about what the situation was. What pitch to throw. He could focus entirely on execution. It simplified the game for him. And, he liked knowing that I believed in him, in his ability to throw good pitches. Because I called pitches tailored to what he did well, Frankie was satisfied every time I worked with him. If we lost, if we gave up some hits, he was okay with it, knowing that we challenged the guys with his strengths and that he had done his best. That I called the right pitches. He didn't have the same outlook if he was working with a guy who didn't rely on Frankie's strong points. The bottom line is, I made him feel comfortable. Most of the time when your pitcher is comfortable, relaxed, you'll get good results. If the pitcher isn't in sync with the catcher, it's funny: what can go wrong usually does.

Another thing I did was to try to keep him from getting flustered. Sometimes, he'd be pissed about a bad play. Like I said, in '91, we had plenty of shitty plays to be pissed about. He'd stew instead of concentrating on pitching. So, I'd go out to the mound and try to get him focused. Tell him to shake it off. "A guy hit a good pitch. Blooped it in there. So what? You got to get this guy out and keep us in the game. Get focused, get this guy out, and we'll win the game for you." That's how the conversation usually went in those situations. Or, I'd make fun of it. Say something like, "Geez, I hope it's not that bad next time." Or, say something completely unrelated to the game to make him laugh. Get his mind off what had just happened. Get him to take a deep breath and forget about it and move on. Of the guys I caught who won the Cy, Frankie got more flustered when things didn't go his way than the others did.

And, I wouldn't bullshit him. If he didn't have his best stuff, I'd tell him. I'd say, "Man, you've got shit today. We've got to figure something out." Or, if he asked, "How am I doing?" and he didn't have anything, I'd just give him this look that was kind of like, "Good luck." Then, we'd improvise and go to a "Plan B" because what he normally threw wasn't there. Frankie didn't mind. In fact, he liked hearing it. With some guys, I couldn't be so blunt. But, he was a no bullshit kind of guy, so I could tell him these things. Couldn't give him false hope. And, hearing it helped him focus on making the adjustments he needed to make. Helped him relax. I'd tell him, "Hey, we'll be okay. We just have to do things a little differently." But, I let him know that I believed in him. That I knew he could adjust, and we'd make it through the game.

Frankie and I worked with some good pitchers' umpires. Harry Wendelstedt and Frank Pulli called the balls and strikes for a couple of Frankie's games. Good guys to work with. I was very demanding of umpires. I expected them to be on top of their games. Give their best effort. So did Frankie. If he got a bad call, he could be kind of a crybaby. But, when I was catching him, Frankie could see my mouth moving. Hear me telling the umpire, "Hey, that pitch was pretty good. He's gonna need that pitch tonight." He knew I'd take care of it. He didn't need to worry about it. Didn't need to start mouthing off to the umpire because I was working on it for him. Kind of like an intermediary. Maybe I could sweet-talk the umpire into calling another five or ten pitches in his favor. Maybe that would turn a five inning outing into a seven inning outing. At the very least, it'd help him out. Calm him down so he wouldn't be distracted by the umpire.

Wendelstedt and Pulli, though, were guys who worked hard. They were fair. Had a good strike zone. Would call a few balls as strikes. This is good. The game can drag if you have an umpire who calls a ton of balls and has a strike zone the size of a shoe box. Plus, Wendelstedt and Pulli were guys that I enjoyed. We could talk about the game, certain situations, pretty girls in the stands. Pulli was a character. Sometimes, during the game, he'd slip me a punch in the ribs. I'd be like, "What was that for?"

"I don't like you," he said.

"Well, hell. You keep hitting me, maybe I'll let a ball get past and hit you."

"Nah," he said. "You won't do that. You're too quick for that."

If a ball did hit the umpire, Wendelstedt and Pulli were guys that you could give some shit to. Catchers get smoked with balls all of the time. Nobody notices. The catcher just keeps rolling. But, when an umpire gets hit with a ball, he falls to the ground. Flails around like he's stepped on a land mine or lost an arm. They have to get their five minutes off the clock. It looks ridiculous, but that's how it is.

I enjoyed Frankie. He had his rituals. Before days he pitched, he always ate a big pasta dinner. If he were on a win streak, he'd do the same routine. Put his uniform on the same way. Kick the rubber the same number of times before he pitched each inning. Eat at the same restaurant for lunch. One time, when he was with Minnesota, he made his wife eat with him at the same TGI Fridays like seventeen or eighteen starts in a row because he had a big win streak going. Threw the same number of warm-up pitches. Same number of long toss throws. Makes sense to me. I did a little bit of this. When I first went out to catch, I kicked out the back line and the catcher's box. They were all neat and pretty when I went out there, clean white lines, but I didn't like them, didn't like being closed in. It just became a habit I did before I played. I started it in high school and did it ever since. The main reason was because I didn't want to get chalk on me while I was blocking balls or moving around. Plus, when I was hitting, I tried to get as far back in the box as I could. If the line were marked out, I might be able to get back a little further. May give you three or four more inches. Give you a little more advantage, just a little more time to hit a fastball.

In the clubhouse, Frankie was a good teammate. Helped create a fun atmosphere. He had a high-pitched voice, New York accent all the way. He was always fun, always laughing. Everybody liked him. He would talk and keep talking, and guys were like, "Gah. He *never* shuts up." He liked to rib guys. Liked to be the center of attention. Sometimes, I swear he'd say stuff just to get a reaction for guys to flip him some shit. He and Johnny Franco bantered, and they entertained me, two East Coast guys who went way back—they both went to St. John's and played together in college—just going back and forth. Brooklyn (Franco) versus Long Island (Frankie). Brooklyn usually won. Franco was quick as hell, and he'd get on to Frankie about how weak he swung the bat. His hair. His clothes. Anything. Franco was one of the team's sharper dressers, but Frankie would wear plaid pants or something you might see on a golf course. That was an invitation for Franco to rag on him. Johnny Franco accepted it every chance he had.

One thing about Franco: he deserves to be in the Hall of Fame. One of the best left-handed relief pitchers of all time. Fierce competitor. Great stuff. One of those guys who'd do whatever it took to get a guy out. And, he was a great leader in the clubhouse. Like I said, the Mets had a crazy atmosphere where guys were having too much fun off the field and not being in shape to play a game the next day. Johnny Franco didn't stand for any of that. He'd jump on guys. Remind them that they were there to play baseball, not to drink, do coke, go to strip clubs, or whatever the hell guys were getting in to. He demanded guys to go out there and bust their ass. He was great for that club. A stabilizing effect.

Frankie and I played together two times: with the Mets in the early nineties and in '96 with the Toronto Blue Jays. When I played with him in Toronto, he'd been released by the Reds. I think he spent some time in the minor leagues to work to get back to the big leagues. He was glad to see me. He felt comfortable around me because I had caught him before. Being in a new situation with a new team, you're on edge a little bit. It's nice to see a familiar face, someone who you can ask how their family is doing and talk baseball: about the situation he was coming from, how the manager was, who he played with, and so on. He hadn't changed at all as a person. He still laughed and had a good time, but he wasn't the same pitcher. His stuff wasn't as hard. He'd lost some velocity. His breaking ball wasn't as sharp and crisp because the arm speed wasn't there. He'd thrown a lot of innings over his career, and the wear and tear just slows things down. I experienced the same thing toward the end of my career. In my mind, I thought I was still throwing the ball well, but I wasn't—the ball wasn't getting to the target as accurately and as fast as it used to. His changeup was still good, though, and I caught him in a couple of games. In one, he got the loss against Boston. He gave up a few hits in the beginning, but then he settled down. Pitched good baseball until the middle of the game. Then he gave up some bloopers but no hard hit balls, and he was pulled. The next game I caught with him wound up being his last big league win. He pitched well. Gave up a few hits and one run. Solo home run, I think. He wasn't overpowering, but he was effective. Later, the club decided to go in a different direction and released him. It's too bad because I think the club brought him in as a veteran pitcher to help mold Sandy Martinez, our young catcher. But, Frankie was coming back from elbow surgery. He was unsure of himself, still getting comfortable. At that time, Frankie really needed some help from his catcher to get him through games. He just wasn't in a position to be teaching a young catcher how to call a game.

I remember talking with him after he found out he had been let go. We were sitting in the players' lounge in Yankee Stadium where they set up food for us after games.

"What should I do?" he asked me. He had tears in his eyes. I understood why. He had busted his butt to get back to the big leagues, but somebody was telling him it was the end of the road. One time, he'd been one of the best pitchers in the league. Now, a club was telling him he wasn't good enough for their roster. I felt bad for him. You hate to see that.

I told him to keep playing. Try to pick up with a team somewhere.

"Do you think I can still pitch? Do I have anything left in me?"

"You've got a lot left in you. You can still get people out."

I was honest with him. His fastball was a little short, but he still had a good changeup. Still changed speeds well. A left-handed guy like him, he could pitch well and get guys out at the big league level. The only thing was that maybe he'd have to accept the fact that his role was changing. Instead of being the number one starter, maybe he'd be a team's number five starter. Maybe more of a situational spot starter, a guy pitching out of the bullpen. A veteran who could work with a young staff. With the way he was pitching and with his experience winning a World Series, he could've played an effective role on a contending team. I guess he didn't want to pursue that. Maybe the offers weren't there. He hung it up after that.

Later on, I asked him, "Man, why didn't you keep pitching?"

Frankie laughed. He said, "You know, you're the last person I talked to in baseball. Last guy I talked to about my situation."

He said that our pitching coach, Mel Queen, had gotten in his head. Convinced him that he couldn't pitch any more.

"Besides," Frankie said. "It all worked out. Got to spend some more time with my kids. Watch them grow up."

I get it. Playing ball, you go for long stretches away from your family. Spring training, first part of the season, the kids are still in school. They stay home while you're gone. Then, when school lets out, they move for the summer and join you. That's good, but even then, the team goes on road trips. You're away for a week, ten days. That time away, the little league games, the everyday things that happen at home, all that stuff goes on without you. You miss a lot. And, you don't get that time back.

CHAPTER 4

DWIGHT GOODEN

Charlie wouldn't be as nice as other catchers when he approached you and with what he said. Other catchers might say, "Come on, Doc. Stay with me. It'll come." But Charlie was more demanding. He'd say, "You're out here, bullshitting around. You got to give me what you got. You've got to tighten up. You're better than this. Let's go." And, if you didn't, he'd fire the ball back at you pretty good. He was very direct. He would get right in your face, basically nose-to-nose, if he felt like you weren't giving one hundred percent out there or that you weren't giving it your all every pitch. It didn't matter if you had a one run lead or a ten run lead.

—*Dwight Gooden*

[*Note: In 1985, Dwight Gooden was baseball's dominant pitcher, winning the Cy Young Award with twenty-four wins, 268 strikeouts, and a minuscule 1.53 earned run average.[1] Only twenty years old and in his second year in the big leagues, Gooden was the face of Major League Baseball and the star of New York City. Fans decorated the railings of Shea Stadium with "K's" each time he rung up a strikeout, and his image, midwindup, adorned a stories-high mural in Times Square.[2]*

A few years later (late 1990 through 1992), Charlie served as Gooden's personal catcher. While he did not match his early career glory, Gooden was still one of the game's best pitchers. Indeed, during some of their early starts together, Gooden averaged nearly a strikeout per inning.[3] In 1991, the dominance waned when Gooden injured his rotator cuff. While he continued to pitch solidly after returning from the injury, Gooden was transitioning from a power pitcher to more of a finesse pitcher, relying on pitching smarts and deception to get hitters out.

After Charlie left the Mets as a free agent, Gooden was suspended from Major League Baseball for violating its drug policy.[4] He missed parts of the 1994 season and all of 1995 before returning as a member of the New York Yankees. He capped his comeback with a no-hitter against the Seattle Mariners on May 14, 1996, and he was a part of the 1996 Yankees team that won the World Series.

In 2001, Gooden retired. He played sixteen seasons with 194 wins, 116 losses, a 3.51 ERA, and 2,293 strikeouts. Charlie caught Gooden in fifty-nine games, with twenty-four wins and twenty losses.[5]]

A fter I was traded to New York, I moved into Dwight Gooden's basement. I'd been in New York for a day at the most when Dwight came up to me and said, "You can stay in my basement."

"What?"

"Until you find a place, stay in my basement. I've got plenty of room. You can have it all to yourself. Stay as long as you want."

So, that's where I lived in September 1990. I spent time with Dwight and his family. Got to know his wife, Monica. She was so down-to-earth and calm. Had this peacefulness to her and was very likeable. Dwight lent me a car to drive back and forth to the yard. It was kind of like a Jeep that had a big picture of a black Bart Simpson on the spare tire cover. Dwight made me feel so at home, and he didn't have to do anything like that for me. From that start, we spent a lot of time together. We'd go to concerts. Shoot pool in his basement. Listen to music. I'm a big soul music fan, mainly old stuff from the seventies like Barry White. Earth, Wind, and Fire. LTD. Dwight liked soul music too. We joked and laughed. Just a good dude.

I think one of the reasons why he and I clicked was because when I played in Milwaukee, one of my teammates was Gary Sheffield. He's Dwight's nephew. I'll bet that, when Milwaukee traded me to New York, Sheff called Doc and told him to look out for me. Sheff was a great teammate. Extremely competitive and talented, one of the best guys I ever played with. He and I got along real well. With Dwight being his uncle, Sheff wasn't real impressed with or intimidated by many players. One time, when Sheff was still pretty new to the league, we were playing against Texas in Arlington. Nolan Ryan was pitching for the Rangers. The first pitch Nolan threw, Sheff yanked a bullet foul. The next pitch, Nolan threw it right at Sheff's head. Knocked him in the dirt. He got up, dusted himself off. Next pitch, he ripped another bullet foul. Then Nolan aimed for his head again. So, it's a 2-2 count, and Sheffield hit another fastball foul. Broke his bat on the pitch, but he didn't leave the box. He was so mad, and he wanted to hit Nolan so badly that he dug in for the next pitch. It zipped in at his head again. 3-2 count. He wound up walking, and when he flipped the bat toward the dugout, the bat split in half. Later, I asked him, "Dude, what happened?"

He said, "Damn, that dude pissed me off. He broke my bat, but I didn't care. I was going to hit him."

That's Gary Sheffield. Phenomenal bat speed. I knew he was going to be a special player. He could hit, run, and throw. Could do nearly anything he wanted to. Wound up putting together a Hall of Fame career.

Inviting me to live in his basement shows you what a friendly and likeable guy Dwight is. I've heard the stories about drug and alcohol abuse. Brushes with the law. I think it just shows you what a pull drugs can have on people, that they affect good people, honest people, just as much as they affect bad ones. Dwight's struggles with drugs have cost him a lot. Part of his career. His family. I hate that for him. For his family. But, he is one of the finer people I've ever met. He is so unassuming. He was one of the best pitchers in the league when I played with him. Some guys, when they're in that position, they think they're better than a lot of people. That they're entitled to special treatment. Not Dwight. He worked with rookies. Taught them tips he'd picked up and how to pitch and conduct themselves like professionals. Some guys, when they reach a certain level, they could be real difficult or even challenging to deal with, but Dwight was just a nice, loyal guy. Good to everybody. And, every single guy on the team loved Doc. You just liked being around him. To this day, I'd be willing to do whatever to help him. Of all the guys I played with, Dwight is one of my favorites, if not the favorite.

At the same time, Dwight could be too nice. He'd be surrounded by some hanger-on and sports memorabilia riff-raff, people who just wanted a piece of him. I'd ask him, "Why are you hanging out with that guy? He's not any good."

Dwight would smile and say, "No, he's okay."

Part of that was his personality. He's a pleaser. Wanted to make everyone happy. Be everybody's friend. With pleasers, if somebody says something you don't like, you just let it go. You don't say anything. You don't want to make waves or create any conflict. That's how it was with Dwight. So, if some losers wanted to latch on to him, Dwight didn't want to hurt anybody's feelings and tell them to get lost. And, he had tons of these guys around him. He was getting tickets for them, they were hanging out in the clubhouse. He was the same way with the media. In one way, he was good with the media. He was honest. Up-front. But, he was too accessible. In New York, they take advantage of nice people. The media would say some shitty things about him. Instead of cutting them off, he kept dealing with them and giving them his time.

You'd see this pleaser side of him on the baseball field too. We didn't disagree much on pitch selections, but, if we did, he'd just laugh about how he kept shaking me off but I kept putting the same sign down. I'll admit: I could be stubborn with him. He wouldn't argue a whole lot. Didn't like confrontation. Guys on the team could be shitty to him, but Dwight would still be nice to them. If he had a rough outing, it ate at him. He'd go to Mel Stottlemyre, our pitching coach, and ask, "How can I fix things?" Then he'd adjust his mechanics. More than any other pitcher I worked with, he was *always* tinkering with his delivery. I think this was Dwight trying to please the coaches or other people when, if anything, he listened to too many people. At some point, you have to please yourself. Be satisfied with how you're doing things instead of trying to please everybody else. I don't know that Dwight ever reached that point. I just wish he would have said, "Screw you. This is how I throw. This works for me, and I'm sticking with it. Leave me alone." And, off the field, if he had said, "Screw you. I'm going home to take care of my family," instead of hanging out with some of the losers he was with. But, he didn't. If he had, and if he kept pitching with what got him to the big leagues and what got him such great results, he would've been just fine. In a way, he was rudderless. A follower. He didn't have the personality to stand up for himself. Which doesn't make sense. He had a *gift*. Had a great arm. Knew how to pitch. Knew how to battle. But, he didn't realize how good he really was. He needed a leader to guide him. Sometimes, he followed the wrong folks and made bad choices. Like Darryl Strawberry. I lay a lot of blame on him. He was a partyer, somebody who'd stay out late the night before and be in no shape to play the next day. I think he contributed a lot to leading Dwight astray.

I tried to help Dwight. When we were on the road, I'd take him out to eat. We'd talk baseball. How we handled game situations. What we should do differently next time. We'd talk about our families. Our hobbies. Dwight liked pick-up basketball games and Nintendo's RBI Baseball. I'd BS and tease him too. Say stuff like, "Black, you better take care of Monica. You don't, I'm gonna make a move."

He'd laugh. "Soul Man, you couldn't handle Monica."

We flipped each other shit. He made fun of me, saying I was the only white catcher in the league with curly hair, that I had a Jheri-curl. I enjoyed being around him. But, there were times when he'd disappear. And, I knew he had past struggles with drugs, but I couldn't tell for sure that he was still battling those demons. I never saw him drunk. Never saw him with cocaine. He did a good job of keeping that under wraps. I think some of the managers turned a blind eye to it and just ignored it. Not Dallas Green, though. I think one of the reasons why they brought him in in '93 was to clean up some of the shit that was going on off the field with some of our guys.

I was excited the first time I caught Dwight. I had worked with Teddy Higuera, our ace in Milwaukee, who had Cy Young Award caliber stuff. One year, I caught Teddy, and he won twenty-one or twenty-two games. He should've won the Cy, but he was hosed out of it. Even so, Dwight was a notch above. He threw real hard. Liked to challenge guys with his fastball, especially those free-swinging power hitter types. His fastball got to the plate in a hurry. He could throw ninety-five, sometimes ninety-eight miles an hour. Electrifying. Threw up and in the zone a bunch. Hitters had a hell of a time catching up with the ball—his arm was just nasty. Few guys could throw as hard. On top of his fastball, he also threw a good curveball and changeup. Dwight was another high pitch count guy with lots of 2-2 and 3-2 counts. This was because he threw high in the strike zone. Some guys swung and missed, but some guys would take these pitches, and some would be called balls. That meant that Dwight would have to throw more pitches. When I played with him, I wouldn't call him a control pitcher. I think he refined his control once he went over to the Yankees and mastered his mechanics, knowing that he couldn't rely on power alone. Even so, with the Mets, he wasn't a big walk guy.

We had one opening day game at Shea Stadium in miserable conditions. Cold and rainy. Not a good day to pitch in, but everybody's excited. Sellout crowd. Our manager, Buddy Harrelson, left Dwight in for the whole game. He threw a ton of pitches, close to 150. That's crazy for any game, much less the first day of the season when pitchers are still getting in to shape. Especially when the conditions were awful for keeping your arm warmed up and loose.

Dwight didn't say a word. Never complained. That didn't surprise me. He wasn't real vocal. But, he was a leader in the sense of "Watch me and how I do my work." He got to the park early. Stayed late. Ran and did his rubber band conditioning exercises. Studied hitters. He was prepared, and he went out to the mound and took the ball every fifth day. And, I guess I think about that game and Dwight going out there inning after inning in the cold and the rain and never complaining about it, and he sent a message to the team. That he'd do whatever it took for us to win. He didn't have to tell us this in a clubhouse speech. He spoke through his actions. He was a gamer. He'd never tell the manager that yeah, he was done, time to bring in a reliever. That's great and all, but sometimes I think about that game, how cold and damp it was, the number of pitches he threw, and I wonder if that had anything to do with his rotator cuff injury later that year. You never know.

Another game with Dwight tested my character. Dutch Rennert was the home plate umpire. One of his last games before he retired. We were playing a day game, and Dwight was in the sun on the mound. Home plate was in the shadows. When you're in the shadows, it's tough to keep a good bead on the ball from the pitcher's hand to home plate because of how the light changes along the ball's path. Dutch was a pretty good age, and we were cruising along in the game when Dutch says, "O'B. You got to help me here."

"What's the deal?"

"I can't see the ball."

"You can't see the ball?"

"Look. Here's what we're going to do. I'm going to trust you. If you catch the ball and hold it there, I'm going to call it a strike. If you catch it and throw it back real quick, that one's going to be a ball."

I said, "Good enough."

And, I tried to do a good job. He was honest with me. I appreciated it. Kept me from getting on to him about missing balls and strikes. But, I felt like I was being tested. That I had to do the right thing. That I couldn't take advantage of the deal we struck. Dutch was right there with me. When I threw the ball back to the mound quickly, he called them balls. If I held the ball for a second, he called them strikes. He was real dramatic in how he called strikes. He'd step from behind the plate, and he had this booming call. A couple of times when we first started, I threw a ball back too quickly, and I was like, "Oh, man. I forgot. That was a strike."

Dutch said, "Better hold it there then."

A couple times, he called pitches balls, and I asked him, "I didn't hold it there long enough for you?"

He said, "No. Got to hold it."

That happened to me that one time only. Dwight pitched great. I don't think it made much of a difference in the game. Like I said, I tried to be fair. Did my best to make the right call for Dutch. And, it doesn't surprise me that this happened with Dwight pitching. Umpires liked him. He didn't bitch about bad calls. He just competed. Earned their respect that way. He usually got a lot of good calls because he threw most of his pitches near the strike zone. His ball was nice and straight, and he was an easy one to call balls and strikes for because his pitches were clear to see and didn't move around too much. It makes sense now: if an umpire was going to give anybody the benefit of the doubt, it'd be Dwight Gooden.

I played with Dwight for parts of four seasons. We reached a point where I caught most of his starts. We got along well. Everybody could see that we hung out a lot. He was comfortable with me, and we had a good chemistry.

Before games, Dwight had his routine. If he was pitching in a night game, he liked to wash his car before he came to the park. That superstition started in the minor leagues. He was having a rough start to the season. His record was something like 0-3 or 0-4. He had a night game, washed his car that day, and then he threw a shutout. After that, he made washing his car part of his ritual. He was particular about what he ate on game days too. He liked an egg white and turkey bacon wrap for breakfast and an Italian sub for lunch. Then something light in the afternoon like half a tuna sandwich.

When he arrived at the park, we'd get together with Stottlemyre and review the lineups. Discuss hitters' strengths and weaknesses and how we should pitch to guys. Unlike a lot of pitchers, Dwight had a great memory of what pitches he threw before to get guys out. He used that knowledge to make pitch selections. He was right on with what he was trying to do, and we'd go with a game plan put together by all of us, really.

After that, Dwight loosened up slowly. He'd play some catch in the outfield, then graduate to some long toss. Then he might work on his curveball. Ask me to move closer to him, not the usual distance of sixty feet and six inches from the mound to home plate. Then Dwight would cut it off and go back to the clubhouse. Drink some juice. Put on his headset and listen to this mellow gospel song, "Optimistic" by Sounds of Blackness. About thirty minutes before the game, he'd go out to the bullpen and warm up. Then he'd come back to the clubhouse and spend a few minutes alone. Think about the lineup he was getting ready to face. Then he'd step out there.

Once the game started, I tried to establish a good tempo. Dwight liked to work quickly. Wanted to get on the rubber and go. Didn't stand around and second-guess the pitches I was calling. My job was to get him going and into a good rhythm early because, if he had any problems, it'd be in the first few innings. Once he was settled in, he wasn't going to give up many runs or lose many games late in the game.

In between innings, I'd sit next to Doc. Talk about what worked well the inning before. Tell him how I thought we should handle the next guys up in the following inning. And, I always asked, "What do you think? You okay with that?" Always asked for his opinion. Some catchers, they'd talk to Doc in between innings only if he was struggling. Encourage him, pat him on the ass kind of thing. But, I did it all the time, good inning or bad.

If he struggled, I'd sometimes suggest minor adjustments. Get him to bring the ball down by bending over a little more in his delivery. Sometimes, he'd throw with his arm too high or too low. So, from behind the plate, I motioned up or down with my hands. Dwight knew what I meant by that and adjusted his arm level. Or, I'd ask him to mix in some more changeups. I picked up on what was working best for him on a given night, and I based my pitch selection on that. If his curveball was really good, I asked him to use his fastball as a show-me pitch, close to the plate but out of the strike zone to set up the curveball for a strike. Really, his only weakness was that he didn't hold base runners on very well. He had a slow delivery to the plate. And, if he had a tough outing, I don't think he forgot about things very well. He had a hard time just taking what he could from a bad game, learning from it, and then forgetting about it and moving on. Some days just aren't meant to be. Things that are out of your control happen, and you lose. And, I think that's one of the reasons why he was always working on his mechanics and trying to improve. But, baseball can be a tough game. My advice: keep things simple. If you keep tweaking and making it complicated, it'll eat you up.

As far as handling Doc, what I did depended on the situation. If he wasn't throwing his best stuff, I'd catch the ball so the glove really popped. Make it sound like his fastball was humming. That he was throwing harder than he really was. That did a couple of things. The main thing was boosting his confidence. Made him think that he had his good fastball. It also kept him from overthrowing or trying to do too much.

Sometimes, if he was trying to find a pitch that just wasn't quite right yet, I'd pump my fist. I didn't have to say anything, but the message was clear: "Come on, man. Stick with it. You've got it" kind of thing. I was pulling for him, and I knew he'd make it work.

If I didn't think he was giving his best effort, I'd fire the ball back to him as hard as I could. Or, I'd pound the hell out of my glove. That message was, "Step it up." And, sometimes, if he was getting hit and hanging his head a little, I'd go out to the mound and tell him, "Hey. Keep pitching. Concentrate on getting the ball where I want it. You're just out here, going through the motions." Dwight responded well when I pushed him. I guess other catchers were softer on him than I was, almost coaxing him. But, I knew that, sometimes, I had to push his buttons. That I needed to get in his face. The bottom line is that we worked well together. He had confidence in the pitches I called. He knew I did my homework, knew the hitters. He saw me as a pitching coach behind the plate. Almost like a security blanket, a guy he could rely on for the right pitch selection, the right location.

––––––––––

Dwight was a tremendous athlete. Could flat hit. Used a big, heavy bat, and he worked on his hitting. Wanted to be productive in that nine spot. Nearly every time he went up to the plate, he said, "I'm gonna take this guy deep." One time, he actually did. Off John Smoltz. I'd figured out a hitch in Smoltz's delivery, and I could tell when he was going to throw his curveball or his fastball. So, when Doc went up to the box to hit, I told him, "If you hear me say 'Doc' or something, it's a breaking ball. If you don't hear me, it's a fastball." I watched Smoltz and could tell it was his fastball. So, I didn't say anything. Dwight started his swing early. Launched it. Later, Doc said he owed me credit for the home run.

You could see his athleticism in how he evolved as a pitcher and dealt with injuries. At first, his stuff was heat. He'd throw high fastball after high fastball. No way hitters could catch up to him. But, after his rotator cuff surgery, he had to adjust. His fastball didn't have the same mid-nineties velocity anymore. That's typical for rotator cuff problems: you lose your velocity. Guys with elbow problems can come back and reach the same velocity they threw before, but, with a rotator cuff injury, it just doesn't happen. And, when Dwight came back from his injury, he stayed stiffer longer. Sometimes, he had a hell of a time warming up—his arm just wouldn't get loose. He adapted, though. He had to become a complete pitcher. Early in his career, if he got behind a hitter with a 3-2 count, everybody in the stadium knew that he'd throw a fastball to strike the guy out. Overpower him. Dwight couldn't do that after the surgery. He had to rely more on location, pitch selection. And, I'd help Doc with these things on his side day, his bullpen session in between starts. Usually, the bullpen catcher works with pitchers on their side days, but every chance I had, I went down to the bullpen and caught Dwight. And, he made a good transition. He developed a changeup and a slider. He still had his competitor's makeup where he battled against a hitter and wouldn't back down. Knew how to pitch. Had a good feel for the right time to throw the right pitch in the right location or when to change speeds to get a guy out. Figured out how to use his curveball earlier in the count. In some ways, he learned how to pitch backward and mix curveballs and changeups in counts where before, he relied on his fastball to put guys away. And, even though his win-loss record didn't compare to his early career, he still pitched well. His ERA was in the threes the years I caught him. He threw 200 innings, piled up a ton of strikeouts. Competed like hell even though we were on a shitty team. The dude was just a winner.

Dwight played the game the right way. The last game I caught him, the umpire tossed him in the third inning because the umpire thought Dwight was intentionally throwing at a hitter. In truth, Dwight was playing the game the way it's supposed to be played. We were facing the Reds, and Reggie Sanders hit a home run in the second inning. Took his time trotting around the bases. Next half of the inning, I got hit with a pitch. Don't know why, but I got drilled. Next half inning, Dwight hits one of their guys. The umpire steps in. Tries to show he knows how to manage the game, so he ejects Doc. That just shows ignorance about how the game should be played. The deal is: you hit one of our guys, we hit one of yours. Tit for tat. That's just how it is, and that's the right way to do things. That's how the game has been played for one hundred years. This tradition is one of the great things about baseball. It's about taking care of your teammates, your friends. Dwight didn't hesitate to smoke a dude to make things right. The umpire really crossed the line in trying to referee the situation. Teams police themselves. In these situations, they don't need an umpire, who's never been in a game, interfering. Players keep other players in check. You protect each other. It keeps the other guys from throwing at you. Sometimes, umpires think they're bigger than the game, and they get involved when they shouldn't.

Another time, I think Jerry Layne was the home plate umpire. It was the damnedest thing, but, if there were a foul ball, Layne wouldn't give me a new baseball to throw back to Doc. Layne had to throw it to him. I liked to throw the ball back to the pitcher so I could keep my arm loose, but Layne said no, he'd throw the balls back to the pitcher. Pissed me off. So, when Layne would throw a ball to Dwight, I'd kind of jump in front of him. Kind of block him and try to throw off his delivery. Dwight said he never saw anything like that. Told me he was surprised I wasn't thrown out of the game. The deal is that throwing the ball back to the pitcher was my job, not the umpire's. Again, sometimes, these guys get involved where they have no business being a part of the game.

Managers were pretty hands-off with Doc. Like Jeff Torborg. Nice guy. His management style worked well with a lot of veteran players. Didn't get in your face. He just expected guys to go out every day and work hard and do their best. How he played. In most situations, that style works fine. Not with our team. Like I said, the Mets had a wild bunch of guys. Guys took advantage of Jeff's trust in us that we'd be prepared to play, and they didn't give it their all. Guys would dick around. Have a good time the night before and not be in any kind of shape to play. It's too bad. Those guys really cheated their teammates, the entire organization really.

When I look back on it, I think Dwight just loved to play baseball, loved to pitch. All around him in New York was chaos and attention, and he liked the spotlight. He tried to play that whole game, of being the man, the marquee player of the team. Maybe even the league. But, part of this didn't fit his personality. After the game, he'd hang out with some shady people who didn't have his best interests in mind. Like I said, Dwight was a pleaser. Didn't want to piss anybody off. It just led to some bad influences that were too much for him. Or, when he got hurt and had too much spare time on his hands, he couldn't handle all of those off-the-field distractions. I think the pull from so many different people and hangers-on was overwhelming for him. He was most at peace on the ball field. If he could have spent more of his time on the field, he'd have been a lot better off. And, I loved playing with him. One of my favorite guys to catch, one of my favorite guys in baseball. Later on, when he was with the Yankees, and I was with Toronto or the White Sox, he always took time out to catch up with me. Since we left baseball, our paths haven't crossed much. It's too bad. Like I said, I know he's had his struggles with drugs and alcohol. I think he's healthy now. I'm glad. He's a great dude. I'm pulling for him.

CHAPTER 5

BRET SABERHAGEN

Charlie is one of the top four guys I worked with. You know, I had a lot of catchers catch me. I played in sixteen active, eighteen overall years in the big leagues. By far, I'd put him up there with Bob Boone, Jimmy Sundberg, and Jason Varitek. One of the best receivers that I was ever around. It was very impressive how he handled his pitchers, and the knowledge that he had. Really on the same page with you. You want to throw a certain pitch, and that's what he's calling for you. Not a lot of shaking off with him. It was a pleasure to have him behind the plate. With him, I knew I was going to get a well-called game and a well-caught game. He made catching look pretty damn easy, and it wasn't.

—*Bret Saberhagen*

[*Note: After Frank Viola departed the Mets as a free agent following the 1991 season, the Mets traded for Bret Saberhagen, sending Kevin McReynolds, Gregg Jefferies, and Keith Miller to the Kansas City Royals. In addition, the Mets signed outfielder Bobby Bonilla to a five year, $29 million free agency contract making him the highest paid player in Major League Baseball. They also picked up future Hall of Famer Eddie Murray to play first base.[1] Despite the roster shake-up, the Mets continued to lose, going 72-90 in 1992 (fifth place, twenty-four games out of first place), and 59-103 in 1993 (last place, thirty-eight games out of first place).[2] The 1993 Mets earned the distinction of being known as "The Worst Team Money Could Buy."[3]*

While Saberhagen posted dazzling numbers in prior seasons that were good enough for him to win two Cy Young Awards (in 1985, he won twenty games, maintained a 2.87 earned run average, and threw ten complete games; in 1989, he led the American League in wins, ERA, and complete games), he suffered a variety of injuries while with New York that prevented him from performing at a similar level.[4] In 1992, Saberhagen won three games and lost five, pitching only 97 ⅔ innings.[5] Of these games, Charlie caught two (both no decisions). The pattern continued in 1993 when Saberhagen's won-

loss record was 7-7 with a 3.29 ERA. He pitched 139 ⅓ innings and threw ninety-three strikeouts.[6] Charlie caught seven of these games (one no decision and six losses).

For his career, Saberhagen played for sixteen seasons with the Royals, Mets, Boston Red Sox, and Colorado Rockies. He won 167 games, lost 117, had a 3.34 ERA, and threw 1,715 strikeouts.[7]]

When I heard the Mets traded for Sabes, I thought it was a great move, even though the trade meant losing Kevin McReynolds who was one of my closest friends on the team. McReynolds liked to hunt like I do, and he was country. Loved to eat frog legs shipped from Arkansas. He'd say, "What's up, Chuck?" Took him forever to drawl those three words out. I hated to see McReynolds go, but I knew Sabes would help our team. He was one of the best pitchers in the league. When he was healthy, he could dominate. If anybody came close to Roger Clemens with the ability to throw hard with great control, it was Sabes. He could overpower hitters with a ninety-seven mile per hour fastball, and he was precise enough to hit a gnat in the ass. When I played with Milwaukee, I hated hitting against him. He was one of the two toughest right-handed pitchers I ever faced (Clemens was the other). Sabes made it hard because he never gave you a good pitch to hit. He threw the ball down and away or jammed you inside. You might face him three or four times. In all of those at-bats, you might get one hittable pitch. I couldn't hit any of them. As a hitter, it was very discouraging. Catching him made me realize why he was so difficult to hit: his pinpoint control. With his placing the ball anywhere I wanted it to go, catching him was fun. No question I'd rather catch him than try to hit him.

Sabes's stuff was electric. Threw a power hook and a great changeup. His changeup was probably eighty-five to eighty-seven miles per hour—slow enough to throw off the hitter's timing. Had a little sink action to it. He was primarily a power pitcher, though. Threw a straight fastball. Didn't have much movement to it, but he could put it anywhere he wanted. And, when he threw, he looked so natural. Some guys, when they release the ball, they grunt and strain. Looks like they're forcing things and working hard to pitch. With Sabes, the ball just jumped from his hand. He didn't look like he was throwing that hard, but after he released, the ball was all over you. He got on top of the baseball well; it was going straight downhill. This downward angle makes it harder to hit—a hitter is going to have to drop the bat lower to make contact with the ball. Makes for a lot of fly ball outs.

Kind of like the naturalness of his delivery, his ball had a soft touch. For guys like Clemens who also threw hard, their pitches pounded the glove. I think it has to do with the number of revolutions the ball makes. With fewer revolutions, the ball feels heavier. Sabes's fastball got to the plate in a hurry but was easy to catch. Felt light. It was effective, too. I'd heard that he was a great curveball pitcher, but when I played with him, he relied on his fastball more than anything. Threw probably eighty percent fastballs and twenty percent breaking balls. It was such a great pitch that my goal was to establish his fastball and then start working the corners of the plate with it.

When I walked in the clubhouse and found out that I was catching Sabes, I reviewed the notes I kept about the other team. What their hitters liked and didn't like. While he was in the training room getting ready for the game, we went over how we'd handle certain guys. He was pretty deferential to my suggestions. He trusted how I called a game. I'd sign for a pitch, and Sabes was right there with me. Rarely shook me off. So, we established a good rhythm and kept the game moving. Worked fast. Some of the guys on the Mets took the opposite approach, like Sid Fernandez. Sid's a talented guy, a great pitcher. But, he liked to work slow. Had a slow rhythm, slow everything. Just drew everything out. It could be agonizing at times.

Because of Sabes's control, I was kind of like a puppeteer pulling strings the way I could ask him to place a ball, and he could hit the glove wherever it went. If I wanted a curveball in the dirt, I could sign for a hook and put my glove on the ground. That told Sabes, "Don't worry. I want this ball in the dirt. I'll block whatever you throw." He had great command of everything he threw. I really can't remember any games when he had control problems. Sure, he had some games when he didn't have his best stuff, but he could always locate the ball well. Put it in places where guys couldn't hit it or couldn't hit it very well. With this, it was easier to improvise. Most guys don't have the luxury of painting the outside part of the plate with an eighty-five mile per hour fastball and keeping the ball away from hitters and still doing all right when they don't have their best stuff.

Sabes was a guy I could challenge. Go out to the mound and say, "Pull your head out of your ass." Tell him like it was—if he kept throwing bullshit up to the plate, he was going to get his ass kicked around a little bit, and he'd be sitting in the dugout in no time. That fired him up. If you told him he couldn't do something, he'd dig deep to prove you wrong. One time, I heard Sabes say that, if he ever got in a fight with a big guy, he might get the shit beat out of him, but the big guy wouldn't want to mess with him again. That mentality carried over to the field. Competitive as hell. Like a bulldog out there. You get in his face, and he'd fight back.

After the game, he was pretty open to hearing my ideas about what he could do the next time around. If it were a good game, I'd tell him good job. If it were an average game, I'd point out some things like, "Hey, in between starts, you might want to work on a couple of things." Maybe a tweak to his delivery. Something that only I could see and that a pitching coach in the dugout couldn't pick up on.

Sabes was a professional. Even though we weren't a good club, he went out and pitched well. We had a few games where he pitched well enough for us to win, but the offense didn't provide good run support or the defense made some errors and allowed some runs to score. We lost a few 2-1 games when he did his job on the mound. Like I've said, defensively, we were unstable with several guys playing positions that were new to them. It's tough to learn a new position at a big league level. These kind of roster moves killed us defensively. Throw in a couple of injuries and a lack of depth at the Triple A level with guys who could step in and play well, and it's obvious why our seasons went south. But, Sabes handled this adversity well. Even though he wasn't putting up the numbers like he did in the past, he pitched well. Putting aside the win-loss record, he had a good earned run average. Had only a few walks (in '93, he had only seventeen walks in 139 ⅓ innings pitched—that's an incredible ratio). He was disappointed that the injuries prevented him from making all of his starts, but he didn't let the negatives weigh him down.

Talking about the losing: after Dallas Green became the manager in '93, I got fed up with the team. We were a long way out of first place, and I saw that guys weren't giving any effort. Going through the motions. Not caring like they should have. I hated to lose, so I went to the coaches and asked if I could call a team meeting. They said sure, so I did. I was like, "Some of us are more interested in getting out of here and going home or hitting the streets than we are in taking care of our work." I just said that we needed to get focused on what we're supposed to be doing. Why were we there? To play baseball. We needed to be accountable for that. I wanted to play and do well, and I hated playing on a shitty team. And, that's what we were.

I'd like to say that my talk ignited a fire under the team. That our intensity improved. But, I don't know that I saw much of a difference. That's part of what you have to do as a leader. Step up and hold people accountable. Tell them to look in the mirror and ask themselves if they were doing all they could to help the team. I felt like I had to do my part and put the issue out in the open. If I didn't, if I just sat there and said nothing, then I was part of the problem. Then I was just blaming everybody else. Then I was getting comfortable with losing and half-assing it. I hated being in last place. We had too many talented people to be in last. I was going to do what I could to get us out of the rut.

Sabes and I worked with some good umpires. John McSherry called the balls and strikes for one game. I liked Big John. So did everyone else. He did a good job behind the plate. Had a fair and consistent strike zone. Plus, he was a nice guy. He'd ask how you were doing. Talk to you during the game. And, you could ask him questions about why he made certain decisions, and he didn't take it personally. He understood that I was just trying to figure out where he was going so I could adjust. He didn't get mad about any of it. He was such a nice guy that I couldn't get on to him like I could other umpires.

Ed Montague, though. Different story. Ed had a real small strike zone. About the size of a shoe box. What I liked about Ed was that he was consistent with it. But, his small strike zone made the game much tougher for the pitcher and the catcher. Unlike John, Ed was not personable. Had a real short fuse. If you asked him a question about why a pitch was a ball, he'd get offended. Kind of a "How dare you question me?" reaction.

A typical conversation with Ed might go something like this. After I caught a pitch that I thought was a strike but that Ed called a ball, I'd throw the ball back to Sabes and say, "Looked like a pretty good pitch there."

Usually, if I said anything to Ed, I wouldn't get a response. So, I'd say something like, "Oh. So I guess I can't ask you any questions?"

"That wasn't even close," he would say.

The conversation would dwindle from there. And, I'd think, bullshit. I've been catching pitches all of my life. I know a good pitch from a bad one. I had a tough time dealing with those cats that didn't respect what I did. But, that's one of the things you learn: which umpires you can talk to and which ones where you need to keep your mouth shut. Games can be long. It helps pass the time, makes it more enjoyable if you can shoot the shit a little with the guy behind you. Have a nice little back and forth going during the game. But, some guys, you just learn not to even try. Don't even waste your time. And, if a ball is in the dirt, well, maybe you don't block it. Maybe you let it beat the fire out of the umpire. That's kind of what you're hoping.

Other guys, though, like Doug Harvey and Bruce Froemming, had the right attitude. Always made a great effort. Harvey was a Hall of Fame umpire and enjoyable to deal with. Like John McSherry, you could ask Harvey questions about his balls and strikes calls, and he wouldn't get offended. You ask him where a ball was, and he'd say, "No, it was outside. Didn't like it. Why? Did you like it?"

"Yeah, I thought it was a pretty good pitch. Did I get in your way or something?"

Then he may say, "Okay. I'll try to watch it a little closer," or "No, I had a pretty good look at it." And, that would be the end of it. Or, he might say, "Ah, you know what? I think I missed that one."

And, I'd say, "Well, good, because I thought the same thing."

He'd laugh. That's what was fun about working with umpires and trying to get things ironed out. I wouldn't bitch about balls that were outside. And, if they didn't like what I said, that fired me up. Then, I'd start asking all sorts of questions. Especially with younger guys.

"That looked like a pretty good pitch," I'd say.

"No. No question it was a ball."

"Oh. So, that's how it's going to go?"

"What do you mean?"

"I know they prep you new guys, tell you that some guys like me are going to push you, say some shit to you."

He'd just listen.

"Let me tell you something: you work hard and do your job, and I'll work hard and do my job, and we'll get along fine. Everything'll be great. But, it's going to be a long game for both of us if you keep up with this attitude."

Most guys listened to me. And, if they had a good attitude, I'd just go along with it.

Like Bruce Froemming. He had a reputation for being a red ass. Real short fuse. Every game I worked with him, he punched the fire out of me. Right in the kidneys. He didn't take any shit. I liked Bruce, though. One off-season, my wife Traci and I went on a baseball cruise. Bruce and his wife were on it too. Got to know him off the field. Figured out that he had a different personality when he wasn't working and was just a good dude. We hit it off. I don't know if that carried over to the field. But, if he missed a pitch, I could tell him, "Bruce, that was a pretty good pitch."

Bruce would say, "Okay. I'll stay with it."

I could also flip him some shit. Look at him at the beginning of the game and say, "Man, I didn't recognize you."

"What?"

"I'm used to seeing you in your Speedo, not this umpire's gear."

I was just kidding around. Never saw Bruce in a Speedo, thank God. But, he'd laugh, and then we'd go about our business. That's what I mean by having a good attitude and being able to work with guys. Some of them really cared about doing a good job. You could ask them questions about the game, and they wouldn't take it as if you were questioning their authority or ability. They just enjoyed umpiring.

But, some guys go out there, and they hate to umpire. They get burned out, but they don't want to give up the good money. I guess it's like anything else. Some policemen are better than others. Same thing with lawyers. And, you know the good ones from the bad ones. If you've got a guy who is a bad balls and strikes umpire, you know, going in to the game, he's going to miss some calls. Jerry Layne. Angel Hernandez. Bad balls and strikes umpires. Layne during the World Series a couple of years ago missed a strike three call. Next pitch, the catcher hits a double and drives in a run and that's the difference in the game. A guy may be a great umpire on the bases, but a shitty balls and strikes guy behind the plate. Some guys are just bad, period. You can't hide them anywhere on the field: they're going to miss calls consistently no matter where they are. That's just how it is. Eric Gregg: pitcher's umpire. Big strike zone. Way bigger than it should be. It could be six or ten inches off the plate, and he'd call it a strike.

Some guys would call games based on how they felt, what kind of mood they were in. One guy I worked with early in my career wanted to get in and out of the game, so he called nearly everything a strike. Made guys swing the bat. And, two hours later, the game was over. I guess he had somewhere to go because that was my experience with him every time he worked home plate. Ridiculous. Most fans watching would have no idea that was happening. But, some guys were more professional than others. The thing is each one of them has a personality. Joe West: he could be an outstanding umpire. Make some great calls. Hustle and be in the right position to get a good angle on the play. But, he also wants attention and to be a part of the game. When that happened, he could be a piece of shit. You have to learn who you can deal with and who you can't. All of these guys have memories. They talk to each other. If you pissed off one crew, that crew usually tells the incoming crew about it, and that new crew, well, they're just waiting on you. That kind of shit happens all the time. And, some of those guys, they'll stick it to you. Like one umpire had a beef with Barry Bonds. Don't know what happened between them, but the umpire hated Bonds. So, when Bonds came up to bat, the umpire told me, "You can set up on the outside for every pitch. Every pitch is going to be a strike to this guy." Okay. You shrug your shoulders on that one and take what you can get.

Still, if an umpire was going to miss balls and strikes and be a dick about it, I'd sometimes catch strikes that they were calling balls and just hold them. The unwritten rule is, if it's a ball, just throw the ball back to the pitcher. But, with everybody watching, everybody screaming, I'd hold the ball in my glove and then take my time throwing the ball back to the mound.

A couple of times, I had umpires tell me not to hold the ball like that.

"Here's the deal," I said. "If you're not going to call it a strike, I'm holding the ball."

"Do it again, and I'm throwing you out of the game," the umpire said.

If it happened again and the umpire called a ball when really it was a strike, I'd hold it again. Just see how the conversation went. I was thrown out of only one game, and that was by a replacement umpire up from Triple A. Generally, you know where the line is and where you shouldn't cross it.

Some of this stuff was cleaned up in the late nineties when a bunch of umpires submitted their resignations as part of a negotiating tactic for a new labor agreement. With some of these guys, baseball just accepted the resignations and never invited these cats back.

Sabes didn't really moan too much about umpires. He just went out and pitched. It makes sense, though. He had a reputation as a control pitcher. Threw a lot of strikes. Hit his target way more than he missed it. Because of that, umpires probably gave him more calls than hosed him.

I mentioned our poor defense as affecting Sabes's pitching, but another problem was injuries. Sabes spent chunks of time on the disabled list. He had some shortened seasons when he wasn't getting thirty or thirty-five starts. I think throwing as hard as he did put a lot of wear and tear on his body. He had a skinny build (he was a little over six foot and weighed around 160). My experience is that guys with that physique don't last year after year throwing hard. It's freakish to have that slight kind of body but to throw a ball with so much power. Eventually, something's got to give. The kid from San Francisco, Tim Lincecum, reminds me of Saberhagen. I worry about his ability to sustain that kind of power, because it takes a toll on your body. Sabes did a lot of things to avoid injuries, but he still had problems. Had good mechanics. Consistently repeated the same delivery. His arm slot was good—some guys have a low arm slot and that can cause elbow problems, but Sabes's was where it needed to be—not too low, not too high. Kept his pitch counts low. Even though he did a lot of things right, he still dealt with injuries. And, he worked his ass off to rehab his arm to come back in top condition. He ran, did conditioning exercises, lifted weights, worked the cuff weights and bands for his shoulder. He did what he could to get back onto the field. He was like a little kid—he loved baseball. Loved to pitch, loved to play. He was athletic enough that he could've been a pretty good outfielder. He ran fast. Shagged balls well. He liked to hit, and he swung the bat pretty well. Just a great athlete. Had quick feet and could step off the mound and throw to first base to pick off runners. And, he was always thinking. He had a couple of different pickoff moves where he stepped off quickly but then threw the ball to first real slowly. Or, maybe he'd just step off and look to first base but not throw. Or, step off and fire the ball to first. Never the same thing. Kept base runners off balance. Because of it, he picked off quite a few guys. He was a complete pitcher, a complete player.

Like most guys, he had his habits or superstitions. In between each inning, he'd change his undershirt. Didn't want to feel sticky, so he'd put on a clean shirt.

Even though we were a bad club and it's tough to find highlights during all of the losing, I had some good experiences while I was in New York and catching Sabes, particularly with the coaching. Midseason in '93, the club fired Jeff Torborg as manager and replaced him with Dallas Green. I loved Dallas Green. He was one of my favorite managers to play for. As old school as you could get. That was a great fit for me. He didn't play games. Was straightforward. You knew exactly what he was thinking, and you knew exactly where you stood with him. He was loud and boisterous and challenged his players to improve. I saw him as the baseball version of Bobby Knight, who I would've loved to have played for. You can learn so much from coaches like that. And, Dallas wanted his guys to play hard. Like I said, we had a lot of guys who'd settled in and gotten comfortable with losing. Dallas shook things up. Pushed guys to work harder. I always played hard, so I was fine with his approach. If you went out there and busted your ass, he wasn't going to say anything to you. Guys who didn't work hard or who weren't prepared to play, shit. Dallas Green would eat you up.

Dallas's becoming manager was good timing for me. Toward the end of Jeff Torborg's tour of duty as manager, I wasn't playing much. I'd probably call it the lowest point in my career. I was playing in a day game in Chicago, and Jeff pinch hit for me in the fifth inning. I remember going into the clubhouse, thinking, "It's the fifth inning, and I'm already out of the game." It's horrible to play for somebody who doesn't have any confidence in you. Gives you a shitty feeling knowing that your manager doesn't believe that you can execute. It starts to affect you mentally. You start to believe that maybe you don't have the talent to handle those game-on-the-line situations. I was very frustrated. Then my wife, Traci, called. She was back in New York. She said she was going to the hospital to have our youngest child. I walked into the trainer's room. Said I was catching a plane for New York. I didn't even ask them. At that point, I didn't care if I were going to get into trouble or not. I was just tired of my situation.

It wasn't too long after that that Jeff Torborg was fired and Dallas Green came on board as manager. Soon after he was hired, he called me in to his office.

"Can you hit left-handed pitching?" he asked.

"Hell, yes, I can hit left-handed pitching," I said. And, it was true. I hit lefties real well, even though when we had the conversation I was hitting like a buck something.

"Good. I'm going to hit you second."

"Okay," I said. I had never hit in the two spot. I was used to hitting eighth. Like I said, I had gotten used to getting pulled for a pinch hitter whenever the game was at a turning point.

That game, I went three for four. Dallas's arrival and his confidence in me was a fresh start. It made all the difference in the world having a guy believe in me. Letting me play. Letting my talent show. I hit close to .300 for the second half of the season. Dallas Green is one of the reasons why I was able to get out of New York and sign as a free agent with Atlanta and ultimately have the second half of my career take off the way it did.

Another guy who helped me out a ton was Tom McGraw, our hitting coach. He asked, "How come you don't hit any better than you do?"

I kind of shrugged and said I didn't know.

"You can hit," he said. "You've got quick hands. You hit the fastball well. You just need a better game plan of what to look for when you're up at the plate." And, Tom and I started talking about hitting, about certain situations, about what pitches to look for, about pitchers' tendencies. He had a library where he had talked to all of the great hitters and wrote down all of their hitting strategies. I would love to have a copy of that now. By far, he was the best hitting instructor I worked with. He got me to believe in me. Before, the message I was getting from coaches was "You can't do this, you can't do that." Instead, Tom told me that, with some adjustments, I could hit effectively. I wished I'd worked with him earlier in my career. That's the disappointing thing. If you hear the message long enough that you can't do this or you can't do that, you start to believe it. Tom built up my confidence, though. Because of working with him and Dallas and later Bobby Cox, I started believing in my abilities more during the second half of my career.

Another bright spot was playing with Eddie Murray. He was our first baseman in '93. Incredible player. He did everything the right way. Worked on his craft every day. Like his first round of batting practice. He used this session to hit ground balls to second base. No matter where the pitch was, he made sure he hit it to second base. It was weird: he made the ugliest hacks to hit ground balls to second. So, one time, I asked him, "Damn, dude, what are you doing?"

He said, "I'm working on hitting the ball to second base."

"Why?"

"If I have a base runner at third, all I need is a ground ball to second, and that's an RBI. I get twenty to thirty of those a year."

And, it had never really dawned on me. How many times do you work on hitting a ground ball to second? He was right, though. I admired the detail he devoted to his game. I started doing the same thing and worked on hitting ground balls to second. He was a great teammate. Funny and pleasant to be with. With the press, he had an icy reputation, but that was because he didn't like dealing with reporters. He'd rather do other things. So, when they asked him questions, he gave pretty short and to the point answers. Or, if they asked him a stupid question, he'd tell them it was a stupid question. I guess that pissed off or embarrassed reporters and made them hold a grudge against him or whatever. I didn't care. On the field, he busted his ass, and he was one of the best hitters I ever saw. In the clubhouse, he was a hard worker who was easy to get along with. I'd want him playing on my team any time.

Losing can make for a long season. Making it even worse, we had our share of drama. Part of it involved Sabes. He was a practical joker, and he horsed around with everybody. He was big on turning off the hot water while I was in the shower and washing my hair. People on the outside took it the wrong way and thought he was a jerk, but he was just clowning. He was a good dude, but he got into trouble with his pranks. One time, he threw a firecracker near some reporters. Nobody was hurt, but folks were startled. That ruffled some feathers. Then, he had a squirt gun, and he was going around spraying some of the reporters' pants with bleach. He'd played around with the water gun before, and everybody thought that he was the one that nailed the reporters, but nobody knew it for sure. The reporters started raising a stink about it. Because we were in New York, something harmless was blown out of proportion and became a story in the papers that wouldn't die down. Sabes wasn't admitting to anything—he was just staying quiet about the whole deal. That's when the Major League Players Association contacted me. I was the Mets' player rep, and they told me that Jay Horwitz, the team's publicist, would lose his job unless someone came forward and confessed to the squirt gun deal. Horwitz was one of the nicest dudes in the Mets front office. Would do anything in the world for you. Everybody liked Jay, and nobody wanted to get him in trouble. So, I went to Sabes and asked for his help. I told him that they said Jay was going to lose his job unless somebody came clean about the deal. Saberhagen said, "That's fine. I'll tell them. It's no big deal." He admitted that he did it and said he was sorry to the reporters.

––––––––––––––––––––

Sabes was a hell of a competitor. After I moved on to Atlanta and faced him as a hitter, he threw me everything he could think of to get me out: curveball, change, inside fastball. And, the whole time, he's talking to me. It was so much fun. It wasn't like a normal at-bat. Reminded me of playing whiffle ball in the backyard with my brothers and sisters. Here was a guy who I caught. I knew what he liked to throw, so I knew what pitches to look for. We had been teammates, friends, and I remember digging in and thinking, "I'm gonna hit this guy." Same kind of deal when your brother's talking shit to you in the backyard, and you get that boost that you're going to nail whatever he throws at you. And, I did. Hit a home run off of Sabes. As I was coming around the bases, he was yelling at me. Calling me a piece of shit. Telling me that the only reason why the ball went over the fence was because he hit the bat with the ball. Next time up against him, I yanked a ball foul like five sections up in Shea. Probably one of the hardest balls I ever hit in my life. There was Sabes, laughing at me. I wound up grounding out that at-bat, but it was fun. I knew how competitive he was. We both wanted to do well, and we were both trying hard and having fun. Playing baseball with the same kind of competition and fun that you have as a kid.

CHAPTER 6

JOHN SMOLTZ

Charlie pulled Cangelosi from out underneath me. And, you know, he did some damage. Like I said, big country strong. You're under a pile, and the guy you had a headlock on was gone. Charlie pulled him out. He was all about everything that was right about the game. Protecting the pitcher and getting after it. Charlie got after it. Maybe he wasn't the most visibly intense guy, but he was intense. Don't let the personality fool you.

—*John Smoltz*

[*Note: After the 1993 season with the New York Mets, Charlie became a free agent. With a strong second half to his credit, several teams pursued him. His preference was to sign with the Atlanta Braves, the team that had just won three consecutive National League Western Division titles and boasting one of the all-time best starting pitching rotations with Greg Maddux, Tom Glavine, John Smoltz, and Steve Avery. During a chance meeting at the Tulsa airport with Jim Beauchamp, the Braves bench coach, Charlie told Beauchamp that he wanted to play for the Braves. Charlie liked the Braves' left-handed pitchers and enjoyed Atlanta's atmosphere and its fans. In fact, Atlanta was his favorite place to play as a visiting player.*

Beauchamp said, "We would love to have you."

Charlie responded, "Tell Bobby [Cox]. That's my number one place to go. I'd love to be in Atlanta."

"I'll tell him," Beauchamp said.

After this conversation, Charlie signed a two-year contract and received a pay raise to play with Atlanta.[1]

The first pitcher Charlie caught in Atlanta was John Smoltz. Smoltz had a reputation for being a big-game pitcher, winning fifteen postseason games, second all-time.[2] In addition, he had one of the best arms in the league. Pitcher Kevin Millwood, who played with Smoltz for six seasons, praised Smoltz as the most talented pitcher he ever saw.[3] One illustration of this talent is Smoltz's being one of only three pitchers in Major

League history to win twenty games in a season and save forty games in a different season.[4]

Despite the postseason achievements and the outstanding arm, Smoltz's results with Charlie were mixed. Charlie caught all of his starts (twenty-one) in 1994, and Smoltz's record was six wins, ten losses, 113 strikeouts in 134 ⅔ innings, and a 4.14 earned run average.[5] Fast-forward two seasons; Smoltz won the Cy Young Award, leading the league in wins (twenty-four) and strikeouts (276).[6]

In total, Smoltz played for twenty-one seasons. Twenty were with the Braves. He won 213 games, lost 155, saved 154, maintained a 3.33 earned run average, and threw 3,084 strikeouts, sixteenth most all-time.[7] He is the only pitcher in Major League history to win over 200 games and save 150 games.[8]]

Catching John Smoltz put me on the cover of *Sports Illustrated*.

In my first game back at Shea Stadium after leaving the Mets, John pitched. He struggled. Had some control problems. Gave up some hits. Threw some wild pitches. Hit some batters. Topping it off, Ryan Thompson hit a grand slam off John. I guess Thompson wanted to savor the experience because he pimped his way around the bases. Took him forever to get to home plate.

John was pissed.

The next guy up was John Cangelosi. Cangelosi had always hit John well, and John, I guess, took advantage of the situation. Two birds with one stone. First pitch, he drilled Cangelosi dead square in the back. John never said if he did this intentionally, and I didn't call for it, but where the pitch was and how Thompson took his time around the bases, it was pretty clear that Smoltz knew what he was doing. You knew something was coming. It was going to be either Thompson next time up or this dude, one of the two.

Naturally, Cangelosi didn't like being hit, so he charged the mound. In fact, that was the second time that day he was hit by a pitch. But, part of the catcher's job is to protect his pitcher. So, I chased after Cangelosi. Got one or two good punches in. Then a whole pile of guys landed on top of us.

At the bottom of the pile, Cangelosi started to freak out. His face was mashed in the grass. I was on top of him. He probably couldn't breathe, so he started screaming at the top of his lungs. It was like panic set in. Hell, I couldn't do anything. I couldn't move. I had a bunch of guys on top of me too. Somebody pulling my hair. It gets crazy in those brawls. You're just stuck there.

Finally, the pile cleared. The umpires tossed Smoltz and Cangelosi. I stayed in the game. Don't know why I wasn't thrown out. Later on, I was fined a little bit for hitting Cangelosi.

After the game, the press stopped by my locker. They asked questions about the fight. If Smoltz meant to hit Cangelosi. If I knew anything about it.

Then, one of the writers said that they talked to Cangelosi. Said that he was most mad at me because I sucker punched him while he was at the bottom of the pile.

I said, "Well, hell. He ran out there. What did he expect?"

The more I thought about it, the more I fired up. So, I walked over to the Mets' locker room. Figured Cangelosi and I could settle this face-to-face. I didn't get too far before I ran in to Dallas Green who was still managing them. He knew something was up, so he stopped me. So did their security guard, Sarge. He was with them when I played there, an off-duty police officer. They held on to me, and I hollered, "Get out here! Dude, I'll show you a sucker punch."

But, like the pile clearing off, that blew over. I went back to the visitors' locker room and cooled off. I was pissed, though. When you charge the mound, a hitter knows that somebody's coming after him. As a catcher, I need to be out there, protecting my pitcher. If a hitter goes out to the mound, you should walk away having something to show for it: a bruise or a black eye or lumps on you somewhere. I can't have a hitter in a free-for-all after my guy out there and just stand there and watch.

A week later, *Sports Illustrated* came out. On the cover, you see me on Cangelosi's back, my fist cocked, pounding him. You see Terry Pendleton with his hands up, playing peacemaker.

A couple of things about this brawl. One is that I think Smoltz was frustrated. He was having a rough day on the mound, and a guy just hit a grand slam off him. He took his frustration out on the next guy up who happened to have a history of wearing him out. Cangelosi would fight balls off and battle, then Smoltz would leave a pitch in the middle of the plate, and Cangelosi would drill him. In some situations, it makes sense to smoke a dude and make him wear a birthmark for a while. (That's how Roger Clemens described it—hitting a dude with a pitch was putting a birthmark on him.) This wasn't one of them. Wait until John had another chance at Thompson somewhere down the line and settle it with him then. That way, it would've been over. Tit for tat. Everybody moves on. Nobody gets thrown out of the game. Nobody gets suspended. But, if you take it out on the guy on the on-deck circle, or, if a pitcher is getting rocked and he decides to hit somebody because he's pitching shitty, somebody on your team is going to take the heat for you. Especially in the American League where the pitcher never has to hit. If you're pitching poorly, get out of there. Do better next time.

Another thing is that Terry Pendleton, our third baseman, grabbed me and tried to keep me from punching Cangelosi. That was bullshit, and I told him. I was like, "Hey, man, don't ever grab me." I was fired up. Like I said, it's the catcher's job to protect his pitcher. If you don't protect your players, then I don't want you. Don't want you as a teammate. Don't want you in my locker room. Some guys don't like hitting other guys, but it's all part of the game. Later, in the clubhouse, I told TP that. He agreed and said he was sorry. He said he saw two dudes fighting, and his natural reaction was to break it up. I didn't think his explanation made a whole lot of sense, but TP's a good guy. Good hitter, good coach.

When a guy is hit as a payback, the hitter who was drilled should go to his teammate who caused him to get hit and say, "Don't ever let me get hit like that again." Cangelosi should have gone to Thompson and told him not to ever pimp himself around the bases and leave Cangelosi next in line to get smoked. A lot of times, guys don't have the balls to say that. It happened to me one time in Toronto. Pat Hentgen was pitching and getting waffled. He was mad, so he hit a dude. Next half inning, I led off for the Blue Jays. In retaliation, I got smoked in the back. Tit for tat. After the game, I told Pat, "I'll choke you out if that ever happens to me again." He felt bad, but I was like, "Look, you don't have to hit, so I have to wear your problem. That ain't gonna happen again." He knew I was pissed, and he was sorry about it. Sometimes, you have to have these conversations. Clear the air and move on. And, with Pat, that's what we did. After that, he never again put me in a position where I was getting smoked for something he did.

The bottom line is that I don't know why hitters run out to the mound. They hardly ever get a good blow in. Hell, they get the fire beat out of them. Like Cangelosi. Think he had a black eye the next day. My buddy, Billy Spiers, played with the Mets then, and later on he told me that Cangelosi said he'd never charge the mound again. He took a thumping for doing it.

———

My first season with the Braves, I caught Smoltz every start he pitched. One reason for this is because we had a rookie catcher, Javy Lopez, who was still learning how to catch. He was a young kid with a huge amount of talent. Very nice. Very naive. His English was real limited, so he had a tough time comprehending everything that coaches were trying to teach him. As far as tools, he had everything to be a good catcher. Big build. Good arm. Moved well. For pure ability, he was tough to beat. He could've been an outstanding catcher if he'd worked a little harder at his defense. And, damn, he could hit the ball. The dude had some big power. Got a ton of big hits when I was in Atlanta. And, he was a great guy to work with. He was real receptive when I tried to teach him things like pitch selection, anticipation, blocking balls. Pat Corrales, one of our coaches and a former big league catcher, spent a lot of time with him too on how to be a better catcher. The whole organization worked with Javy a lot because they knew he was going to be a special player. I was surprised he didn't stay in Atlanta and play longer there than he did.

Another reason why I worked with John so much in '94 is because, when you caught him, you had your work cut out for you. He was definitely going to beat the fire out of you. A few seasons, he led the league in wild pitches. That should tell you something. He threw a lot of balls in the dirt, and they were hard to catch. To block his pitches, you wound up getting hit everywhere: arms, shoulders, hands, elbows, legs. I'd guess that, during a game with Smoltz, you'd block the ball twenty times. Maybe ten of those are no big deal. But the other ten, man. You don't stop them with the glove—you stop them with some part of your body. When the day was over, you hurt. You knew you'd just caught John Smoltz. It wasn't like this with Glavine and Maddux. With those guys, you never had to block anything. Because of that, the coaches didn't put Javy with John. Javy needed a season to adjust to being a big league catcher. They'd be throwing him to the wolves if they asked him to catch John as a rookie.

I enjoyed the challenge of blocking so many pitches. I took pride in my ability to do it. That's just one of those things you have to do well if you want to be a good catcher. You have to work at it. Have coaches or other players just throw you dirt ball and after dirt ball. You learn to be ready and anticipate where the ball is going and prepare to block the ball with your whole body. If you know it's coming, it's a little easier. So, if I knew John was throwing a forkball, I knew I needed to be ready to block—chances were good the ball would bounce in the dirt. Same thing when I went to Toronto and caught Juan Guzman. He was another guy who threw a lot of dirt balls. You just had to be ready for them. Some, you can't do anything about. Most of them, you can stop. And, the good catchers figure this out. Like Bob Boone. He was real quick. Some guys have more range than others and can cover more ground—quickness is a major factor here. Very few balls got past Boone. He could read the ball out of the pitcher's hand and guess where the ball was going and get to it. Same thing with Johnny Bench. He was real nimble the way he dug out balls in the dirt. He played the position like a shortstop.

As far as talent on the Braves staff, Smoltz had the best stuff. He was a big strong dude who threw the shit out of the ball. Had great arm speed. Explosive fastball. Like ninety-eight miles per hour. His slider or slurve or whatever you want to call it was unhittable if he was hitting his spots with it. He threw it hard, probably eighty-eight to ninety miles per hour. Balls thrown that hard usually don't break much, but his had a big break to them. And, he had an amazing forkball. Most guys throw a forkball in the eighties. About the same speed as a changeup. John threw his at ninety-two miles per hour. Not many guys can throw a forkball at this speed. Roger Clemens could, but his was more of a split-finger fastball. John threw more of a true forkball—holding the ball deeper in his hand than guys who throw splitters. His forkball looked like a fastball that just tumbled forward and the bottom fell out of it. Totally dominating pitch. Best forkball I ever caught. It wasn't a pitch that he threw for called strikes. Definitely a two-strike pitch that guys chased and missed. He was a lot like David Cone: he struck out a lot of guys with breaking balls. A lot of balls in the dirt. He reminds me of Justin Verlander, too, a guy with no-hit stuff nearly every time he goes out there. I'd watch John's pitches and see how good his stuff was and think, "How in the hell is anybody ever going to hit that?"

Athletically, he was the best pitcher I ever caught. He fielded so well that he was fun to watch. He could make some defensive plays that most middle infielders couldn't make. I remember one play. The hitter laid a bunt down the third baseline. John ran toward the ball. In one motion, he fielded it, jumped, and threw the ball to first and got the base runner out. Great play. I can still see it. So good that it ought to be an MLB Network highlight. Off the field, Smoltz was a well-rounded athlete, too. He could play football, tennis. Great basketball player. He organized charity hoops games during the off-season. Looking back on it, I wish I would have come back from Tulsa to Atlanta to play in one of those. People wouldn't think that I could play basketball, but I could. Loved playing. Had a scholarship offer to play at a small school in Kansas. When I was at Wichita State, I'd play pick-up games with some of the dudes from the basketball team. We had some studs then: Xavier McDaniel, Antoine Carr. Guys who went on and had good careers in the NBA. Anyway, Smoltz was a good basketball player, and I should've taken the time to shoot some hoops with him. Great golfer too. He's playing in some high-level tournaments now. In a couple of years, you may see him on the Senior PGA Tour. If anybody could do that, excel on the baseball field and start playing professional golf, it'd be him.

So, with Smoltz having such great stuff and being such an excellent athlete, why did he win only six games and lose ten the year I caught him? Part of it was health. John wound up having surgery on his arm after the season. He wasn't one hundred percent.

Part of it was because he was still figuring out how to pitch. Sounds weird because he'd been in the league for five or six years when I caught him. But, I think John would tell you the same thing. We knocked heads a bunch about throwing his fastball more. He wanted to focus on his breaking pitches—his forkball and his slider. They were dominating, so he wanted to throw them all of the time. But, he didn't understand that he needed to set these pitches up with his fastball. Then, following the fastball in a pitch sequence, those breaking pitches would be totally untouchable. He'd have the hitter behind in the count, and he could put the hitter away with his breaking stuff. I had a pretty good feel for how a guy could best take advantage of his tools. And, I could see how John could be absolutely dominating with just a slight change to his game plan. I'd talk to him before the game, during the game, after the game, trying to convince him to throw more fastballs. "We've got to use our fastball more," is something I repeated over and over. Most guys, they just go with you. Not John. I don't know why he wouldn't listen to me. He was hardheaded as hell about throwing his breaking pitches and not throwing his fastball. Reminded me of a horse that I kept trying to pull but he just wouldn't follow me. He shook me off a bunch. He was one of the few guys that I just couldn't get through to. Or, when he'd finally give in and throw his fastball, he'd be upset with me and not give his best effort behind the pitch. I couldn't get him to understand how good his fastball was. He was so talented, and I wanted to be there once he brought it all together and pitched to his potential. Later on, after I left the Braves, I saw that it clicked for him. Located his fastball well. Used it early in the count to get ahead of the hitter and set up his breaking pitches. I was like, "Dang, John, how come you didn't do that when I had you?" Look at his numbers after I caught him—24-8 one season, 17-3 another. Fifty-five saves a few years later. Dominating. When guys improve like that, there's a rhyme and a reason to it. They've figured something out. Usually, it's because their control is better. They're not behind in the count as much. They're throwing their breaking balls for strikes. I knew he'd figure things out eventually, but his reluctance to throw his fastball more was his biggest weakness when I caught him. If he'd learned how to pitch earlier in his career, he would have won three hundred games, easy.

He was right that his breaking pitches were nasty. Some of the best in the league. Maybe *the* best in the league. But, breaking balls are hard to throw for strikes consistently. What would happen to John is that he would lean on his breaking pitches, bounce one in the dirt for a ball, get behind in the count, and then he'd give hitters a good pitch to hit. Kind of like Bert Blyleven. Blyleven had a great curveball, but he always seemed to give you a good pitch to hit. Same thing with John. He'd go to his fastball once he was behind in the count. Unless he put the ball exactly where he wanted it, he was at a disadvantage because the fastball is a predictable pitch at this count. Hitters are looking for it. You're a different pitcher when you're behind in the count. That's why I wanted him to throw his fastball earlier. Get ahead in the count with it, *then* go after guys with another fastball, his forkball, or his slider. But, he was always pitching backwards. The bottom line: the pitcher has the final say. He gets the win or the loss. And, after years of catching, you figure out that if a guy is committed to throwing certain pitches and you can't change his mind after you make suggestions to him, it's hard to help. That was my case with John. It got to the point where I was frustrated with him. I'm sure he was frustrated with me too.

Another thing holding John back when I caught him was a lack of concentration. He could zone out. He had too many lackadaisical moments when he threw instead of pitched. What I mean is that he wouldn't try to change locations and speed. He wouldn't stay focused on every single pitch. Some innings, it was like he was getting bored out there, and he'd wind up giving hitters some good pitches to hit. With guys like Maddux, Glavine, and Clemens, this didn't happen. Inning after inning, pitch after pitch, they'd grind it out. Missing one pitch pissed them off. Talk about tunnel vision and concentrating on the game. With Maddux, it started in the bullpen. I never saw anything like it—from warming up to the end of the game, he was locked in. If he missed one pitch in the bullpen, he'd drop an f-bomb and you knew his next pitch would be perfect. Clemens was the same way. John just didn't have that intensity. And, things could turn to shit so fast for him. We could be sailing along. Next thing you know, the wheels would come off. He'd give up a walk, a hit, and then a guy would homer just like that. Happened so fast that you didn't have time to react or do anything to stop it. Usually, when that happens, it's because a guy loses focus. That's how it was with John. Nothing was wrong with his stuff. But, his lack of focus led to his giving guys some pitches that were easier to hit, and it'd snowball on him.

One of the reasons why I think he was such a great closer was because it forced him to focus. Going in to the game during an on-the-line situation, he couldn't zone out. Had to be locked in. It was a one inning deal, and it suited his makeup perfectly to go in knowing his job was to get three outs, period. Out of all the guys I caught, he was the ideal closer. Perfect for his psyche, perfect for the stuff he threw. Look at his bullpen stats. Phenomenal. He played during an era of dominant closers, and he was as good as any of them. If he'd spent his career in the bullpen, he would've been the most dominating closer of all time because his shit was so good. It was better than Mariano Rivera's, who I think is the best reliever of all time, a guy who's so good that he's in a class of his own. And, if John had started his career earlier in the bullpen, I think he would've worked through his focus problems sooner.

When I caught John, it was a tough season for him. Hands down, he had the best stuff on the staff. Hell, he probably had the best stuff in the league, but he wasn't getting great results. He'd have some games where he'd give up two hits and have ten punch outs. The next time out, he'd give up a lot of hits and get pounded. He didn't meet expectations. Didn't pitch like he had the best stuff in the league, much less the staff. He was 6-10 with a four something ERA. That wears on you. Especially when he was way better than that. Few guys could come anywhere close to touching his ability. But, I don't think he understood how good he was. It was almost like he had to go out there and invent something different, that what he ordinarily threw wasn't good enough. Yet, it was amazing. Maybe it was because he was playing with Maddux and Glavine and having to follow them, guys who were so dominant. Maybe he felt like he needed to match them. When, really, all he had to do was just be John. But, I think those were the demons that he had to live with. And, I don't think he was confident enough in his ability or understood how good he really was to say, "You know what? I'm just going to do what I do. Let me pitch the way I want to pitch. Let me go do what I do." And, then, not worry about the other guys.

As far as comparing John to Maddux or Glavine, I see one big difference. Those guys had figured out their game plans. John hadn't. Maddux and Glavine understood what their ability was. What their strengths were. They built game plans around that. When I caught John Smoltz, he hadn't pulled that together yet. He didn't know what he wanted to do. He didn't know if today he was going to throw his fastball or if today he was going to throw forkballs. Then, maybe he'd decide that he wasn't going to throw any forkballs—he was going to throw sliders. Maddux and Glavine didn't have the luxury of having as many options. Greg knew that he had to rely on movement and location. Same thing with Glavine. He knew he'd throw 110 pitches. Ninety of them would be fastballs, and the rest he would mix in his changeup. But, when I caught him, I don't think Smoltzie had a good feel for what he was doing. After I left, he figured it out. Sometimes, that's how it works. Guys grow up or develop after you've worked with them. The message sinks in later.

Being around guys like Maddux and Glavine made Smoltz better. Maddux helped him by teaching him to pay attention during the games when he wasn't pitching so he would learn more about the hitters and watch for certain pitches, certain locations. Those things helped John. He had so much natural ability that he just went out and threw. But, once he started pitching with a game plan, that's when he really turned it on.

John was a great dude to be around. Real likeable guy who was good to everybody. He liked for people to mess with him. You could pick on some of the things he said or did. Just a fun guy. Clean cut. Never cussed. If he said anything close to salty, it was "frick." Like most pitchers, he had his game day habits or rituals. Tried to sleep in as late as he could. Ate pancakes the days he pitched. If he were at home and starting and the weather allowed it, he liked to mow his yard before he came into the park.

John is special. Not many guys win twenty games in a season and then save forty games in a season. John has. No one else has won 200 games and saved 150. That tells you how unique John and his talent are. That versatility to start and close and be one of the best pitchers in the league for both. People ask, "Is John Smoltz a Hall of Fame dude?" My answer is "Hell, yeah." No doubt. I put him up there with all the other great pitchers I caught who should be in the Hall of Fame: Maddux, Glavine, Clemens. For some reason, Hall of Fame voters don't place a lot of importance on the closer's role. I disagree. Guys like Johnny Franco who were effective closers deserve to be in the Hall of Fame. But, when you have a guy like Smoltz who was dominating as a starter and a closer, come on. He's definitely one of the best pitchers of all time, no doubt.

CHAPTER 7

STEVE BEDROSIAN

Charlie was one of the better catchers I had the privilege of teaming up with. The one thing that sticks out in my mind about Charlie was that he made you accountable for your pitches, of hitting your spots, of doing the job you were supposed to do. When he put down that finger, he expected you to hit that spot or make that pitch. Now, you're not going to do it every time, and when you didn't, he let you know. I think that's very important in catchers, and in coaching high school for the past fourteen years, that's one of the big things that I stress to the catchers. Jump that pitcher if he doesn't do what he's supposed to do. If he doesn't hold a guy close to first. If he doesn't hit his spot. Let that pitcher know in a good way, in a positive way. Not to make waves and disrupt the game and the flow but to make him accountable for the things he's supposed to be doing. Charlie always did that. And, he was brutally honest with you. If you threw a pitch and the guy hit a home run, he didn't feel sorry for you. He would tell you, "You've got to make a better pitch right there. You left that curveball up." That's what I remember about Charlie as a catcher. He expected the best out of you all the time—if you were in a game or throwing a side session.

On the other hand, he would praise you when you made a good pitch. It could have been anything from his pointing his glove at you and telling you good job, to coming over to you in between innings in the dugout and saying, "That was a great pitch right there. Good thinking," or "Good job holding that guy on." I had a high leg kick. I had a hard time holding guys on close. I would rather make a good pitch and try to strike that guy out than to try to quick pitch and slide step and give up a double, and sometimes, I wouldn't give catchers the best chance to throw runners out. But, when you did, when you threw over two or three times, or then made a good pitch where he could throw a guy out, he let you know good job in doing it. I think that's important. Confidence breeds confidence. When you know your catcher has confidence in you, you're going to be a better pitcher.

—*Steve Bedrosian*

[*Note: One of Atlanta's set-up relief pitchers was Steve Bedrosian. Bedrosian began his career as a relief pitcher with Atlanta, converted to a starter, and then returned to the bullpen as a closer. In 1987, he won the Cy Young Award while a member of the Philadelphia Phillies. That season, Bedrosian's record was five wins, three losses, forty saves, and seventy-four strikeouts in eighty-nine innings.[1] During this season, he broke Sparky Lyle's record of most saves in consecutive appearances (twelve).[2] He continued to pitch as one of the game's best closers, but after the 1991 season, he retired when his son Cody underwent treatments for leukemia, including a bone marrow transplant, and Bedrosian started experiencing numbness in his fingers. In 1993, with his son in remission and the feeling returning to his fingers, Bedrosian made a comeback with the Braves. Charlie caught Bedrosian in several games during the 1994 and '95 seasons (eighteen games in 1994 and eleven in 1995). Highlights include Bedrosian striking out the side (July 10, 1994 against St. Louis) and shutting down the heart of the Cincinnati Reds' potent offense (in two innings, Bedrosian had Hal Morris, Kevin Mitchell, and Reggie Sanders tap ground balls for outs and Tony Fernandez line out).*

For his career, Bedrosian pitched in fourteen Major League seasons. He won seventy-six games, lost seventy-nine, earned 184 saves (tied for fifty-second all-time with Kent Tekulve), and posted a 3.38 earned run average. He threw 1,191 innings and 921 strikeouts.[3]]

All good clubs have chemistry, and the Braves teams I played with gelled, especially the '95 club that won the World Series. The Braves had a lot of great teams, winning fourteen division titles. But the '95 team: that group was special. Everybody working in the same direction. You can put twenty-five talented guys together on a roster but not have the atmosphere like we had. For some reason, like with the Mets, guys sometimes don't mesh. But, in Atlanta, our top guys pushed other players to improve. How you create this environment, I don't know. It's almost magical: it was all about the team, not the individual players. Steve Bedrosian compared us to an old Viking ship where everybody had their oar in the water, all of us pulling in the same direction. Everybody did their work. Got along real well. Total contrast to New York where guys like Darryl Strawberry might have a little nag and decide not to play. You didn't have that on the Braves. Every single guy wanted to be on the field every day.

I think this chemistry started from the top. Bobby Cox was so well-respected that guys wanted to play hard and please him. Nobody wanted to cause him any problems. Bobby was straightforward. Old school. He had some funny rules like not allowing music in the clubhouse and having a certain dress code. On the field, players couldn't have any color on their shoes. Black and white only. No Oakley sunglasses. Really, nothing stylish at all, just a traditional baseball uniform. When the hockey-style catcher's mask I designed came out, he didn't want his catchers using it. Didn't look traditional enough for him. This was different from most managers. Most managers let you do what you want. You want to wear colored cleats? Fine. Funky sunglasses? Whatever.

Bobby had his rules, but he did a lot of things the right way. First off, he treated everybody the same. Didn't matter if you were Greg Maddux or Tom Glavine or the twenty-fifth guy on the roster. He gave everybody the same amount of respect and room to prepare for a game. He was hands-off. Didn't require stretching or extra batting practice. He treated you like a man. Didn't try to force-feed anything down your throat. He trusted that you would do what you needed to do to be ready to play. And, if he had a problem with you, he'd speak to you about it privately. Never bad-mouthed players in the press.

Bobby also stayed positive, which was amazing because, in baseball, you fail more times than you succeed. And, with coaches, what you hear is mostly negative: "Next time, you need to . . ." or "What you should have done is. . . ." Not Bobby. He'd praise you. Or, if you struck out, he would say, "We'll get 'em next time." Like with Steve Bedrosian. Toward the end of his career, he came into a game with the bases loaded and got hammered. Gave up a grand slam and the lead and just didn't pitch very well. A few games later, Bobby put Bedrock right back out there in a similar situation: a short lead and the bases loaded. This time, the hitter popped up to end the inning. Bobby understood that baseball has its ebbs and flows, and he wouldn't give up on his players. He wasn't afraid if you had a bad game the day before. He believed that a player would get people out and get hits and make good plays. Guys thrived under Bobby Cox because he believed in his players so much.

Better than anybody I ever played for, Bobby understood the importance of putting guys in situations where they'll succeed. I wasn't a fast runner, so it didn't make sense to ask me to steal bases. But, as a right-handed hitter, I could put together some good at-bats against left-handed pitching. When I first joined the Braves, Bobby asked me to pinch hit in a close game against a lefty. What a change. When I was with Milwaukee and later the Mets until Dallas Green came along, I reached the point where, if the game were on the line and I was up next to hit, the manager would pinch hit for me. I didn't even have to look at the dugout because I knew that I was coming out of the game. That disappointed the hell out of me, not having the chance to win games. But there I was, having played only two games for the Braves and Bobby was looking for me to be the guy in the clutch to help the team. We were behind 3-2, with a runner on base and two outs. Bottom of the ninth. If I perform, I keep the team in the game. If I fail, we lose. Kevin Rogers was pitching for the Giants. I hit the first pitch for a single between shortstop and third. Mark Lemke scored and tied the game. Sent it into extra innings. I loved it. You never know what you can do unless you're given an opportunity to do it. Bobby let me know that I was an important part of the team and that I could contribute. That I was a player they could count on. That's all a player wants. It's the same thing as when you're a little kid: everybody wants to be the one to get a base hit to win the game.

Bobby's expectations were simple. Be ready to play. Play hard. Be a team player. As long as you followed those rules, he had no problems with you. But, if you were a me-first guy or if you loafed, you were gone. If you were a problem on the field or in the clubhouse, he didn't keep you around. Didn't matter how much talent you had. Bobby didn't take any shit off anybody. If a player violated one of his rules, there were consequences.

The bottom line is that Bobby Cox was an excellent manager. I played for some guys, and they were good managers. They had to be good because they made it to the Major Leagues and earned a managing job, and there's only thirty of those positions. But, it's funny. It's like some of them were so fearful of losing their jobs that they had to do everything by the book. They had to pinch hit or change pitchers instead of trusting their players and letting them play. That's what set Bobby apart from some managers. Same thing with his treatment of players. Simple respect to players is key. When you don't receive that kind of treatment, it dampens a team's spirits. Just makes the atmosphere tense. And, baseball's a tough game. You grind out 162 games in a season. To the extent a manager can stay positive and treat his players well, like men, that helps a team a lot. And, the good managers that I played for, guys like Dallas Green, Cito Gaston, and Bobby Cox to name a few, did these things. Some of the guys who weren't as good didn't do these things as well.

Bobby surrounded himself with good coaches. Good guys to play for, and Bobby gave them plenty of room to do their jobs. Leo Mazzone was a good pitching coach. His big thing was to pitch inside for effect but to get guys out by working the outside part of the plate. A good pitching coach adapts to his staff. Leo did that, especially with guys like Maddux and Glavine who wore out the outside corner. I'd argue with Leo that guys needed to pitch inside more, but he didn't budge much on his stance. He was away, away, away. Likeable guy. Funny guy who could tell some great jokes and stories. Could bullshit his way through some things. But, if you have a staff like he had, you can bullshit your way through things pretty well. And, while it was fun for me to catch guys like Glavine, Maddux, and Smoltz, I think the guy with the best job in that situation would be the pitching coach. To work with guys like that: incredible. These guys knew their mechanics. Knew how to pitch. Sometimes, all Leo would have to do is put their name in the lineup and then sit back and watch them do their jobs as well as anybody else in the league. Or, as well as some guys have ever played the game.

Jimy Williams ran spring training. Made sure that guys got all their work in. The manager's in the dugout, spending time with the media, but Jimy was out there, hitting ground balls, fly balls, keeping batting practice running smoothly. He was the practice coach on the field. Great baseball guy. Very knowledgeable. Real no-nonsense about "Hey, let's get our work in." He was always the first guy on the field. I loved to beat him out there. He was pissed when guys would get out there before him. And, I'd give him shit. When he hit fungoes, he hated for balls to be around his feet. So, from the outfield, Mark Lemke, Jeff Blauser, and I lofted balls in so they landed around his feet. Like a golf shot. Or, if we were close to him, we'd roll balls in as close as we could to him. If he saw a ball near him, Jimy would kick the shit out of it. He knew somebody was messing with him, but he couldn't tell where the ball was coming from. I messed with him for two years.

With the '95 team, the coaches and the players meshed really well. We had twenty-five solid guys who were typical Bobby Cox-type players. Guys who knew how to play smart baseball. Played it hard. Put the team ahead of themselves. You had a solid defense with guys like Lemke at second base. He wasn't the flashiest dude, but you could count on him to be in the lineup every day and catch every ball hit in his range. Do all the little things, the grinding part of the game to help your team. Hitting the ball or getting a walk to get guys over. Get guys in. Turning double plays in the field. The things that don't ever show up in a box score but that mean so much to win. Same thing with Fred McGriff and David Justice. Solid guys who went out there every day and played hard. Guys might get dinged up with little injuries, but nobody took days off. They wanted to go out there and play as much as they could, and they did. The coolest thing was that *every guy* on the roster had this attitude.

We had talented young guys too, like Chipper Jones. Chipper had all of the tools. Could hit, run, field, throw. Switch-hitter. He could do everything. Hit for average. Hit for power. As a rookie, he was confident in his abilities. Wasn't cockiness. Wasn't out of control. But, he knew he could play. Knew he belonged in the big leagues. And, he went out there and played like it. He liked the media. May have talked too much to them. We used to call him "Chirper." Some of the older players told him, "Don't worry about talking. Just play." Because, when you deal with the media, they tend to misconstrue things. That's why I always gave simple "Yes" or "No" answers. Was blunt and to the point. At the same time, if I had a bad game, I stood in front of my locker and answered their questions about it. Was accountable for it. Didn't hide out in a back room away from the media. Just told the truth, good or bad game. You can't be a phony and be willing to talk only if you have a good game. You have to be available, either way. Be honest if you had a bad game. Accept it. You'll gain respect that way. Because of that, sometimes, the media will give you the benefit of the doubt.

A few times, Chipper wasn't too excited about infield practice. He'd say that he'd sit one round out. So, I challenged him to see who could field the most grounders and throw the ball to first with the fewest errors. The throws had to be good because a coach was usually acting as the first baseman, and he wouldn't move a lot to catch the ball. If we tied, the win went to whoever had the most service time. Chipper was a rookie, and I had been in the league for close to ten years then. I won nearly every time, so Chipper had to provide service. Bring me a Snickers or a drink or something. By making it a game, that got him out there, practicing, honing his skills. Later, I had this same contest with Robin Ventura in Chicago and Troy Glaus in Anaheim.

Like I said, Javy Lopez was one of the best young catchers to come into the game in a long time. Ryan Klesko was there with a ton of ability. Big power hitter. Nice left-handed presence in the lineup. Talented guy. Wasn't the greatest outfielder, but his defense didn't kill you either. The mix of guys was fantastic. Rafael Belliard: great shortstop. Maybe he didn't hit very well, but he could hit guys over and get them in. When Blauser got hurt at the end of the season, Raffy stepped in and hardly made any mistakes. On the bench, we had Smitty (Dwight Smith) who could pinch hit, and the club made some smart moves toward the end of the season to pick up Luis Polonia and Mike Devereaux, guys who had been around the game for a while. Guys who were professional hitters. Could come in and get some big hits for us. On paper, we weren't the best team, statistics-wise. We didn't have a bunch of all-star hitters, but we walked a bunch. And, because our pitching was so good, we didn't need to score a lot of runs.

The real difference maker, in my mind, was Marquis Grissom. The club traded for him in early '95, and he gave us Gold Glove defense in center field. Gave us speed. Gave us that good lead-off hitter that we needed. At the time, he was the best defensive center fielder in baseball. He could throw. Played real shallow and caught a lot of flare hits that most guys miss. Because of his speed, he ran down balls that were hit over him too. He accounted for so many outs because of the range he covered.

The pitching staff was cohesive too. Pitchers shared a healthy competition. If Maddux had a good game, then Glavine wanted to follow it with an even better game. Same thing for Smoltz, Steve Avery, and Kent Mercker. They pushed each other to improve and to play at a high level. They laughed and joked about it, but there was no doubt that each of them wanted to be the best at whatever they were doing. If they golfed, it wasn't like, "Hey, let's just knock some balls around." It was about being the best. They would bet, and they'd come in to the clubhouse talking about who beat who. In the clubhouse, they'd have putting contests. And, they were intense: screaming and hollering over who was the best. Same thing with playing cards.

You could see this friendly competition in this batting practice game pitchers played to see who had the most hits or who hit the ball the best. Our coach, Pat Corrales, threw it. They'd split the pitching staff in half, usually five starters versus five relievers. Corrales would give them so many points for laying a bunt down, getting a run in, hitting a home run. Like my infield practice contests with Chipper, the losing team would serve the winning team by bringing them a Dr. Pepper or a bag of chips or something. Bring it to their locker and set it on their stool. During the game, there'd be some bitching about how this guy cheated or whatever, but Corrales had the final say. He was the judge who would say, "Hit" or "No hit," and then they'd be all over him: "What do you mean that wasn't a hit?" It was a lot of fun. Broke up some of the monotony of a long season. And, it was one of those things where the entire staff worked together.

A lot has been said about how great Atlanta's starting pitchers were, but we had a solid bullpen too. A lot of depth. Gave Bobby a lot of options. You had guys out there like Greg McMichael with a three-quarters delivery and his changeup as his out pitch, getting guys out throwing in the mid-eighties. Some lefties like Pedro Borbon and Mike Stanton. Brad Clontz had a submarine delivery. changeup specialist. On top of that, Mark Wohlers was one of the hardest throwers in the league. To win games, you need a good bullpen. Atlanta had a great one. The Braves' starting pitchers were some of the best I ever played with, guys who'd typically go six or seven innings into a game, if not longer. Pair these starters with the bullpen, and you had a great pitching staff top to bottom. Made it tough for the other team to score many runs.

Not only was the pitching talent rich, but, like the team's overall camaraderie, pitchers were a tight group. Atlanta had the only group of pitchers I ever saw with that kind of closeness. With other teams, a lot of guys would just go their own way after the games, but the pitchers especially and the Braves as a whole were close-knit. Probably the closest team I've ever been on. I think a lot of it has to do with the fact that most of the team came up through the minor leagues together. Guys knew each other well. Off the field, guys would go out to eat. If we were on the road, they'd hang out by the pool or get a group together and go see a movie. One off day, a bunch of guys went to a NASCAR race. Our bullpen coach, Ned Yost, served on Dale Earnhardt's racing crew. That created a connection for us, and some of the guys became interested in racing. All this off-the-field stuff means something. Builds chemistry. And, it carries over to the field.

Even though I didn't come up through the Braves system, I felt like I was part of the team. Guys like Blauser and Lemke made me feel welcome. I lockered near them. They were the team's smokers, so we put up a shower curtain between their area and everybody else's. Blauser had posters of half-naked girls up. I'd bring my kids in to the clubhouse, and one time, my son Chris pointed to one of the posters and said, "Dad, why is she showing her boobies?"

I was like, "I don't know. Why don't you go ask him?"

So, Chris went over and asked his question. Blauser lost it.

Lemke was great about keeping the team loose. He was from New York, up around Cooperstown, and we were playing in the Deep South. I loved being in Atlanta because the people there are more like they are where I'm from in Oklahoma than they are in other Major League cities. Country. Friendly. But, around Atlanta, we'd sometimes run into some real thick southern accents. Lemke could imitate them perfectly.

"How're yew?" he'd say, raising his voice real high. You couldn't even tell that he was from up north. He'd crack guys up. And, sometimes, he'd make it even better. He'd lost his front two teeth, so he'd slip out his false teeth and turn his cap to the side and do a few "How're yew's," and everybody'd be laughing.

The funny thing was, this spread across the team. When guys first walked in the clubhouse, they'd call out, "How're yew?" with some twang. Rafael Belliard spoke real broken English, but he was big on doing the southern accent and saying, "How're yew?" Raffy sounded Japanese when he said it, though.

They were just a bunch of good dudes. Family guys where you were comfortable bringing your kids around the clubhouse. Bedrock did that, and the Braves treated him and his boys well. I remember his son Cody, who was recovering from leukemia, throwing out the first pitch for a game. I credit Bobby Cox for creating such a good atmosphere to play in. I credit the organization as a whole, too. The Braves' scouts knew what kind of talent the team was looking for. They were just better than other clubs at evaluating talent and drafting it. I don't know if they did their homework better or if they were better scouts. On top of that, there was a lot of stability there. Not a lot of turnover. Scouts weren't coming and going. Same deal with the front office. It was put together better than any other team I've ever been on. This stability led to the results on the field. Fourteen straight division titles while Bobby Cox was the manager. That means a lot to an organization's success. The Braves did things the right way. Because of it, they won a bunch. They didn't win a bunch by luck. It was by design.

Everybody plays a different role on the club, and I saw Steve Bedrosian as a kind of player-coach. Earlier in his career, he was a dominant closer, but when I caught him, he'd shifted into a set-up role. Relief pitchers, or at least closers, tend to follow a cycle for their careers. They start out in long relief, move to set-up man, and then closer. When they lose some velocity and their stuff isn't as sharp as it once was, they step back into that set-up or long relief role. That's where Bedrock was. When he was closing games with the Phillies and winning the Cy Young a few years earlier, he was throwing hard fastballs and sliders with a velocity in the high nineties. When I caught him, he'd lost some speed. So, Bobby Cox mainly used him or Greg McMichael to face left-handed hitters and Pedro Borbon for righties to set up Mark Wohlers to pitch the ninth inning.

Bedrock taught the young guys in the bullpen the right way to prepare for a game. There's an art to warming up, and he showed them how to gauge situations. Figure out whether they needed to get hot in a hurry because they were getting ready to go in to a game. Or, once a guy was loose, he may need to back off a little bit. Take his time between pitches. Not tire his arm out. He was good about paying attention to the situation on the field to anticipate when Bobby would call a new pitcher into the game. What pitches you should warm up. Analyzing what you have. The mental preparation. Because, sometimes, you get up and throw five pitches, and you're in the game. Or, you get up, throw three different times, and you don't get in the game. You're at the mercy of the manager's whim. It takes a special person to handle that uncertainty. You can't let your guard down because, depending on how the game develops, you may be out there pitching just like that.

Some of this preparation varies depending on your role in the bullpen. A long reliever's out in the pen the whole game. He's staying loose by playing a little long toss with the outfielders between innings. Watching the game and telling some stories to pass the time. It's different for closers. When Bedrosian was a closer, he'd watch the first three or four innings from the dugout. Then he'd go into the training room and heat his arm. All the while, he's watching the game on TV and gauging whether it's a close game and the chances of being called in. The last few innings, he'd walk down to the bullpen and be there in case they needed him. Closers are all different, though. Like starting pitchers, they have their own routines.

Some guys hang out in the clubhouse most of the game. Hell, some nap until late in the game and it's time for them to warm up.

Bedrock worked with Mark Wohlers a lot. Wohlers was a young guy who'd been in the league for only a couple of years. Incredible stuff. A power arm, probably the hardest thrower in the National League at that time. Good forkball. Good slider. And, he threw 100 miles per hour, 102 miles per hour. With his stuff, he had the makings of a top-notch closer. But, the closer is a pressure position. If your starter fails, maybe your bullpen bails you out. Keeps you in the game by not allowing the other team to score any runs. If your team scores some runs, you may win. The flipside: if your closer fails, you usually lose. At the end of a close game, if your closer gives up the lead, you don't have much time to score any runs and get that lead back. Sometimes, there's *no* time. It's not a good spot for a young guy because of all the pressure. And, at times, Wohlers could let a blown save bother him the next day instead of just saying, "Screw it," and moving on. The bottom line is you can't change what happened: you blew a game, but you have to go out with a good frame of mind next time. If Wohlers was whining around after a bad game, Bedrock picked him up. Tried to work with him on the mental aspect of the game, to develop that thick skin and learn to put the bad things behind you. Keep an even keel where you believe in yourself. Don't get too high when you succeed. Don't get too low when you fail. If you're gloating because of how you pitched in one game, you may get your ass handed to you the next because you're not focused. If you're hanging your head about a bad game, then you take that negative attitude with you into the next. You can't do that. You have to shake off tough outings. Closers need a fearlessness, a strut that they can go into a game and it's theirs. Execute their pitches and attack hitters night after night with a brazenness that they'll get the job done even if they're not throwing their best stuff on a given day. That's a make-up thing. Some guys, like Bedrock, they have it. They're wired to come to the park every day, ready to pitch a few innings, and they're in charge. They're getting after it. Not everybody can do it. Not everybody can stand that pressure. You either have that fearlessness or you don't.

When Bedrock was a rookie, he had some veterans like Al Hrabosky and Gene Garber take him under their wings. If he had a bad outing, those guys picked him up. Taught him lessons about what it takes to come into games in relief situations. How to deal with the stress of it. That you can't get caught up in the moment and let your adrenaline overwhelm you, that you have to control it. Breathe deeply and slowly. Relax. Harness that excitement so that it helps you execute your pitches. Like any good veteran, the same as Pete Vuckovich, Don Sutton, and Tommy John did with me early in my career, Bedrock did a good job of passing the baton to the next generation. Veterans are usually willing to teach young guys. If they pay attention and listen, young guys can learn so much. Bedrock tried to reassure Wohlers that he wasn't perfect, that he was going to make mistakes, but he needed to learn from them and move on. It's a hard thing to do, especially for younger players, and Wohlers was a pretty young guy at the time. Fortunately for Mark, his situation was ideal in having a veteran like Bedrock pull him aside and teach him about the mental aspects of closing. Add Bobby Cox to this mix and his faith in his players. If Mark had a bad game, Bobby would put him right back out there. A lot of managers give you one or two shots. You don't do well, he won't use you any more. Not Bobby. He understood the pressure surrounding the closer's role. He didn't want it to be too much for Mark, so he didn't run him out there every time. With some experienced arms in the bullpen, guys who had closed games before and were used to late inning situations, Bobby could put Bedrosian in there. Alejandro Peña. Relieve some of the strain so Wohlers wouldn't crumble under the pressure day in and day out. And, in '95, Mark grew in to the closer's role. Started pitching more instead of just throwing. Understanding that you get guys out not just because you throw hard but because you pitch to locations. Change speeds. Use all of your pitches. I think watching Maddux and Glavine set up hitters had a big impact on Mark. Eventually, he took the ball and did a good job of closing games for us.

Bedrock had been around the league for a long time, and he approached the game the right way. He was well prepared. Was in great shape. Ran a lot. A few years before I played with him, he retired from the game. As I've said, he was having some health issues, and so was his young son. He needed some time away to deal with these things. Once those were taken care of and he decided to come back to baseball, he trained to get back into playing shape by working out under an intense Olympic weight lifting regimen. Russian squats and power cleans. All leg and back muscle work. As a relief pitcher, he couldn't do that kind of intense weight lifting during the season. You'd waste your leg muscles because of a workout that day and not be able to pitch that night. But, when I played with him, the weight training had paid off. He was a big guy anyway—six foot three—and the dude was strong. And, he played the right way. He'd throw inside if he needed to. Wouldn't hesitate to hit a guy for the right reasons—if a guy was swinging the bat real well or having a great series and just wearing us out. If a pitcher didn't throw inside when he should, Bedrock was up-front about chewing on the pitcher's ass. Letting him know that he disagreed. He'd say, "How come you didn't hit the dude? He went out there and smoked our cat, and you let him get away it. You can't do that. You've got to protect your own." Outspoken. Full bore all the way, on the mound and in the clubhouse.

Bedrosian put the team ahead of himself. His peeve was to come into a game with runners on base and give up a run. While the run didn't show up in his ERA, Bedrock felt like he was letting guys down when he gave up somebody else's runs. And, even though he worked with Mark Wohlers on controlling emotions and not letting a bad outing affect you, Bedrock didn't exactly practice what he preached. He hated to give up a hit to anybody. Didn't matter if it were a good hit or a broken bat dribbler. If somebody hit his fastball, he'd try to throw it harder, but this overthrowing affected how he located the ball. Overthrowing makes the ball stay in the middle of the plate more. Elevates the pitch. Makes it easier to hit instead of being where it needs to be: down and toward the bottom of the strike zone. That's the hardest place to hit a ball, and it was one of the lessons I tried to drill into all pitchers. If you don't know what to throw, throw it down and away.

I've said that one of the things Tommy John taught me was using humor to lighten a stressful situation. Bedrock did a great job at this. One time, he came into a tie game against the Giants at Candlestick in the bottom of the ninth, base runners on. Steve threw one pitch. The hitter launched it. Walk-off home run. That was the ballgame. They win. We lose. After the game, the clubhouse was quiet. Everybody's moping because we lost. We get on the bus to drive back to the hotel. The quiet continues. To break the tension, Bedrock calls out, "Hey, Leo," to Leo Mazzone.

"Yeah, Bedrock."

"What was my pitch count tonight?"

We lost it. Everybody was laughing. It took the edge off. Some games or experiences are bad. Some sting more than others. But you have to learn to let them go.

Maybe it's something about how you have to have a certain attitude to be a relief pitcher. Bullpen pitchers kept the team loose. Our stadium in Atlanta, Fulton County Stadium, attracted a ton of moths. Don't know why, but every time you went into the bullpen dugout, moths would gather on the ceiling. Bedrock told me that, one time early in his career, the guys decided to have a little fun with the moths. A pitcher, Bob Walk, stuffed like thirty of them into his mouth. Then he stepped outside, went to the railing separating the field from the fans, and started talking to this lady. Moths flying out of his mouth the entire time. Freaked her out.

Another time, Bedrock was telling me that, when he played with Kent Tekulve in Philadelphia, Tekulve was the main set-up man for Bedrock. Teke had a clause in his contract where he received $5,000 for every appearance he made after forty appearances. Once he passed that appearance mark and it was a good time for the set-up guy to come in and the bullpen phone rang, the relief pitchers knew that Teke was going into the game. They'd say, in unison, "Cha-ching," ringing up the cash register for Teke and his five grand. One year, Teke really raked it in when he made ninety appearances.

———————————

When he came into games, Bedrock made me think that he was pitching with his hair on fire. He wasn't one of those guys who saved a little bit when he pitched. He put everything he had out there on the field. He wanted to step in and pick dudes up and get them out of jams. And, he was confident that he'd keep the game where it was and that the other team wouldn't score any runs off him. Outstanding arm. Threw hard. Located the ball well. Threw strikes. He was a power pitcher who wanted to dominate guys with his fastball and slider. Toward the end of his career, he developed a good forkball too. One time, he threw a forkball, and it was dirty. Dropped like eighteen inches. Amazing. Good pitch to keep hitters off-balance, especially left-handed hitters. He liked that I could block pitches. That was a good thing, because, nine times out of ten, if we had two strikes on a guy, Bedrock liked throwing a slider in the dirt to finish off the hitter. A slider down and away is a great pitch that fools hitters. If a slider is thrown hard, it breaks late. Hard to see. Looks like a fastball, but at the end, it keeps sliding away from the head of the bat and drops. Great pitch for righty on righty situations. You get a lot of strikeouts this way, and Bedrock had confidence in his slider. Threw it with command in 2-0, 3-1 counts when the hitter is thinking fastball. That screws hitters up. They don't know what's coming. Leaves them guessing. They don't have much time to react when they're seeing a high nineties fastball or a ninety-one mile per hour slider. Put a little wrinkle in there, and hitters are really in trouble.

Unlike starting pitchers, we didn't have meetings with relief pitchers about the opposing lineup and hitters' tendencies. We'd have these meetings on the mound right after he came into the game. That's why you see pitching coaches out there. We'd talk about who's on deck. Who to pitch to. Who to pitch around. How we'd pitch to certain guys. Bullpen pitchers need to rely on their catcher to know the hitters and how they should be handled more than starting pitchers do. Like the other pitchers, Bedrock knew that I had a good reputation for pitch selection. Ninety-nine percent of the time, Bedrock went along with what I called for. Most of the time, we were in sync. In that pitcher-catcher rhythm where Bedrock's thinking, "Man, I want to throw a slider right here," and that's what I signal for.

But, he had real definite ideas about which pitches he wanted to throw to certain hitters. He liked to throw his fastball, and he wouldn't hesitate to shake me off.

Mechanically, he had a real herky-jerky motion that was all over the place. It was like seeing all elbows and assholes when he delivered the ball to the plate. It wasn't the prettiest or smoothest delivery, but he still threw hard and with good control. And, the way he finished his delivery left him in a good position to field the ball. He fielded well. Covered first well.

Bedrock had some superstitions or quirks, but by the time I caught him toward the end of his career, he had quit following most of these. At one point, he had to wear his favorite underwear, put his left sock on first, take so many swallows of water in between innings. If he pitched well, he had to eat the same thing for lunch as long as he kept pitching well. All that had tamed down, and he had only one superstition when I caught him: never stepping on the line when he walked on or off the field. Always stepped over it with the right foot first.

Like I said, Bedrock was intense. Very competitive. Hot-tempered as hell. If he had a bad night, he could go into the clubhouse and smash some bats. Blow off some steam. When that happened, I'd go over and tell him to keep pushing. I knew he was locked in and doing everything he could to execute his pitches. I knew he was a competitor and he'd shake off the bad outing. Let it go and be ready to get back on the mound the next day. I nudged him that way, but he didn't need me to get there. He was a veteran guy, and he'd figured out how to accept a loss and deal with it. Not take it out on the people around him. During the game, though, if he was getting hosed with some calls, that intensity would flash. He could get fired up at umpires. If Bedrock caught a bad call, he'd holler, "Come on!" or "Get on it!" The best umpires, you can say something like this. They just let it go and move on to the next pitch or the next play. They may say, "Okay. That's enough," and they end it. Other umpires jaw back to the pitcher instead of just diffusing a tense situation. Then the pitcher responds, and the two of them are in a testy conversation. These umpires just don't understand why they're there.

If Bedrock had any weaknesses, his delivery was slow to home. This opens the door for base runners to get a jump on stealing a base. But, in Atlanta, Leo Mazzone didn't push pitchers to work on their slide step to hold runners on.

Toward the end of '95, Bedrock's stuff was getting a little short. It didn't have the same velocity and pop that it had at the beginning of '94. Location wasn't as crisp. If he didn't have his best stuff, I'd try to help him by telling him to fake it. Act like he could make that pitch so the hitter wouldn't know that Bedrock didn't have a sharp fastball, a good slider, or whatever that night. And, I tried to help him focus on hitting his spots. Relying on location and putting the ball where it's tough to hit. This was an adjustment for him. Sometimes, he'd just let it rip. Throw instead of pitch. With his arm not the same as what it was eight years earlier in his career when he won the Cy, he had to concentrate on making his pitches. It happens to all of us: physically, you just can't do what you used to. It's hard to see, and it's difficult to deal with, not being able to do what you did earlier in your career. Bedrock spent a long time in the big leagues, fourteen years, but it can't last forever. Your skill definitely starts to slip when you're in your late thirties, and I caught his last game, a short outing against Cincinnati. He was lit up pretty hard. Bedrock was in his late thirties then, and he retired the first part of August. He was so well-liked in the clubhouse, and starting pitchers appreciated his contributions of coming into games and getting them out of jams so much that, when he left, guys were like, "We've got to win this for Bedrock." When he left, no question there was a void.

Bedrock liked playing in Atlanta. He was an all-around good guy, very likeable. Talked to everybody. Your typical Bobby Cox-type player where no one is better than anybody else and everybody is working hard and doing their best to play their role. He's a humble man. Not a guy who toots his own horn. He was named the best pitcher in the National League one year. But, he never made a big deal about winning the Cy. Good family man. Very close with his kids. As I said, brought them around the clubhouse. He was in the perfect situation, playing in Atlanta and living in the area. I think he's still around Newnan, Georgia, now. He's very involved in his community. Always has been. When he was playing in San Francisco and they had that big earthquake during the World Series, he was out there, volunteering for the Red Cross, passing out blankets. Now, he hosts an annual golf tournament to raise money for SAFE, a program to teach kids about the dangers of drugs and violence. For several years, he served on his local school board. Did what he could to help the kids in his county have the best educational opportunities. Wasn't about him. It was about the kids. That doesn't surprise me at all. He'd always do the right thing, and I could see him getting involved in politics. I could see him standing up if a change is needed. Getting after it to make sure it happens no matter how difficult the circumstances are. That's just the kind of guy he is.

As a senior in high school
at Bishop Kelley in Tulsa,
Oklahoma

On the Oklahoma team for the 1978 California-Oklahoma series. I'm number sixteen, on
the back row. I hit the first homerun by an Oklahoma player in the series. Six future big
leaguers are in this picture.

(*Top*) Mound meeting where I'm sharing my worldly knowledge. Notice how no one is listening. (Bernstein Associates / Getty Images Sport / Getty Images)

(*Above*) My friend, Dwight Gooden

(*Left*) Game Three of the 1995 National League Championship Series, circling the bases after hitting a three-run home run off David Wells. (Rick Stewart / Getty Images Sport / Getty Images)

(*Above*) Five of the greatest pitchers I worked with: Greg Maddux, Pat Hentgen, John Smoltz, Roger Clemens, and Tom Glavine

(*Left*) Thumping that ass for John Smoltz (*SI* Cover / *Sports Illustrated* Classic / Getty Images)

(*Below*) My World Series ring (1995)

Sports Illustrated

Another round of ugly brawls gives baseball and basketball a black eye

Enough Already!

The first hockey-style mask that I developed and produced with Eric Niskanen and Stan Jurga. All-Star Sporting Goods deserves tons of credit for making the mask a reality.

Behind the mask

Walking from the bullpen for Roger Clemens's first game back at Fenway. I was afraid I was going to get shot. I took off running right after this picture was taken.

Fieldin Culbreth and I having a pleasant conversation after he threw me out of the game. That was the only time in the big leagues I was tossed from a game. (Henny Ray Abrams / AFP / Getty Images).

(*Left*) The great lefty, Tom Glavine

(*Below*) Firing bullets in between innings (Otto Greule Jr. / Getty Images Sport / Getty Images)

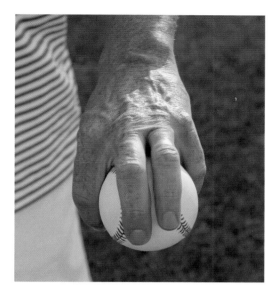

(*Left*) Glavine's changeup grip. Should be trademarked.

(*Below*) Picking up a bunt and throwing to first (Jonathan Daniel / Getty Images Sport / Getty Images)

Greg Maddux and I at a Braves alumni game

Today at home in Tulsa, Oklahoma

CHAPTER 8

GREG MADDUX

We were struggling with signs a little bit. The lighting was bad, and I couldn't see the signs too well. And, you're always worried about crossing up your catcher, especially with guys on base. And, Charlie comes out, and the way he says it is, "Hey, man, just fuckin' throw what you want. I'll catch it. Fuck it." Goes back to the plate. And, it kind of went from there. The freedom to cross up your catcher: it frees up your timing, your tempo, your rhythm. And, you have confidence that, if the pitch is close, he'll still be able to frame it, and if it's a brutal pitch, he'll still be able to block it.

Probably the biggest difference between Charlie and other catchers is that Charlie would tell you what you needed to do. Most of the other catchers would ask you, "Well, what do you want to do?" Charlie always seemed to have an answer, though. Other catchers tried to ask you what the answer was. That's what separates him. He knew the hitters as well as any catcher I've ever thrown to. That's where he excelled. And, he'd pat you on the back or kick you in the ass, depending on what you needed that day. It was obvious that he wanted you and the whole staff to do well. It was sincere. That gave him the right to get on to somebody when they were fucking up or being lazy or not giving a good effort. Because he cared. That's what separates a good catcher from all the others: how much does this guy actually care how a guy pitches. A lot of catchers say it, but few mean it. And, Charlie was one of those guys that meant it. A lot of catchers will say, "Oh, I'd rather catch a shutout than go four-for-four." And, it's kind of bullshit for four out of five catchers. But, with Charlie, you knew it was true. He would say things to make you better, not to kick you when you were down.

—*Greg Maddux*

[*Note: Greg Maddux is one of baseball's greatest pitchers. A model of consistency, he holds the record for most seasons in a row (seventeen) with fifteen wins or more.*[1] *Three times, he led the league in wins.*[2] *Four times, he posted the lowest earned run average.*[3] *Five times, he led the league in shutouts.*[4] *When comparing Maddux's statistics with other pitchers', some of the game's all-time greats become a part of the conversation. In 1994 and 1995, Maddux became the first pitcher since Walter Johnson to post back-to-back ERAs lower than 1.80.*[5] *During these same seasons, baseball writers unanimously selected Maddux for the Cy Young Award. Before that, the last pitcher honored with consecutive unanimous Cy Young Awards was Sandy Koufax.*[6] *In his career, Maddux won four Cy Young Awards (1992, 1993, 1994, and 1995). The other pitcher to win four Cy Young Awards: Steve Carlton.*[7] *The only pitchers to win more than four are Randy Johnson (five) and Roger Clemens (seven).*[8] *Maddux is the only pitcher in Major League history with 300 wins, 3,000 strikeouts, and less than 1,000 walks.*[9] *He also won more Gold Glove Awards (eighteen) than anyone else in Major League history, including Brooks Robinson (sixteen).*[10] *Unsurprisingly, Maddux was a first-ballot Hall of Famer, inducted into the National Baseball Hall of Fame in 2014.*

Charlie caught Greg Maddux during the 1994 and 1995 seasons. In 1994, Maddux posted a 16-6 record and a 1.56 ERA. He led the league in wins, ERA, shutouts (three), innings pitched (202), and complete games (ten). In 1995, Maddux was sterling, going 19-2 and again leading the league in wins, ERA (1.63), shutouts (three), innings pitched (209 ⅔), and complete games (ten). He earned Cy Young and Gold Glove awards each season.[11]

Charlie caught Maddux for three games in 1994 and twenty-seven in 1995, including five postseason starts when the Braves ultimately won the World Series, defeating the Cleveland Indians in six games. Maddux earned a World Series Game One win by pitching a complete game two-hitter (giving up no walks and striking out four), and he narrowly lost Game Five.

Following the 2008 season, Maddux retired with a career record of 355 wins, 227 losses, 3,371 strikeouts, and an earned run average of 3.16.[12] *All-time, he ranks eighth in most wins, and tenth in most strikeouts.*[13]]

In pressure situations, most pitchers try to reach back and fire the hardest stuff they can throw. Greg Maddux did the opposite. When the game was on the line, he slowed the game down. Took a little off of his pitches or relied on his changeup. His theory was that, in pressure situations, the hitter's amped up. He's looking to get a big hit and crush the ball. He's going to speed up his swing. To counter that, Greg would take a little speed off of the pitch. Maybe add a little more movement to it. Throw the ball down and in to right-handed hitters or down and away to left-handers.

One game, we were playing the Giants. We were leading 1-0 or 2-1, just barely ahead, toward the end of the game. Eighth inning or so. The bases were loaded with two outs. Barry Bonds was the hitter. It was a 3-0 count, and Greg signaled for me to come out to the mound. I trotted out to talk strategy.

Greg said, "I'm going to throw him three straight changeups."

Most guys won't throw a 3-0 changeup. They may throw one off-speed pitch, but then they'll go to their fastball. Greg had a lot of confidence in his changeup, though. Makes sense. It's a hard pitch to keep fair if the pitcher throws it in the right spot, and Greg could hit any spot. If he walked Bonds, Greg didn't care. Didn't have a fear about walking guys. If Bonds hit him, it was going to be off a fastball, so Greg was like, "I'm throwing changeups." He was throwing *his* pitch. Wasn't going to give in. He was going to throw strikes, and the hitter was going to get himself out.

"All right," I said, and I went back to the plate. Slung on my mask. Squatted down and waited for these changeups. The first one was a strike. Bonds fouled off the second change. Then, Bonds watched the third one cross the plate for a strike. He struck out in three pitches, and we won the game.

Greg surprised hitters with this slow down approach. It typifies Greg Maddux. He understood the game well. Understood his strengths and weaknesses, hitters' strengths and weaknesses. Had a good feel for the right pitch to throw in certain situations. Earlier in his career, Greg would rare back and try to blast the ball past hitters. Got beat that way. He's a smart guy, though. He learned from his mistakes and his losses and figured out that he had to change some things. Figured out a different approach that worked great for him.

———————

Catching Greg Maddux in '95 was catching a master in his prime. I've worked with a lot of talented cats. They all impressed me with their ability, their determination. But Greg was something different, something special. The dude was just locked in all season long. It was like he was pitching as well as anybody can pitch. Looking back, I realize what a gift it was to work with a guy who is one of the game's all-time great pitchers. Not only that, but to catch him during a season when he was at his peak. Pitching the best baseball of his life. I'm honored I saw it so close and firsthand. It was a privilege, and I don't know that there will ever be another pitcher to play as well as Greg did in '95. Ever. And, working with him that season, that's one of the coolest things I did in my career.

I became his catcher in part because he pitched on rhythm. Once he was in the flow of the game, he wanted to keep throwing, keep the game moving. He didn't want the catcher to take a lot of time in between pitches to figure out the next pitch to call. I was in the right place at the right time, because Javy Lopez was still learning how to call a game. He hadn't mastered the intricacies of pitch selection and reading scouting reports, keeping straight who's hot and what the hitters' tendencies are. It's a lot of information to remember and apply during a game. I had been around the league for a while. Knew how to call a game. Knew the hitters. I wouldn't slow Greg down, so Greg was like, "Why not throw to this guy?"

A year or so ago, Leo Mazzone and I were talking about Maddux. Leo remembered the first time I caught Greg. It was in spring training, my first season with the Braves.

After Greg pitched a bullpen session to me, Leo asked him, "Well, how was he?" You know, seeing how the new guy is.

I guess Greg said something like "I tried to fuck him up, but I couldn't. He's good."

That sounds like Greg. Seeing how I would adapt when he threw a pitch different than what I signed for. I appreciated the compliment.

Once I started catching him, I found out a few things that he liked. For one, he wanted you to set up early. Liked having a target to zero in on. Some pitchers want you to set up at the last second when they're making their delivery home to reduce the chances of tipping pitches. Not Greg. He wanted his target established before he started his delivery. So, I set up low and wide to the ground, creating as large of a target as I could. Some catchers would set up higher on breaking balls, lower on fastballs. I didn't do that. Tried to offer the same low, wide target regardless of the pitch. Pitchers like this because it looks spread out and easy to hit.

Another thing he liked was the way I caught the ball. I wouldn't move. I tried to sit there and be still. Some catchers are kind of herky-jerky and stab for the ball or lunge their bodies to catch a ball. All of this jostling can make the umpire think that the pitcher is off target and that the catcher is having to reach for the ball outside the strike zone. Makes it easier for an umpire to call the pitch a ball. But, if the umpire doesn't perceive any movement, he may think that the pitcher hit his target. You improve your chances of him calling it a strike. So, I tried to be still. Relaxed and calm. Know the pitch that's coming and read the ball from the pitcher's hand and anticipate where the glove should be. Move my glove slightly and do my best for it to appear that the pitcher hit his target. Growing up, I always liked how Bob Boone received the ball so quietly, and I tried to model this part of his game. In between pitches, I might move a step one way or another, but once I set up, I sat there. Plus, by being still, you create an easier target for the pitcher. It's the same thing as when you're shooting something: it's harder to hit a moving target than it is a still one. Pitchers loved my stillness. By my moving only slightly, they felt locked in because it looked like they were hitting their target nearly every time.

Greg had the best control I ever saw. Talk about a guy hitting his spots pitch after pitch. One way I took advantage of this was how I set up behind the plate. I positioned my hand on the corner of the plate and caught the ball with the tip of the glove actually off the plate. Doing this made pitches that were balls look like strikes. Kind of like an optical illusion. With Greg consistently hitting his target and me being perfectly still, it pressured the umpire to call strikes. Greg had a reputation for throwing strikes. He was hitting his spots. I wasn't moving at all to catch the pitches, so they must be strikes, right? The other team couldn't complain because I caught the ball so it looked like he was throwing strikes. The combination of Greg's control and the tricks I learned about framing pitches was lethal. Meant he could wear out the corner of the plate all day long. It's fun now to watch replays of some of those games and see how many of his pitches were called for strikes that were really balls.

Don't get me wrong: framing pitches or stealing strikes is neat and everything, but it works only if the pitcher can hit the target. Greg could do it nearly every time. His control was unlike anything I've ever seen. He was a hell of a pitcher, one of the two best pitchers I ever caught, and I caught just about all of the great pitchers of the nineties with the exception of Randy Johnson, Pedro Martinez, and Mike Mussina. Greg could place a ball anywhere. With most pitchers, the ball tends to tail to the side that the pitcher is throwing from. What I mean is that, if the pitcher is right-handed, the ball will tend to move to the right side of the plate. Greg, though, could place the ball so it moved five feet in front of home plate either to the left or the right. And, his accuracy was phenomenal. During the game, he might miss one or two pitches. I'm not exaggerating too much when I say that I could've caught him while I sat in a rocking chair. All I had to do was hold up my glove, and he'd hit it. And, he was very demanding of himself. If he missed a spot during his warm-ups, he'd scream, "Fuck!" I was like, "Dude, we're just warming up here." During a game, though, he maintained his composure. If he gave up a hit, he might holler a little, but he wouldn't let it fluster him. Some guys, they fire their gloves. Kick shit around. Not Greg. He moved on to the next hitter.

The big question is how did he have such great control? What could other pitchers mimic and have the same results? I don't know the answer. A lot of it was that he had a unique talent. Another thing was that he understood how his mechanics worked better than most pitchers. When Greg was coming up with the Cubs, Dick Pole was his pitching coach. Dick made Greg understand why certain pitches worked. What they were supposed to do once Greg released the ball. What in his mechanics caused this. Dick's thinking was that, every time Greg got into a jam, Dick couldn't get into Greg's brain and help him figure out what wasn't working. Greg needed to do this on his own. Needed to make adjustments while he was pitching and not wait until between innings to hash it out with his pitching coach. So, he had to explain to Dick why some pitches worked and why others didn't. Greg learned to understand what his body was doing to cause these differences. From that, he figured out what adjustments he needed to make.

While we're on mechanics, I'll add that Greg had good ones. His delivery was consistent. Dick worked with him on the positioning of his head, chin, and stride. How he removed the ball from his glove. His tempo. For all the fundamentals that he used in the big leagues, Greg credited Dick Pole with most of these. He used his legs properly. Avoided placing stress on his arm and the rest of his body. Pitched with a good arm angle. His front shoulder closed when he delivered the ball to home plate. Had a smooth finish where both feet landed square to home. His finish placed him in a perfect position to field the ball. That's part of the reason why he won so many Gold Gloves. He expected the ball to be hit back to him, and he'd make five or six fielding plays a night.

On top of Greg's outstanding control, he also threw the ball with incredible movement. Could make the ball do amazing things. He proved the point that movement is more important than velocity. Greg was a big believer in that. He didn't worry about the radar gun. He focused on the ball's movement during that last ten to fifteen feet toward home plate. Like his cutter. Was three to four miles per hour slower than his fastball. Looks like a fastball, and when you start to swing, the ball will cut in to a lefty and away from a righty. Breaks maybe about a third as much as a slider. When you start swinging at it, it looks like you'll hit the head of the bat on the ball, but the ball moves enough so it hits off the end of the bat or toward the handle. You don't make solid contact that way. Most cutters start cutting as soon as the ball is released from the pitcher's hand. The hitter can spot it and adjust. Greg's, though, would stay straight for so long and then cut five or eight feet in front of home plate, in to left-handed hitters and away from right-handers. Weirdest thing. I've never seen anything else like it. Could totally stymie hitters. Same thing with his changeup: incredible movement. It looked like his fastball except it would drop. The drop is what set Greg's changeup apart. Most changeups look like a fastball with less velocity, but Greg's was incredible in how the bottom would just fall out from under it. Tough pitch to hit. His fastball had great movement too. On left-handed hitters, the ball would almost be at the hitter's hip, then it would zip in and cross the inside part of the plate for a strike.

Because his pitches moved so much, some hitters squawked that Greg scuffed the ball. He didn't. I checked. His pitches moved so much that *I'd* look at the ball to see if it were scuffed. If that's why it was moving like it did. But, the ball was clean. I'd show it to the umpire, the hitter, anybody who asked. Now, if the ball was beat up a little, like from somebody hitting a ground ball, Greg knew how to use it and make it move even better. And, I kept my shin guards sharp. If we had a critical situation, I might rub the ball against the shin guard. Try to slip him a ball here or there that he could use to his advantage. But, that wasn't something that Greg knew about. His movement was all in his finger pressure and grips. In his mechanics by changing his arm angles or flexing his wrist. It had nothing to do with scuffing the ball.

With his movement and location, Greg could place the ball in spots where it was difficult for hitters to get good wood on it. They just couldn't hit his pitches hard. He didn't throw overpowering stuff like Roger Clemens or Nolan Ryan, but his ball had so much movement on it that hitters would be out in front of the ball on one pitch, behind on another, and jammed for the next. He could run his cutter inside and jam guys where they hit the ball on the label or below it. He could throw his changeup to lefties, and if they made contact, they'd hit it off the end of the bat and the ball would barely go anywhere. I used to give Greg hell that he didn't have to make any hard plays to win all those Gold Gloves because the ball practically stopped once it left the bat. Sometimes, the ball would be hit so weakly that Greg had to run to get the ball and turn around and toss it to first base. In some parks, like Wrigley Field and Atlanta, where the grass was kind of long in the infield and the dirt was a little wet around home plate, the ball *really* slowed down. Giving him hell wasn't far from the truth.

Greg was one of the most cerebral guys I worked with. Had an intellectual approach to the game. He analyzed hitters. Our lockers were next to each other, and in the clubhouse, some guys don't want to talk about baseball. That's the last thing they want to talk about. Not us. We spent a lot of time talking shop. If a game was on TV, we were like, "Why is that guy throwing that?" Or, we'd talk about hitters, what pitches we'd throw in certain situations. Greg would pick apart how other pitchers got guys out. Ask, "How did you get so-and-so out with that pitch? I never get him out with that pitch."

I'd say, "That's great. But, this is what we did. This is how we had success in getting a guy out."

We'd analyze how a certain hitter was a breaking ball hitter. To get him out with breaking pitches, we'd need to throw these outside of the strike zone because, if Greg threw a breaking pitch for a strike, we had a good chance the hitter would hit it. We went round and round about how to pitch to guys. Greg would pick my brain and ask, "What did Cone do?" "How did Viola get that guy out?" "What kind of pitch did Gooden throw?" It was interesting to see the different approaches. To see how one guy got one hitter out and how another guy got the same hitter out going a different way. There's not just one way to skin the cat. But, as far as taking this information about how Smoltz or Gooden or whoever got guys out, Greg didn't use that to adjust how he faced hitters. He stuck with his game plan unless a guy started having success against him. Then he adjusted. And, I think that's one of the things that made him so good. He didn't bounce back and forth. He just went with what was right and what worked for him.

Mark Wohlers was a young player with Atlanta then. Grew into the closer's role in '95. He moved his locker next to Greg's and mine. When Greg and I had these conversations about pitch selection and how to get guys out, Mark listened. Sometimes, his mouth would be open, jaw dropping, and after Greg and I dissected how we'd pitch to a hitter, Wohlers would shake his head. "Man, I didn't realize that much was involved in pitching." But, this kind of goes back to what I was saying about older guys being available to work with younger ones. Mark had the right attitude of wanting to learn, to absorb as much as he could. Greg and I were happy to help him. Share what we knew and help make him better.

When he wasn't pitching, Greg watched the other team's hitters, seeing what they hit, what they missed. He wouldn't jack around while the opposing team was hitting (he'd wait until in between innings or when we were hitting) because he was studying hitters. He liked watching games when finesse guys like Glavine were pitching, not power dudes. Greg didn't have the kind of stuff that guys like Smoltz had—Greg knew he couldn't go out there and throw five sliders in a row like Smoltz could. So, he preferred watching a guy like Tom Glavine and seeing what kind of results he had by pitching outside.

He knew the scouting reports too. Before the games he pitched, we'd go over these. Talk about the guys swinging the bat well. Who we needed to pitch around and not give them something they wanted to hit. Greg had definite ideas about what would work and what wouldn't, and he was headstrong as hell about it. His theory was to stick with his strengths. He wouldn't change because it was a day game or a night game or because he was playing in a park with short or deep fences.

He was confident in, maybe even stubborn about, his game plan based on what he did well. He'd stick with it even on the days when he didn't have his best stuff. At times, I'd try to suggest something to him, and I'd have to present it like, "You might want to think about this. . . ." He wasn't big on taking advice, though. Look at his record and try to argue with those results. ERAs in '94 and '95 that were under 2.00, the best since Bob Gibson in 1968. And, this was during the height of the steroid era when offenses were exploding. Unbelievable numbers. But, a few times he was wrong. Like during the World Series, Game Five, with Jim Thome up. From the scouting reports, I knew that Thome hit the changeup well. Greg threw a changeup, and Thome had a good swing. Just barely missed it. Next pitch, I signaled for a cutter on the inside of the plate. Greg shook me off. He wanted to throw another changeup. That's what he threw, and Thome waffled it right past Greg's ear into center field.

When I say Greg had definite ideas about how to succeed, I can't emphasize this point enough. Unlike any pitcher I ever caught, Greg called his own pitches. Before games, we'd go through the signals. If he wiped his head, he'd throw a slider. Holding his glove to his chest meant a fastball inside. Adjusting his cup meant changeup. Our thought processes were alike, in that we both thought several pitches ahead in the game. What I mean is, when I signaled for a pitch, I already knew the next pitch or pitches I'd call depending on if the pitch I just asked for was a ball or a strike. I knew this by studying the scouting reports and knowing which pitches dudes liked to hit, knowing which guys were hot. And, knowing my pitcher. What he did well. What his weaknesses were. Same deal with Greg. He liked certain patterns of pitches depending on the situation. No other pitcher was as structured or rigid as Greg was in how he had these series of pitches he liked to throw. He had a certain rhythm, and it worked for him. One time, after I left Atlanta and was playing in Toronto, I told Shawn Green, a left-handed hitter, that if he were hitting against Greg with no base runners on board, he should look for a pitch sequence of a fastball away, a cutter inside, a fastball that runs back inside, and a changeup. If there were base runners, Greg might throw a cutter inside, then two changeups.

Sure enough, Shawn spotted the pitches. Hit a home run. Shawn thanked me for it. I felt kind of bad about that, but at the same time, I'm competitive. I wanted my team to win. I'd help however I could.

Greg's whole approach to pitch selection was that he'd throw you what you didn't want. Most guys are good at hitting a fastball either in or away. Greg would avoid those pitches the hitter wanted to hit *unless* there were a base runner on or the game were on the line. Then, he'd throw what the hitter hadn't seen before:

the pitch he wanted to hit. The example is that the hitter is a good inside fastball hitter. For his first three at-bats, Greg would throw him fastballs away. Then, on the fourth at-bat, with runners on, the game on the line, and with the hitter expecting to see more fastballs away, is when Greg would throw him a fastball inside. He'd confuse hitters. Major Leaguers are good at adjusting. Most guys, you can't get out the same way three or four times in a game. Greg understood this. So, he'd give guys different looks depending on the situation.

One time, Greg said he'd take the heat for me as far as calling pitches. It was in the playoffs against Colorado in '95. Eric Young was the base runner on first. I could tell when EY was going to try to steal second because he'd wiggle his fingers if he was getting ready to run. If he wasn't running, his whole body was still, even the fingers. An 0-2 count. I saw Young's fingers wiggling. So, I called for a pitch out. Greg threw it. I fired the ball to second, but EY didn't go anywhere. I guess he got a bad jump or something. Decided not to go. Anyway, I look over to the dugout. Bobby Cox is having a fit. Mad as hell about this pitch out that he didn't call. The batter wound up hitting a blooper, and the runner scored.

I went out to the mound. Greg was like, "Bobby's pissed."

"I know."

"Well, I'll tell him that I called for the pitch out. He won't get mad at me."

I said, "Okay."

So, we finish the inning. Go back to the dugout. Bobby jumps all over me. Chews my ass out about calling for the pitch out.

Greg sat right next to me and never said a word.

When Bobby walked away, I looked at Greg and said, "Thanks a lot, asshole."

He laughed.

Greg's calling pitches was something that he started with me. Later, he said that it was something he tried to do with the other catchers he worked with after me. Like I said, Greg was a big tempo guy. You really slow the game down if base runners are on and you go through a more elaborate series of pitching signs. Shake off the catcher a few times, and you wind up with fifteen signs for one pitch. I was like, "Just throw what you want to throw. I'll catch it." That saved Greg time. Made the game move faster. I know this helped Greg out, not only when I caught him, but for the rest of his career.

———————————

Greg tried to throw as few pitches as possible. His body wasn't built for stamina. Wasn't a big workout geek. Hated to run and lift weights. He didn't have thick legs, which most pitchers rely on for speed and stamina. Didn't have the strongest arm either, but when I caught him, he threw ten complete games. He could go the distance by maintaining a low pitch count. One way he did this was by getting ahead of hitters and avoiding three ball counts. Going for the strikeout at an 0-2 count. Some pitching coaches cringe at the idea of giving up an 0-2 hit. And, some pitchers, when the count is 0-2, they like to knick and nibble, throwing some trash and seeing if the hitter will chase it. Greg wouldn't. He figured, with this count, the hitter was at his most vulnerable, so he'd go for the strikeout by hitting a corner. If the hitter got a hit, well, tip your hat to the guy and go on to the next hitter. But, by not wasting pitches, he could pitch complete games and not even break a sweat.

One knock I heard against Greg was that he wasn't a big game pitcher. I disagree. Look at the guy's entire body of work. He won over three hundred games, had a career ERA of just barely over 3.00. I'll take that any day against anybody. He was one of the toughest pitchers to face because his control was so precise and because the ball moved unlike anything else hitters faced. Maybe he lost some big games because his team didn't play well behind him. Didn't give him good defense or good run support. And, I point out one other fact: Game One of the '95 World Series. Greg threw a two-hitter against the Indians, a team loaded with hitters: Kenny Lofton, Jim Thome, Albert Belle, Eddie Murray, and Manny Ramirez. That was a big game, and he dominated it. Two hits.

That World Series game: we prepared for it the same as we did every other game. By keeping it normal and on a regular pattern like you do other games, you take away some of the butterflies. Go do what you've always done. That way, I wasn't nervous. And, my mind was occupied in trying to get tickets for family who came into town for the game. Making sure they're taken care of. This irritates some guys, the increased media, the pull for more tickets. I had fun with it, though. And, Maddux did his bullpen work before the game just like any other. Bobby Cox was calm. The whole team was workmanlike. We had a mix of young guys with veteran guys who'd been there before. Even though it was my first and ultimately only World Series, I had played enough baseball to understand that you've got to keep things simple. Treat it like another game.

Some of that game stands out. In the first inning, Lofton stole second base without a throw. I really didn't have a chance at him. But then, a pitch or two later, he broke for third, and I threw him out. The umpire called him safe, though. Lofton wound up scoring that first run of the game. I was like, "Oh, man." Because the Indians came in to the game with the best offense in the big leagues. But, we came back. Scored some runs. And, Greg gave up only two hits. Pitched an outstanding game.

After the game, there was no conversation between Greg and me of like, "Wow. I just pitched a two-hitter against one of the best offenses, maybe of all time. What a hell of an accomplishment." He was very low-key. Didn't get excited about anything. Glavine was the same way. Unemotional. Didn't want anybody to acknowledge their good job or bad job. They just wanted to go out and pitch. Workmanlike is the way I think of those guys. And, that's how I liked to play. I wasn't one of those real emotional guys. So, to play with those cats, with that kind of approach to the game, it was a good fit for me. And, I never thought much about that kind of stuff until after my career was over. That I had played this game all my life. Busted my ass in the minors. Made it to the big leagues when I was twenty-five, an age where most guys have washed out of the game if they haven't made it by that point. Played ten years in the big leagues and just caught Game One of the World Series with one of the game's all-time great pitchers. A complete game two-hitter. Holy shit, what an accomplishment. Not many people can say that. But, when you're in that moment, when you're playing, you don't think about it like that. I didn't anyway. But, I think that's one reason why you're successful: you don't have that kind of emotional attachment to what you just did. If you do, your body wants to do different than what it normally does. You have to have an even keel to handle the ups and downs of baseball. Like I've said, the game involves a lot of failure, and you can't let it affect you too much. Can't carry your last bad game with you out on the field, or you won't last long. You have to be able to say, "Forget about it; I'll be a lot better player than I was yesterday," and put it behind you. Or, act like you didn't even play yesterday, if you were really bad. Same thing with your last good game. If you keep your composure and don't get too high when things are going well, it keeps you steady. And, it was Game One. Yeah, it was great that we won, but we had three more games to win. That was one battle, but the war wasn't over kind of thing. There's not time to sit there and pat yourself on the back. You're playing the best team in the American League, and they're gunning for you the next day and the day after that. They'd won four games in a row a couple of times that year. You didn't want them to get on the same kind of tear against you. You have to stay focused on the big picture, not just playing one good game.

Greg started Game Five, and it had its dramatic moments. Eddie Murray was hitting. Greg pitched inside. The ball got away from him and wound up around Eddie's head a little bit. Eddie started barking at Greg: "You don't have to throw at my head! You know where the ball's going!"

He thought Maddux was trying to throw at him. Benches cleared. I stepped in between Eddie and Greg.

I said, "Eddie, the ball just got away. He ain't trying to hit you, bud." Like I've said, I think the world of Eddie Murray. Great dude. Great player. Great teammate.

It may have looked like I was jawing at Eddie, but I was just talking to him. I knew Eddie wasn't going to go out there. Eddie wasn't going to fight anybody.

"Yeah, he threw the ball up at my head," he said.

"Come on, dude. Trust me. He's not trying to hit you. If he wanted to hit you, he'd hit you right in the head."

"He ain't got to throw a ball right at my head."

I said, "I understand. The ball got away from him, man."

I think that diffused Eddie. And, it's true: I don't think Greg was throwing at Eddie. Maddux wasn't the kind of guy to throw at hitters because he was pissed off. Not his style. He'd throw at guys if they needed to get hit or to protect his teammates. But, he didn't have a reason to hit Eddie Murray.

Eddie got on base, though. Greg walked him. Right after that, I picked him off at first. He was mad at me for that more than anything, probably.

I mentioned that Greg called his own pitches. I had fun when I walked out to the mound and he said, "My brain is fried. I'll just throw whatever you call." He did it only two or three times. I was like the puppeteer pulling the strings then. With his calling the game, he took away part of my fun. I got part of it back when he told me to call the game. He could throw whatever I wanted wherever I wanted it: high, low, inside, outside. Most guys can't do that. It was the coolest thing. But, I also understood what he liked to do. What he was good at. How he had the most success. Patterns of pitch sequences that he liked to throw. So, it wasn't like I completely changed pitch selection and his approach to hitters. I just enjoyed being able to think through situations, know the hitters, know which pitches to call, and see him execute them, usually perfectly.

And, I enjoyed Greg. Liked to mess with him. Pinch his arms because he was such a skinny little dude. He was a geek in the clubhouse. Loved playing video games. Big golfer. Loved eating McDonalds. And, he was a goofball. Great teammate because he was always joking around and messing with people. Could figure out how to get under guys' skin and ride them and give them hell. Gave Smoltz and Wohlers shit about their golf games. One time, I brought my son into the clubhouse. He must've been three, maybe four years old. Greg yelled at him, "Hey, Cameron!" My son looked over at him, and Greg's mooning him. Crazy. He'd be talking to you in the shower and be pissing on your foot at the same time. Our bench coach, Jim Beauchamp, was one of Greg's favorite pissing targets. He'd wipe his boogers on you. Shake your hand all weak and limp-wristed and say, "Hey, Hot

Rod." Goofy shit, but he was fun to be around. You kept an eye on him because you didn't know what kind of shit he'd pull.

On game days, he stuck to a routine. Ate about three or four hours before the game. For day games, he'd load up on pancakes. If it were a night game, he'd order a room service cheeseburger on the road, or he'd stop by Arby's or Burger King on his way to the park if he was at home. If it were a 7:40 p.m. game, he'd walk down to the bullpen at 7:17 p.m. so he could start throwing at 7:20 p.m. Be done at 7:35 p.m. He'd play cards before the game with the other team's lineup in front of him. On his side days, he knew the next team he was facing, so he'd mentally pitch to that upcoming lineup. He wasn't down there just throwing. He was thinking about that next lead-off hitter he'd face. And, one other thing: no golf the day before he pitched.

Around the press, he was real stoic. Hated the limelight. Very unassuming. He didn't want to deal with the media, but when he did, he gave the credit to others, complimenting the offense for good hitting or the defense for good fielding. He just wanted to go out and pitch and compete and not have any one know about it. He wanted to play his game, and then, after the game, he loved to put on his glasses and this old baggy suit and slide out of the clubhouse unnoticed. He didn't want people to recognize him when he went out in public. A regular guy.

On the mound, he was unflappable. He could be in a jam, in a big game. Fifty thousand people screaming. All eyes on him. He'd be so cool about it. Not even break a sweat. He'd be so calm and say, "All right. Let's throw this pitch here and get out of here." And, he'd do it. This was so different from some of the other guys I caught. Guys like Pat Hentgen and Roger Clemens, guys who were so fired up and intense, you could see the veins in their neck pumping.

During the two years I played with him, he was locked in like no other. So accurate. So easy to catch. I rarely had to block a ball because his control was so precise. Wherever I went with the glove, he'd go with me. I wouldn't have to dive over here or dive over there because he was wild. I look back and think what it would've been like to play with him for five or six years. That would've been some-thing. Could've done some great things. But, I'm glad I had the chance to play with him for two seasons. Because, if I were able to pick a team from scratch, the first player I'd choose would be Greg in his prime. I say this partly because he was such a dominant pitcher. I also say it because he was such a student of the game. Could teach other guys on the staff tips that helped him achieve so much success. Make the other guys around him better. I saw him do that with Glavine and Smoltz. He taught them how to get better by watching the other team, studying their tendencies and their weaknesses. This made Glavine and Smoltz better pitchers, and I know it'd help other guys too. That's kind of what Greg is doing now with Texas. Consulting work where he visits the Rangers a few times, their minor league teams for a few days, and is another set of eyes for the coaches. Lets them know what he sees and how pitchers can improve. Just a smart, smart baseball guy. And, one of the best ever to pitch a baseball.

CHAPTER 9

TOM GLAVINE

Charlie was tremendous in calling a game in terms of knowing the hitters and the scouting report. The thing I always looked forward to when Charlie caught me, and I don't mean to say this the wrong way, but I felt like I could turn half of my brain off. You knew you didn't have to think too much because Charlie was going to help you get through the game. You knew you weren't going to have to recall scouting reports or sequences of pitches by yourself because Charlie was there to help you out with it. You knew he remembered what happened the last at-bat. He had a good grasp of what the hitters were good at and also what you were good at as a pitcher. From a mental standpoint, he took a lot of the workload off of you. I knew he was going to do his homework and help me with that part of the game.

—*Tom Glavine*

[*Note: While the 1995 season belonged to Greg Maddux as one of the finest pitching performances in baseball history, Tom Glavine stepped into that postseason's spotlight. A self-described soft-tossing lefty, he started and won Game Two of the World Series by allowing three hits in six innings and giving up only two runs. He topped this performance in the final game of the Series, Game Six, when he pitched eight innings and allowed one hit, leading the Braves to a 1-0 win over the Cleveland Indians that brought Atlanta its first World Series trophy.[1] His performances were so sublime that Glavine was named the World Series Most Valuable Player.[2]*

Charlie caught Glavine over two seasons. In 1994, Glavine was 13-9. Charlie caught nine of these games, six of which were wins, and two were losses. In 1995, Glavine was 16-7. Charlie caught three games: one win, one loss, and one no decision.

Overall, Glavine pitched for twenty-two seasons, seventeen of them with the Braves, winning 305 games, losing 203, striking out 2,607, and maintaining a 3.54 earned run average.[3] During his career, he won the Cy Young Award twice: first in 1991 when he won twenty games and led the league in wins and complete games (nine), and again in 1998 with a 20-6 record. He retired in 2008 and was inducted into the National Baseball Hall of Fame in 2014 in his first year of eligibility.]

Winning a World Series is something you dream about as a kid. It's what you play for, what you work toward every year, what you want to accomplish in your career. To finally make it there, it's hard to describe. Everything is elevated. Every game means something. Not only that, but every play means something. Hell, every pitch seems like it means something. Because this is it: you've played an entire season, and it's down to who wins four games. During the regular season, it may be game one hundred. If you lose, you have another sixty-two to go, and you think, "Well, we'll try and win the next one. We can turn it around." In the playoffs, though, it's win or go home. You want to get that edge and win the first game. Or claw back and tie it up if you drop the first one. Everything is magnified. Concentrated. Not only with the games, but also with everything else that surrounds them. The media attention is greater. Family is in town and staying with you. The vibe from the fans that this would be the year we finally won. People you don't know coming up to you and thanking you for getting the team to the World Series. It's an electric atmosphere. The first pitch of Game One: all these flashbulbs went off at once. Incredible. Like 50,000 diamonds sparkling around you. You've reached the top, and you're after that ultimate prize: a World Series Championship. To be there is extremely gratifying. It's something you always watched on TV, and you wanted to be in that situation, in those games. And, now, you're in it. You've worked with twenty-five other guys and the coaches for eight months toward a goal and achieved it. Nothing was more satisfying in baseball than that. You win it, and you're ecstatic, running around on the field like a bunch of twelve year-olds.

During the '95 World Series, Tom Glavine carried the team. We were on the biggest stage, all eyes on you and a lot of pressure, but he was so cool about it. Pitched like it was no big deal. Kept his emotions in check. Stuck to his usual game plan. Changed speeds. Moved the ball around. Didn't throw all that hard, but got in and out of innings. From a technical standpoint, he executed his mechanics, his pitches. He didn't miss his spots, or if he missed, he did it in a situation where it wasn't critical. Wasn't going to hurt him. His performance was amazing to watch. He just shut down the Indians. We wouldn't have won without him. How he pitched in Game Six: I don't think I've ever seen a better pitched game. Pressure situation, one win away from finally bringing a championship to Atlanta, and a nothing-nothing game for most of it until David Justice hit that home run. Threw eight innings, and gave up only one hit. That shows what good pitching will do against one of the greatest offensive clubs of all time. Like I said, the Indians had a hell of lineup. A lot of free swingers. They didn't have a lot of guys who slapped the ball and put it in play. Tom just ate them up, those bangers swinging for the fences. It was a good matchup for us. And, Tom made it look effortless. The pressure of the moment never got to him. Looked like he never broke a sweat.

I guess during the Series the Indians made some comments to the press that they knew we couldn't win a World Series. There was talk about how this disrespect fired us up. May have for some guys. Not me. Media quotes and stories had absolutely no effect on me. My thought was we had outstanding pitching. Most of the time, good pitching beats good hitting. So, I figured we were in pretty good shape. All we needed to do was figure out a way to score three runs, and we'd win. Offensively, we were a middle-of-the-pack team as far as batting average and stats go. But, we had some guys who were professional hitters who'd come in and get guys over and in by laying down a bunt, hitting a fly ball, whatever it took. We took advantage of walks. We did all the little things to score a few runs and scratch out ways to win behind our outstanding pitching. And, because our pitching was so good, I figured the Indians had to be sweating, thinking there's no way in hell that they could beat us. And, at the end of the day, I was right. We beat them in six games mainly because of Tom Glavine. He won two games in the Series and just shut down their offense.

When I think about who used their talent to the fullest, two guys stand out: Pat Hentgen and Tom Glavine. Hentgen pitched real well in '96 when I caught him and he won the Cy Young Award. He didn't throw real hard, but he won a lot of ball games. Same with Tom. For a left-hander to win 300 games with a fastball that doesn't go ninety miles per hour and a changeup: astounding.

Tom was the master of the changeup. Used a three-finger grip, kind of a modified circle change grip. That's different from most changeup grips, and it's a grip that Tom discovered by accident. Early in his career, he knew he needed to develop an off-speed pitch. He experimented with a bunch of different changeup grips, but one time, when he was shagging flies in the outfield, he picked up the ball the wrong way with this three-finger grip and thought, "You know, this might work for throwing a changeup." It felt good. From there, he refined the pitch. Saw that it offered him a good change of speed. He learned to throw it for strikes and really made it a cornerstone of his game. With this grip, he took about five miles per hour off his fastball. That's slightly faster than most changeups. His would sink a little bit at the end too, kind of fade away. Most people will tell you the perfect changeup is ten miles per hour slower than the fastball. Tom's was harder than that, but it still threw off a hitter's timing. He'd get hitters to step out on their front foot, fooling them to think that he'd thrown a fastball. By throwing off the hitter's timing, Tom would get them to shift from their power base when they swung the bat. They were off balance just enough so they wouldn't hit the ball cleanly but would dribble one off the end of the bat. Or pop up. Tom kept the ball away from the bat's sweet spot. Didn't rack up a ton of strikeouts that way, but he sure as hell racked up the wins.

Like Greg Maddux, Tom didn't want to waste any pitches. He wanted to throw one pitch and get a guy out with it. He and Maddux had a competition to see which one of them could throw a complete game in eighty pitches. Greg threw a complete game one time in like eighty-two pitches. Glavine came close to matching it. And, it was the damnedest thing, but Tom could pitch a complete game and never break a sweat. He made pitching look effortless. His delivery and his mechanics were smooth and fluid. Didn't look like he was working hard out there, wasn't straining to blast the ball to the plate. He didn't have Dwight Gooden, Nolan Ryan, or Saberhagen-type stuff where his shit would just blow you away. But, he kept guys from getting comfortable and being able to hit. He just made pitches to get people out.

With Tom, a typical at-bat might start off with two fastballs away. Just off the plate. Then he'd throw a 2-0 changeup or a 3-1 changeup and get you out with it. He set up hitters with his fastball and got them out with his changeup. And, his control was so good that he could place the changeup perfectly. By dropping the ball from ninety to eighty-five miles per hour, or later in his career, from eighty-two to the high seventies, he threw off the hitter's timing. He wasn't a guy you watched and said, "Man, I can't catch up to that." He just fooled hitters. Crafty. You'd go 0-4 against him and be pissed, thinking, "I should've hit him." Guys would see a pitch but barely miss it. His effectiveness shows that you can get guys out without having a heater in the mid-nineties or the most wicked stuff. If you know how to pitch, you can succeed without having the best arm.

The best part about his game: he never gave in to a hitter. His confidence made him so much fun to catch. Had a huge set of balls out there on the mound. Never threw a pitch that the hitter wanted to see. To guys who like a first-pitch fastball, he threw them changeups. Some guys cave and leave a pitch over the middle part of the plate for the batter to hit. Not Tom. He threw *his* pitch. A 2-0 changeup: fine; 3-2 changeup: he'd throw it. He didn't care if he walked a guy, but he wasn't going to give the hitter a pitch that he wanted to hit. He was going to pitch *his* way. He knew what the hitters liked, and he refused to give them those pitches. He spent a lot of time with Maddux, discussing hitters, and those guys were some of the smartest pitchers that I've been around. Tom knew the art of getting them out, and he was methodical about doing it.

Tom didn't really have any weaknesses. The only thing I can think of is that he didn't have a third pitch that he could throw when he was in trouble. He had a good curveball, but he hardly ever threw it. But, when you win 300-something games, there's not a whole lot of weakness there. He was an outstanding fielder. Outstanding hitter. Knew how to handle the bat and get bunts down. Held runners on well. He didn't throw ninety-five miles per hour like some of the other guys I caught, but like I said, Tom figured out a way to use his talent to the fullest and pitch effectively with it. He was one of the most complete pitchers I caught.

Tom and I had some things in common. We're both Catholic. Enjoy hockey. He was from up North, Massachusetts, so he played a lot of hockey growing up. He was such a good athlete that he had to choose between being a professional hockey player or baseball player. Every time hockey was on TV in the clubhouse, I'd watch it. He would too. I'd been the Mets player union rep for parts of three years, and Tom was the Braves rep. But, we didn't really have a whole lot of conversations or exchanges. I didn't get to know Tom as well as I did some of the other guys I caught. He was kind of aloof. Kept to himself. Kind of a loner and didn't hang out with the guys a bunch. But, he never caused a problem in the clubhouse.

Describing Tom as aloof applies to how he was on the mound too. Of all the pitchers I caught, he was the most unemotional. So calm. He never showed anything on the mound, if he were pissed off or happy. Stone-faced. When we won or lost, he acted the same. Composure, I guess is the way to describe him—he always maintained his composure. Almost robotic-like. He was out there to get the job done. Never seemed to lose control. Wouldn't get too upset if he walked a guy. He just moved on and faced the next hitter. If he had a bad outing, it didn't affect him. I liked that even keel. Part of this is Tom's calm personality. But, part of this is something he worked on: taking the emotional aspect out of the game. One time, Tom said that pitching is an emotional position. That pitchers get either too much credit if the team wins or too much blame if the team loses. He said that he could be pitching really well and executing but, because you're not catching any breaks, it looks like you're having a horrible game. Tom learned that, no matter what was happening, he needed to keep things in check. Act like he had things under control and that he was doing the things he wanted to do. Not send any messages to the other team that you're rattled, or that you don't have it today, or that they've gotten under your skin. Don't give them that advantage.

He kept his cool before games, too. Maybe he was nervous. Had the jitters and wouldn't settle down until he was in the flow of the game. He wouldn't show that nervousness, though. Part of that is being a professional. Knowing that you've prepared for the game. Knowing that you've had success before. Trusting that and going out and executing.

Tom and I talked a few times about the players' association labor dispute with the owners. From my experience as the Mets player rep, I'd heard the message from Donald Fehr, the Executive Director of the MLB Players Association, and his guys that the owners weren't interested in negotiating a new deal. They wanted to break the union. One time, in '94, the labor guys had a conference call with all of the player reps. The Braves were in New York, and I went with Tom for the call. I was interested in hearing the message. Maybe five guys were in the room. Everybody else is on a conference call listening in. Fehr starts talking about how we need to start planning for a strike with six weeks left in the season. That way, we'll have plenty of time to negotiate a deal in time for the playoffs.

I stepped in. "You're wrong," I said. "The owners don't want to negotiate. They don't give a shit about playoffs. They want to get rid of the union."

Fehr didn't like that. He's an arrogant guy. I guess he didn't like having me disagree with him in front of everybody. He told me, no, I was wrong, there's no way the owners would want to have a situation where no World Series is played.

I was like, "Why not? They've waited this long and haven't reached a deal. Why wouldn't they go through with it?" This is a common sense thing. If we've heard the message for two or three years that the owners won't negotiate, why are they going to start negotiating at the last minute? Why are they going to ignore all that they've been doing over the last few years just to say, "Ah, forget it. Let's talk now." Nothing was different. Nothing had changed. And, I told Fehr that. He didn't like it. I didn't give a shit. It was true.

After that meeting, Tom and I talked about waiting to strike until the end of the regular season. My thought was, if we played until the last week of the season, we'd get paid for the full season. Then we could get some leverage against the owners. We'd send a message to the owners that they couldn't break the union if we went on strike at the playoffs. Tom said, no, we need to strike now; that way we'd have six weeks to work out a new deal with the owners, get everything settled, and be back playing in time for the playoffs. Said it'd be bad PR if we went on strike right before the playoffs. Tom was very knowledgeable about the labor union stuff. Very articulate in explaining the situation. He did a good job. Kept us filled in about what was going on. And, he liked serving as a player rep and doing all that labor stuff. He's a polished, corporate-type guy. Serving on committees or being involved with the Players Association suited him. But, hearing him say that striking during the season gave us a chance to negotiate made me think that he was one of Donald Fehr's boys. I knew it didn't matter if you gave owners five days or two months to negotiate. Tom and I disagreed about that. He said, "They'll negotiate."

I told him, "No, they won't." I didn't see how a strike would be resolved quickly. Shit, Ted Turner came into the clubhouse one time before the strike. He was one of the owners who leaned more on the players' side, but he told us he wasn't putting up with any strike bullshit.

"You strike, and we'll break you. I've got more money than all of you put together. I'll wait you out, and I'll break you."

He wasn't far off from the truth. Hell, if it wasn't for that judge that ruled that the owners couldn't lock us out, the owners still wouldn't be talking to us. They were fine dragging it out as long as they could.

Anyway, we went on strike toward the end of the '94 season like Fehr said. Missed three paychecks. And then the '95 season was shortened. It was just a bad deal. Wound up costing a lot of people a lot of money. Fans were alienated. Thought we were a bunch of overpaid prima donnas.

While guys like Tom did a good job explaining the ins and outs about labor union stuff to the team, I wish the Players Association had more reps like me. Guys making close to the league minimum. Guys who depend on the benefits more than the players making millions of dollars. Guys who are more in the trenches—your blue-collar players. For some reason, the Players Association doesn't want that kind of guy as the rep, the guys who need the Players Association the most. They want the Tom Glavines, the high-profile players who everybody knows but who depend on the Association the least. I guess that elevates the Association's profile. Gives it more attention. But, the collective bargaining agreement helps the low-end guys with the minimum salary, free agency, the pension plan. Spend one day in the Major Leagues, and you get a retirement pension. It's all prorated up to ten years. At ten years, you're fully vested. You can start drawing at forty-five. Or, you can wait until you're sixty-five and draw more. Offers health insurance, too, but the premiums are astronomical.

When we played in New York, the visiting team had a clubhouse attendant named Icky. For whatever reason, the visiting clubhouse in New York is kind of like the fair. You see all types of people there that you don't normally see. Icky was one of those guys. He wasn't all there. If you said something like "Where are the towels?" or "Would you mind getting me a baseball?" he'd laugh real loud.

Most guys were entertained by Icky. He wanted to be liked, so he'd do anything to make the players laugh or to get their attention. Guys made him jump around the clubhouse like he was a dog or a rabbit. Have him run around with his underwear on his head. He'd do tricks. And, Icky loved it, I guess because the players would laugh, and he thought that meant that they liked him. He was just odd, and I didn't like it. I wouldn't laugh at him. Wouldn't smile at any of his shit. I thought it was sad. He'd be laughing and having a good time, and I'd say, "Icky, that shit's not funny. Put your clothes back on."

He'd stop and look all sad and start putting his clothes on. Then, the other players would say, "Man, don't let him do that to you, Icky. Go ahead! Run, run, run!" Off he'd go again.

"Icky! Stop!"

He'd stop and look around. I'd say, "Goddamn it, get your clothes on." But then, players would start flipping him shit, and he'd start running around again. So, I would leave. He was a nice guy, but guys just abused him.

The weird thing was, I was trying to look out for the guy, but because I wouldn't laugh or smile at any of his tricks, Icky was afraid of me. He'd say in this real gravelly voice, "I don't like him," meaning me. If you said my name to Icky, he'd leave the room. And, during all this kind of thing, Tom wasn't the kind of guy who was amused by Icky's antics. He didn't take any part in these kind of deals. Too classy. Always did the right thing. Said the right things. I saw him as the face of the organization. He was concerned about his image, and he liked being the spokesman. Liked dealing with the media. Where Maddux wanted to avoid them, Tom was happy to step up and talk with them. And, as our spokesman, he wasn't the type to get a kick out of guys like Icky and egg him on to keep running around half-naked.

Tom was easy to work with. We never had a set-up where I was his personal catcher. Usually, if I caught him, it was a day game after a night game to give Javy Lopez a rest or because I hit the other team's starting pitcher okay. Tom was fun to catch. Liked to work fast. Wanted to get the ball back so he could get back on the mound and make his next pitch. He never shook off. Would do whatever I wanted. But, this goes back to the catcher figuring out what a pitcher does well and relying on his strengths. I knew what he wanted to do. I knew he loved throwing his changeup. I knew how he pitched. It wasn't like I was trying to guess and figure shit out. I called the pitches he wanted to throw, asked him to do things that made him successful. Maddux pitched differently. So did Smoltz. My job was to figure out each one. And, the fun part was calling different games for different people. With Tom, I did a lot of the tricks that I used with Maddux. Tom threw balls on the outside corner or off the plate, so my biggest thing was to make every pitch look like a strike. Frame his pitches with part of the glove on the plate but catch the ball with the tip of the glove off the plate. Moving the glove quietly if he missed his target instead of jostling my body around. With his throwing the ball on the outside part of the plate and me making these pitches look like strikes, he forced umpires to call outside pitches for strikes.

Some umpires were harder to fool than others. When I was in Toronto, I overheard a conversation where a veteran umpire was prepping a younger one for working behind the plate.

"You've got to watch him," meaning me, the older one said. "He'll trick you. He'll make you think it's a strike, but it's not. Be careful."

That made me smile. I took it to mean that I was doing a good job.

Like everybody else, I heard the grumbling about how Tom and Greg had a bigger strike zone than other pitchers. That's all talk. I didn't see that the Braves pitchers had a greater advantage and got more calls in their favor than other pitchers. The day before a pitcher starts, he charts all of the pitches for both teams. Maddux would keep track of how many pitches the umpires missed. He told me it was pretty even. Same strike zone for both teams. If we had a wider strike zone, the umpire gave the same wide strike zone to the other team too. I think it was more a question of guys like Glavine and Maddux taking advantage of it better. They had great control. Hit their spots on the outside part of the plate consistently. There's a big difference between a guy who hits his spots over and over compared to the guy whose control isn't as good, and he's all over the place. The other guy isn't going to get the same borderline calls that the control pitcher will get. You're not going to get that call if you haven't established with the umpire that you're able to throw to your target consistently. Glavine and Maddux: they could wear out the corner pitch after pitch if they wanted to. Where we would throw five or six pitches there and get those calls, the other team threw there only once or twice. Yet, everybody perceived that we were getting an unfair advantage. Not true. We were just more effective at pitching outside than others. Made more pitches there than others made.

One thing that was kind of funny with this strike zone stuff: Tom thought he didn't get as big of a strike zone as Maddux. More than once, he'd bitch, "Doggie gets strikes out there. How come I can't?" I couldn't see much difference between the two, though.

While he had great results pitching outside, I tried to get Tom to pitch inside more. He was reluctant to do that. He had so much success getting guys out away and off the plate that he wanted to stick with this formula. He could get lulled into thinking fastball/changeup, that this was the only way for him to pitch. But, it wasn't. Tom was a hell of a pitcher, so I'd ask him to slip in a slider or a hook here or there. Make him use these as more of a weapon than he did in other games. He was so good that he could mix these other pitches in well. And, I think he liked that I asked him to do something a little different. I think Tom would come out of those games thinking, "Okay. I can do that. I can make these pitches a little more of my game plan."

With his personality, I could get on Tom. Chew on his ass a little bit and get him going in the right direction. Sometimes, first innings could be tough for him. Give up some runs and some hits. Once he settled in, though, you knew that, most times, he was going to give you a good start.

In one game, I think it was in St. Louis, the first inning was shaping up to be one of those nightmares. He wasn't getting guys out one, two, three. He was giving up some hits. Some runs. It wasn't out of control yet, though, and I didn't want him to sink into a "Uh oh, here were go. Another bad first inning." So, I went out to the mound.

I was like, "Hey! Let's go! Don't give in to this. Let's get through this."

He nodded. After that, he turned things around. Got out of the inning. I don't know if airing him out a little or giving him a little break in between hitters helped him get out of the rut. But, he pitched a solid ball game the rest of the way.

Tom was a good teammate. Took care of his responsibilities and was there for guys if they needed him. Answered the bell every time he had a start and went out there and pitched his ass off. Can't remember him spending any time on the disabled list. If he had to hit somebody, he'd do it and take care of his teammates. Some guys looked to do this more than others. Did Tom like doing it? No. But he knew that was part of the game and playing it the right way. And, he did things the right way. Worked hard. Ran. Watched what he ate. He was real committed to his workout routine of running one day and lifting some weights the next and so on. He found a pattern that worked well for him, and he stuck with it—didn't matter if he won or lost his last start. For pitchers, I think there's a lot to be said for that. On top of that, Tom was well-prepared for games by watching the other team. On game days, he tried to sleep as late as he could. Like some guys, he could have some restless nights before a game. On days he pitched, he showed up to the park later than usual. He didn't want to be cooped up in the clubhouse, preoccupied and getting worked up about what was facing him. Once he left the clubhouse and stepped onto the field, he calmed down. To cut the nervous energy, he came to the park later. That helped him relax. Kept his mind off the game and kept him from overanalyzing things.

As far as the pitching rotation of Glavine, Maddux, and Smoltz, I don't know that there's ever been a group of pitchers who played together and was that dominating for that long. I know the Dodgers had Koufax and Drysdale in the sixties. The Orioles had some great pitching staffs. The Mets guys that I worked with in the early nineties were outstanding. But, these guys with the Braves went to the post every day. One right after the other: one, two, three. You had a chance to see a well-pitched game every night. I can't see three people being better, three people on the same team in that same class. Think about what they've done. Two guys won 300 games. Another guy won 200 games and saved 150, and no one else has done that. They all did something a little better than the others. The cool thing is that these guys all got along well. Were good teammates. Good friends, too. Never had any problems with egos clashing or one guy needing more spotlight than another. And, I think that's because they kept each other grounded. They did so much together—go out to dinner or spend a morning together on the golf course. If you had put these guys on different teams by themselves, they might not have done as well. But, as a group, they made each other better. They pushed each other. Fed off each other. The competition of matching up with Glavine or Maddux or Smoltz drove them. It was kind of like, "I'm going to do what he did . . . no, I'm going to do *better* than he did." At times, one had the hot hand and was pitching better than the others. But, no one wanted to be the weak link in the chain. If one of them had a bad game, the next guy wanted to step in and turn things around and get things back on track. They all wanted to win twenty games apiece. They all wanted to lead the league in innings pitched and strikeouts. Even with these individual goals, they all wanted the team and the other starting pitchers to do well. Friendly competition.

One time, Maddux said that the reason why they got along so well and there weren't any ego problems was because the three of them played golf together so much. I asked him what was it about golf that made them click. He said, "Do you play golf?"

"No."

"If you play golf with someone, you find out real quick what kind of person they are," he said.

"Yeah?"

"You find a group of guys who can spend a day together on the golf course and get along, they can do anything together. That's the beauty of golf."

I pressed him. I asked what was it about the game that made them get along so well. Greg just said there's something special about the game. By the second hole, you can spot an asshole or tell if a guy's a good guy. Glavine, Maddux, and Smoltz: they're all good guys, and that game was their outlet. A break from eating, breathing, and sleeping baseball. The season can be a grind. A lot of ups and downs through the course of the year. Golf was a separation from all of that. Of thinking about mechanics. Of dwelling on things if they were struggling on the mound and lacking their usual confidence. Golf gave them a few hours of distraction. A time for some trash talk. Some screwing around. It kept them fresh. Kept them grounded, too. There were times when things were going really well for those guys, and you could get caught up in yourself. Start thinking you're really something special. The three of them golfing, ragging on each other, kept that in check. It recharged them.

Those Braves starters. When I think back on catching all of these guys, I was there during a snapshot of baseball history. Probably the best starting rotation ever, and I caught them in their prime. Amazing. Just makes you shake your head in wonder. I don't see how three guys on the same team will ever be any better. They can't be topped.

CHAPTER 10

PAT HENTGEN

The first thing that I think of when I think of Charlie is that he opened my eyes to the outer third of the plate, to righties and lefties. And, it's no coincidence that I had my best season and won my Cy Young that year. He obviously became my personal catcher and caught me that whole year. And, it was just one of those relationships that, as a coach I preach this all the time to our minor league guys, you have to know when to light a fire and when to pump a guy up and when to give a guy some encouragement. And, I think that Charlie, although he was a great catcher and a great defensive catcher to boot, he was very good at knowing the personalities of the pitchers he was catching. He knew my personality. He knew he could get on my butt a little bit and chew me out a little bit, and it was going to work in a positive way for us. He knew when to light a fire under a guy and when to pat him on the back. That was his best asset. And, it all comes down to time spent with a guy on the bus. During batting practice. In the locker room. On the plane. All these times when we're not in uniform. And, when we're in uniform, when we're in batting practice in the outfield shagging. After batting practice when we all come in and we're sitting in our lockers and talking shop. These are critical, critical moments. And, it's a shame because I think a part of that is not in the game today for a lot of players, the shop talk. You can learn so much from each other, and yet it's just a sign of the times with how baseball is today with the iPads and the iPhones. The Twitter and Facebook. It makes for less verbal communication among teammates than there was when Charlie and I played together. We didn't have smart phones and all that. We relied on face-to-face conversation and going over lineups and watching games together from the dugout when he wasn't playing and I wasn't pitching. Those are the times when you really can grow as a player.

He was the best catcher I ever had. Without a doubt, and I had some good ones. I'm not throwing the rest of those guys under the bus. But, as far as calling a game and getting the best out of me, he was the best I ever had.

—*Pat Hentgen*

[*Note: After the 1995 World Series, Charlie became a free agent. Returning to Atlanta was unlikely with Javy Lopez as the everyday catcher and younger and less expensive Eddie Perez from Triple A ready to step in and catch an occasional start. One team that expressed an interest in Charlie was the Toronto Blue Jays. At first, Charlie was reluctant. When he started his career, he was adamant that he did not want to play in Canada. "It's too different," he said. "Different money. Different language. In Montreal, most of them speak French. They use the metric system. You buy milk in a bag. You bring it home and pour it into a pitcher. Everything's different."*

Nevertheless, Toronto pursued Charlie, inviting him and his wife to visit the city. The team toured them around the SkyDome. Charlie met with Paul Beeston, the club's president, and Gord Ash, the general manager. They explained that they wanted a veteran catcher to mold Sandy Martinez, a young catcher new to the Major Leagues. They wanted to re-create the situation in Atlanta where Charlie tutored Javy Lopez with catching skills and tips. They wanted Charlie to work with a young pitching staff. Charlie fit the Blue Jays' needs perfectly, and they courted him and convinced him to join them. He signed a two-year contract to play in Toronto.

One of the first pitchers Charlie worked with on his new team was Pat Hentgen. Hentgen achieved success early in his career, winning nineteen games for the 1993 Blue Jays team that won the World Series. In 1995, the year before he worked with Charlie, Hentgen struggled with a 10-14 win-loss record and 5.11 earned run average. Hentgen was looking to bounce back from this subpar year, and in 1996, his first year with Charlie, he bounced back boldly, going 20-10 and winning the American League Cy Young Award. He led the league in complete games (ten), shutouts (three), and innings pitched (265 ⅔).[1] He had a streak of pitching seven complete games in a row.[2] During this exceptional year, Charlie worked closely with Hentgen, catching twenty-six of his thirty-five starts (fourteen wins, eight losses, and four no decisions).

Hentgen continued to pitch strongly in 1997 with a 15-10 win-loss record, 3.68 ERA, and 160 strikeouts. He threw thirty-nine consecutive innings without giving up an earned run.[3] Of Hentgen's thirty-five starts, Charlie caught fourteen (eight wins, three losses, and three no decisions).

After playing fourteen seasons in the Major Leagues, Hentgen retired in 2004.[4] He won 131 games, lost 112, maintained a 4.32 ERA, and struck out 1,290.[5] In addition to Toronto, he played for the St. Louis Cardinals and Baltimore Orioles.]

My best friend in Toronto was Pat Hentgen, but one time, I told him I would beat the piss out of him.

We were playing against Boston. Pat was pitching shitty. He gave up a three-run home run, and he was mad as hell, so he hit the next batter.

Next half of the inning, I led off. Like I've said, it's tit for tat. You hit one of our guys; we hit one of yours. So, I knew what was coming. Sure enough, I got smoked in the shoulder.

I was pissed. Taking the heat because he was getting his ass handed to him.

Usually, after a game, Pat and I would talk. Especially if our families weren't in town and there wasn't a rush to get back home. We'd sit in the training room or go out to eat and go over the game, at-bat by at-bat, sometimes pitch by pitch, and break it down. What worked. What didn't. What we could do better next time. He was thinking that we should've thrown this pitch, but I called that pitch. Both of us were baseball junkies, and we loved to analyze games and pick them apart. He was a lot like Greg Maddux in that he could talk baseball all the time. Pat was very aware of where the defense should be positioned and when guys should've gotten to balls and made some plays. He'd key in on that.

After that game, I avoided him. Didn't say a word to him. He knew I was mad. But, when I walked into the shower, he was already in there. So, I went over to him. Showed him my shoulder. It was starting to welt up. You could tell there was going to be a big bruise.

"Do you see this?" I said.

"Yeah, man, I'm sorry. . . ."

I interrupted. "Dude, let me tell you something right now. If I ever get hit again because you're getting your ass handed to you, I'm gonna beat the piss out of you."

I was dead serious.

He was quiet. He just looked at me. Then he said, "I'm sorry."

"Man, I don't want to hear an apology. I'm just letting you know. I'll do whatever I can for you, but I'm not ever taking your beating for you. Don't do it again."

Later on, he told me that, the way I was looking at him, he thought I was going to tear his head off right there in the showers.

I've gone over this, though. There's a right way to do things. There's tradition. There's loyalty and friendship and looking after your teammates and hitting a guy to right a wrong. But, just because a pitcher is pitching badly doesn't mean that he can start plunking guys. That's ridiculous. I told Pat that. And, he understood. Hell, he knew he was wrong. Kind of like your mom catching you with your hand in the cookie jar after she's told you no more cookies. I don't think he ever took his frustrations out like that again because he wasn't getting the job done on the mound.

––––––––––––

Of all the guys I caught, the things I did helped Pat's game the most. Before I caught him, he liked to pitch inside. Pound hitters. That's fine, but Pat's fastball had a natural cutter movement to it. What would happen is that he'd pitch inside, but, because of the way the ball moved, it tended to wind up over the plate, especially against right-handed hitters. That really reduced his margin of error. If he missed his location by a little, the ball cut right down the middle. Made it easier for guys to hit, if not waffle it.

The first game we worked together was against the California Angels. They had a real good team back then. Several good hitters like Tim Salmon, Chili Davis, Jim Edmonds, J. T. Snow, and Garret Anderson. For some reason, I hadn't caught Pat at all during spring training games. Wasn't planned or anything—that's just how it worked out. But, this game against the Angels, I think, was Pat's first or second start of the year. From catching him in bullpen sessions, I knew he was a good pitcher. Had a good fastball. Good location where he could place the fastball in all four quadrants: up and in, down and in, down and away, and up and over the corner. He changed speeds well. Good curveball, good breaking ball. I saw how he could be effective as hell. So, I set up and called for a lot of pitches down and away. Like I've said, if a pitcher is ever in a bind and doesn't know what pitch to throw, he needs to go down and away because that's the toughest place for hitters to hit the ball. That's my philosophy, anyway. And, with the way his ball naturally cut away from right-handed hitters, it was a good fit for him to throw more on the outside part of the plate than it was to go inside.

Pat had never pitched outside like that. I didn't realize his normal approach was to pound guys inside. I never asked him to go inside, though. Working the outside part of the plate, we had easy inning after easy inning. Later, Pat told me that, during the sixth or seventh inning, he looked up at the scoreboard and saw that he'd given up only three hits. And, I was signing for more pitches down and away. Pat said he thought to himself, "Man, I can't believe we're going away again. They're gonna hit it. They've got to be looking away." But, then he thought, "Well, how can I second-guess this guy and shake him off? I'm not shaking him off until I give up some hits and a run."

He wound up throwing a complete game shutout. Gave up five hits.

After the game, he said, "I kept waiting for you to call a pitch inside. I was thinking, 'He'll have to call a ball inside.' You never did. You kept going away, away, away."

It's true. But, why argue with the results? Pat went up against Mark Langston who was an All-Star, one of the better pitchers in the game at that time, and he won. Not only did he win, but he threw a shutout.

Pat said, "I've never pitched that much down and away in my life."

That game opened his eyes. I showed him the outer third of the plate that he hadn't been taking advantage of. I showed him another way to get guys out. And, it was a way that worked real well for him.

That game set the tone for us that year. We hit a good groove, and he had a great year. Won twenty games for a shitty team. We weren't even .500—hell, we were 74-88, which is pretty bad no matter how you put it. The fact that he won twenty games for a team like that is amazing in itself. But, Pat pitched great. Kept the ball around the plate. Because he was always near the zone, hitters couldn't take pitches. Had to swing the bat. If a guy is all over the place, hitters can sit on some pitches. Wait for what they want to hit—that one pitch in a certain location. They couldn't do that with Pat. They'd chase some pitches out of the strike zone because they knew he'd throw strikes.

When Pat pitched, he was intense. Real focused on the pitch in front of him. His body language projected that intensity. He scowled a bunch. Pulled his hat down real close to his eyes. He was a big tempo guy. Liked to work fast. Hated it when hitters stepped out of the box to take a time-out. I'd throw the ball back to Pat, and he'd catch it and be ready to go. He wanted guys to stay in the box so he could work them, pitch after pitch. But, sometimes, he'd be too amped up, too pissed off if something didn't go his way. Then, he'd want to work faster than he needed to, like if he hurried up, that could get him out of a jam. When that happened, my job was to go out and tell him, "Okay, Pat. I'm going to give you a breather right here. Let's slow down. Your heart's going one hundred miles an hour. Clear your mind here. Get your breath under you. Get your legs ready to go. Here's how we're going to get this guy." He was kind of like a horse that wants to run too fast and you have to rein him in. Slow him down so he can finish the race. That's part of your job as a catcher. Remind the pitcher to step back and clear his mind. Because, sometimes, if things were going bad, he wants to go harder. Work too fast. Steve Avery and Mark Wohlers in Atlanta were like that too. But you have to calm them down. Help them focus on what's in front of them. Do it in a real calm voice. Not like when I'd go out there and chew on guys' asses. Just get them to slow down and focus. If you keep going faster, faster, faster, things can go haywire.

Pat was a gamer. Never wanted to give up the ball. Took a lot of pride in throwing a lot of innings. I think the years I played with him in Toronto, he led the league in innings pitched. One of the ways he was able to do this was good mechanics. Used his legs well. Kept his arm in the same slot and didn't put a lot of stress on it. Another thing was, during the second half of the season, he wouldn't throw a lot of bullpen sessions. You usually throw a bullpen session two or three days after a start. A lot of times with Pat, though, he wouldn't even pick up a ball in between starts during the second half. That way, he'd try and keep his arm fresh. Or, at least fresher. All those guys: their arms hurt all year long. The first and second days after a start, most of those guys don't want to move their arms, much less pick up a baseball.

Pat was real adamant about not wanting to come out of games. Toward the end of the season in '96, Pat's nineteenth or twentieth win, our manager, Cito Gaston, went out to the mound. He had somebody from the bullpen warmed up and ready to go. Our bullpen had a lot of good arms in it. Mike Timlin had great stuff. Became a great set-up guy when he moved on to Boston a few years later. We also had Paul Quantrill. Outstanding. Good sinker and slider guy. And, there was Dan Plesac. One of my favorites. A guy who I worked with early in my career in Milwaukee who was just a really good guy and a left-hander you could bring in for certain situations. Kelvim Escobar was a young kid when I caught him. Great arm. Developed into a closer. Like all bullpens, we had our share of ups and downs. But, they were a good group. Talented guys. Got the job done well. I had no problem with any of them coming in to the game.

Cito asked Pat how he felt.

"I'm great. Feel great."

Cito nodded.

I stepped in. "He's done, Cito."

"No, no, I feel great," Pat said.

Like I said, his tendency was to stay in longer than he should have. But, I wanted the team to get the win more than I wanted a pitcher's record to be good. So, I pushed. "He's done."

Cito usually listened to his catcher. Most managers would. Bobby Cox did. And, I was honest. If the pitcher still had good stuff, I'd say, "His shit's still good." I don't know if other catchers were as honest as I was, or if they just went along with what the pitcher said. I wasn't out there on the mound for those conversations.

When Cito signaled for someone to come in from the bullpen, Pat got all pissed off. But, those guys usually came in and did a good job. This game, I think Timlin came in, got somebody to hit a ground ball for a double play. Got us out of the inning. After the game, I went back to the clubhouse, and Pat was sitting there. He said, "Hey, dude. Thanks for saying that. I was done."

"Then why in the hell are you saying you feel good? Why are you running your mouth knowing your shit's already wasted out there?"

"I don't want to come out."

"I understand," I said. "But, you've got to be honest."

"I ain't ever telling anyone that I want to come out of the game."

"Well. It's about time you start doing it."

He was stubborn. We'd have situations where I'd call the same pitch three or four times. He'd shake me off. Finally, I'd call the pitch again and just set up. He'd throw it, and we'd get the guy out.

In between innings, I'd be like, "Why are you so hardheaded? Just listen to me. I'm not going to get you hurt."

"Man, I just didn't think we could get him out like that."

"Well, we got him out."

"Yeah, but I didn't think it was going to work."

He could be kind of nervous too. One of the first times I caught him, we had a base runner on second base. Some catchers go through multiple signs so the base runner can't steal signs. I didn't. I just put down the sign, set up, and was ready to go. Pat stepped off and looked at second base. Pointed at the runner and then motioned me out to the mound.

I said, "What are you doing?"

"Man, we have a runner on second. We always do a last pitch indicator or first pitch to every new hitter. We always have different signs and mix it up all the time. I mean, you only gave me one sign."

I said, "Come on, dude! That guy's not looking. He's looking behind him to see if they're going to try to pick him off. He's not even looking at me. Trust me."

Pat was like, "Oh. Okay."

"We'll speed things up if we stick with one sign."

"Yeah, you're right. That's a great idea."

"We'll keep your rhythm going and your tempo up that way."

Another thing I did during our mound conversations was lighten things up. Like I said, he was very intense. But, I could get him to crack up so fast. If Pat was mad because he kicked a ball and missed a defensive play or threw a ball away that he was trying to throw to second base, I'd give him shit. Say something like, "Jesus, dude, do you have *any* motor skills at all out here? You look like a retard. Please do me a favor. Next time, make sure they hit the ball to somebody else. I don't want to see that shit again." This was all sarcastic. That usually lightened things up for him. Got him to laugh and move on from what had just happened and concentrate on making his next pitches instead of dwelling on a bad play. His emotions could change from A to Z just like that. How you handled him made a big difference in how he did. He could get so uptight, and sometimes, a catcher just needed to go out there and help him relax. Get him to laugh and realize, "Hey. This is just a baseball game."

And, I liked to rag on guys when they made mistakes. They'd get all fired up when they got back to the dugout. Throw their gloves against the wall and kick shit around. To break the tension, I'd chime in, "Hell, at least you threw that one over the plate." Or, "How come you can't throw a ball that hard?" Some guys, they'd be pissed. Tell me to fuck off. But, when they said it, at least they were laughing. When I got on to guys, I tried to do it in a way that was funny. Use humor to diffuse a tense situation and not piss anybody off. But, at the same time, the point's been made that a guy needs to step it up.

Because of Pat's intensity, I didn't jump on him too much. But, once or twice, I picked up that he wasn't as locked in as he usually was. So, I told him, "Dude, if you're just gonna heave the ball, throw as hard as you can down the middle, then why don't we just go to the bullpen right now? This is bullshit." That pissed him off. Got his attention. Fired him up, and he started pounding the glove. Hitting his target. Making his pitches. But, that's one of the things that a catcher has to figure out: his pitchers' personalities and when they need stroking and when they need a kick in the ass. Some guys, if you crawl on them like I did with Pat, they just crumble. Other guys, that challenges them. Pumps them up. And, I wasn't afraid to say anything to anyone. If a guy needed somebody to get in his face and tell him to get his shit together, I'd do it.

If Pat had a bad outing, he moped around. More so than other pitchers. It really ate at him. And, the guy would get so worked up and stressed before games. Have trouble eating. He was less sociable. Didn't talk as much with teammates. And, he'd shit like four or five times before his starts. That was his ritual. He'd shit, read the paper, go back to the shitter. Before games, he spent most of his time in there. I gave him hell about it. I'd go into the bathroom and say, "Pat, is that you in there again?"

"Yeah. It's me."

A little later, I'd walk by again. "Pat?"

"Yeah. I know. I've got to go again."

Even later, I'd go in and ask, "All right, Pat. So how many times has it been?"

"Four. I've got one more."

He didn't seem nervous. He always wanted the ball. I guess this was his stomach's way of coping with what was in front of him. Better he took care of all that before the game than during the third inning.

In '96, as the season went on, we became great friends. If we were on the road, we'd share a cab and get to the park early before the bus left the hotel. When we were in Boston, we'd walk back to the hotel from Fenway after the game, going over the game, what happened. We'd go out to eat. Talk shop. One time, we had already played. I was back in my hotel room, flipping through the channels. Saw that the Braves were on, playing a West Coast game and that Maddux was pitching. Pat was a big Greg Maddux fan. He always wanted to get in my brain to share what I had learned from catching Greg. So, I called Pat.

"Dude. Doggie's pitching on WTBS. Come on over."

Pat came to my room. We ordered some Domino's Pizza and some Dr. Pepper and watched the game. Before each pitch, we'd talk about what Greg was going to throw. I was calling pitches from two thousand miles away. Explained why he was throwing it. Pat ate it up. We were like two college kids, guys who loved the game.

During games, I'd sit next to Pat. One time, we were in Toronto and in the third baseline dugout. There was a left-handed hitter and hard-throwing righty pitching. The hitter kept fouling off pitches late, late, late. So, I said to Pat, "Hand me my glove, would you?"

He passed it to me.

I put it on.

Next pitch, the guy hit a one-hop pea into the dugout. I caught it. Pat died laughing. He said, "Damn!"

I said, "Come on, dude. You know I was watching the game."

Our personalities meshed. We got along so well that, one season, he needed to move out of his apartment early. I said he could crash with me. So, for the last month of the season, he lived in my place. Fun guy, great sense of humor. Good to everybody. Didn't think he was better than anybody else. Never big-leagued anybody and made somebody feel like Pat was superior to them. That was something that really stuck in his craw. He treated guys with respect. He knew how hard it was to play in the Major Leagues. And, he never took anything for granted. He knew he was one pitch away from having it be over.

After he won the Cy Young Award, he bought a Porsche. I guess he had a bonus clause in his contract where he'd get extra money if he won the Cy.

When he told me that he bought this car, I was like, "Dude, you mean you bought a dick extension?"

I wouldn't drop it. I really stepped it up after Roger Clemens won the Cy in '97. After that season, Roger thanked me for the help I'd given him that year and gave me a custom-made rifle. Real nice. It was all inscribed: "From 21 to 22. Catch Ya Later." Twenty-one was his number. Twenty-two was mine. Anyway, I told Pat about it.

"See how Roger treats people?" I said. "That's the right way to do things. Give your catcher something nice. You? You don't give me shit. You just go out and buy a dick extension. I see how you are."

Pat said, "Man, I should've gotten you something."

"Yeah, you should have. But you got yourself something. You got your Porsche, and I got nothing."

He laughed.

He was fun to mess with. And, I liked him. He was a smart guy. Good organizational guy, loyal to the team. He's done some coaching for Toronto. He'll do well as a coach. He knows a lot about the game. Learned a lot from guys like Dave Stieb and Jack Morris when he first came up to the big leagues. Stieb was good about working with Pat about the mental and physical preparation and being ready to play every fifth day, even if your arm didn't feel great or if you had some distractions away from baseball. Morris taught him to keep the same routine on the days he pitched. For most games, Pat would show up to the park at 1:30 p.m. or so. Go out and play catch, shag a few balls. For games he started, though, he would show up at 4:30 p.m. Jack was like, "Why don't you try sticking with your same routine? Why are you changing things on the days you pitch?" Pat followed his suggestion and responded well. And, I can see him sharing with a pitching staff the mistakes he made and lessons he learned along the way. Help them avoid the pitfalls that he ran into, from dealing with the press or a pitching coach to how a guy should throw a bullpen session. What your thought process should be. Understanding what a pitch does. How to change your mechanics. Making adjustments quickly. On that point, guys need to realize that you don't get the luxury of making adjustments from one game to the next. Sometimes, you need to adjust in between pitches. That can be your key to success. There's a lot to teach, a lot for guys to learn. But, Pat worked with a great pitching coach, Mel Queen. Mel was real good about talking to you like you were a man, not talking down to you. Real good about emphasizing the positive, which builds up belief in yourself. If you threw 120 pitches, seven innings, and gave up five runs and walked away with a six and a half ERA, some guys would look at it as a terrible game. But, Mel was good about looking at it from the perspective that the pitcher threw 110 good pitches. You made some mistakes, and it just so happened that, when you did, guys were on base and scored some runs. Focus on the good pitches and move on. Pat has those same people skills. He'll help guys improve.

I still keep in touch him. We talk baseball, about games we played or stuff guys are doing now. He tells me to watch for certain players in the Toronto system, and I tell him about some of the guys from around Tulsa who I coached or who played with my kids, guys like Dylan Bundy, the Orioles top pick a few years ago. We also talk hunting. I have a place south of Tulsa where I raise and hunt deer. Pat has a place up in Canada where he hunts deer. Moose and bear too. The bass fishing up there is supposed to be phenomenal. One time, he said that all you had to do was throw a hook in the water, and you'd catch a beauty. We've gotten together in Illinois to hunt, but we need to figure out a time when I can go up to his place and he can come down and hunt at mine. It's one of those things that we always talk about, but we need to quit talking and just do it.

I caught most of Pat's starts in '96 when he won the Cy, but I didn't catch him a whole lot in '97. Maybe one out of every three or four starts. I don't know why. That's really a question for Cito. I guess part of it was because the club signed Benito Santiago as their primary catcher to a two-year deal after '96 and they knew I wouldn't be around after '97. They knew that Pat needed to get used to working with Benny.

Benny was a tremendously talented cat. He could do things that I just wasn't capable of. Amazing hitter. He was lazy, though. Wasted so much talent. He had no idea how to call a game or get pitchers out of trouble. Killed a pitching staff. Pat told me that one time he was in a jam and Benny was catching him. So, Benny came out to the mound to talk to him.

Benny said, "Hey, Holmes, what do you want to do?"

Pat sized up the situation and said, "Let's throw a slider here."

"Okay."

So, Benny goes back behind the plate. Calls for a fastball. Not even thirty seconds earlier, they'd agreed that he'd call for a slider. So, Pat shakes him off.

After the inning, Pat goes up to Benny and is like, "Why are you calling a fastball? We just said I'd throw a slider."

"Damn, Holmes. I forgot."

Embarrassing. When I say wasted talent, I mean it. He had all of the tools to be a Hall of Fame player. If he busted his ass and tried to reach his full potential, he could've been an amazing player. Who knows why he didn't put forth more effort. But, I know Pat was discouraged to be working with a guy who wasn't tuned in all of the time, using his ability to the fullest to help out the guy on the mound do as well as he could. Especially when the year before, Pat had pitched his ass off for the team, and now they won't let him throw to the catcher that he wants to work with. I wasn't the best player, but it meant something to me to go out there and do the best I could. Call the best game I could. Do everything I could to help the pitcher. If something went wrong, I tried to figure out how I could help my pitcher.

Make it better for him next time. You went from that to a guy who was just going through the motions. I think Pat felt slighted. He asked me what the deal was, and I said, "Dude, I have no idea." Pat was loyal to his team, though. Even though something like this may have bothered him, I don't think he brought this up to Cito or raised a stink about it. I don't know if it was because he was afraid to say how he really felt or if he just plugged away and did his job. It was under his skin, though. He'd bring it up to me: "How come I'm not getting to work with you?"

And, Pat was the same way with umpires. He knew to hold his tongue, that if he made a big deal out of a missed strike call, most umpires wouldn't take too kindly to it. But, one time, we were in Boston, and the home plate umpire called a pitch that was up and in a ball, but it was definitely a strike. Pat peppered it right where it needed to be, but most umpires have a blind spot where they miss balls either on the inside or the outside. The umpire missed this one, and Pat leaned in and said, "Is that up?"

The umpire didn't take his mask off, but he said, "It was up!" The way he said it, you could tell he was pissed.

Next pitch, I called for a fastball down and in. Set up with a low target. As long as you get the ball in, you really don't have to worry about the up and down location of the pitch. If you make your pitch and hit it in on the black, not too many guys are hitting the ball with authority. Pat executed the pitch perfectly. In his lane and going right for the black. Right at the knees.

"Ball!"

Pat walked halfway to home plate. "That's down?"

"That's down!" the umpire barked.

Pat said, "I've got to have one of them. One of them's got to be a strike." Then he turned around and walked back to the mound.

Eventually, he got out of the inning. Stayed in the game and wound up pitching a complete game and winning 3-2 or something like that. Most times, when a game ends, the umpires take off from the field and head to the showers. This umpire, though, went out to the mound. Tapped Pat on the shoulder and said, "I used to think you were a nice guy. But, the next time you pull that kind of shit on me again, you won't last past the fifth." Then he turned and walked away.

Pat was fired up. I could tell he wanted to rip into the ump. He was real intense, but I don't how much of that was for outside show. He turned to shit the minute umpires gave him any kind of grief. He was one of those guys who was like, "Man. He got onto me. I better be quiet." And, I'd give Pat hell about that. If he was so fired up about the calls he's getting, he should say something to the umpires about it.

"Man, they'll throw me out of the game."

"For what? Saying he missed a pitch? Come on."

I just liked to give Pat hell. That really was my job, not his. Like I've said, I could get away with it a lot easier than he could.

Umpires, though. They could be difficult to deal with. One time, in Yankee Stadium, we were in a close game. Andy Pettitte was pitching for New York. We were behind 1-0. Runners on base. One out. I was hitting. I hit a line drive to center field. I watched the ball, and I saw that Bernie Williams didn't catch it. The ball bounced up into his glove. I could see it from the first base line. A run should've scored, but the first base umpire, Dan Morrison, said Williams caught the ball. He called me out, and Williams threw the base runner out. Inning over.

I didn't like the call. First off, it was wrong. Second, Morrison didn't take one step off the first base line to get a good angle on the play. If Morrison had gotten out there and gotten a good angle, he would've seen that the ball bounced. But, because he missed the call, he cost us a run. Ended our rally. Cito went out and argued, but nothing changed. They threw him out of the game, I think.

I didn't say anything. Went back to the dugout and put on my catching gear and came out. Our pitcher was Huck Flener. First pitch he threw was a ball on the corner of the plate. The home plate umpire was a guy named Fieldin Culbreth. At that time, he was a Triple A umpire who was called up as a replacement umpire because one of the regular umpires was going on vacation. Culbreth called the pitch a ball, but it was a strike. I didn't say anything to Culbreth. I just threw the ball back to the pitcher and said, "Come on, Huck. We'll beat 'em all."

After I said that, the umpire said, "Hey. One more word out of you, and you're gone."

I said, "You're telling me I can't even talk to my pitcher?"

"You're out of here."

Just like that. That fast. Never been thrown out of a game at the big league level ever before.

I let him have it. Called him a Triple A cocksucker. I said, "I'm not mad at you. I'm mad at the son of a bitch who brought you up here and put you in a position where you're in way over your head. You're overwhelmed, and you ain't worth a shit. You're nothing but a Triple A cocksucker."

A few days later, I received a letter from Bob Watson on behalf of Major League Baseball. Said I'd been fined $100 or whatever.

I called Bob. I had worked with him when I first came up in Oakland. He was our minor league hitting instructor, so we had a relationship. I said, "Bob, I ain't paying that fine."

He asked me to explain myself.

I told him I never said anything to the umpire to get thrown out of the game. All I did was talk to my pitcher. Not a cuss word. Not anything else, and he tossed me. Completely uncalled for. There's no way that I should have been thrown out of the game. Now, once I got heaved, yeah, I lost my temper. Said a few things.

Bob said, "You're right." He said that some of the umpires talked with Culbreth after the game. Told him he was out of line for throwing me out of the game and that he'd need to handle the situation differently next time. That's not how it's supposed to work.

Bob said, "Don't worry about the fine." He also told me, "Next time you get thrown out, you don't have to act like that."

"I never would've acted like that if he hadn't thrown me out of the game."

I worked with Culbreth a few games after that. To his credit, he didn't hold a grudge against me or my team. Gave me a fair shake. Which is the right thing to do. There's a lot of umpires, though, if you ever do something wrong to them don't forget it. And, if they get a chance to stick it to you, they will. Call bad pitches just to test you. A lot of those guys are gone now, though. That's good.

But, with the bad you get the good. Pat and I worked some with Durwood Merrill as the home plate umpire. I always liked Wood. During the game, we'd wind up talking about OU football. Wood knew I was from Oklahoma, so he liked to talk about the Sooners. He was from Hooks, Texas, and he was always telling me that he was the one who convinced Billy Sims, OU's running back who won the Heisman Trophy, to go to Norman. Sims was also from Hooks.

You could give some shit to Wood. I remember a few at bats where I was hitting, and the pitcher threw a pitch and Wood called it a strike when it was a ball.

"What was that?" I asked.

"Hall of Fame pitch," he would say.

"Shit. This guy ain't going to the Hall of Fame."

"Hall of Fame pitch, O'B."

I also saw one of baseball's uglier umpire moments up close. Paul Quantrill was pitching for us. I was catching. Roberto Alomar, who was loved in Toronto for all that he did for the World Series teams, was hitting for Baltimore. Early in the game. John Hirschbeck was the home plate umpire. Quantrill threw a pitch, and it was a little bit outside. Hirschbeck called it strike three.

Alomar freaked out. Called Hirschbeck a faggot. Spit in his face.

I don't know why Alomar snapped, but he did.

The League suspended Alomar, and the Players Association was going to appeal it. They contacted me, wanting to know if Alomar said anything because they were trying to make a case that the suspension was undeserved, that he never said anything to the umpire.

I didn't go into the details of what was said, but I said, "Hirschbeck didn't do anything. Alomar said something."

"He says he didn't say anything."

"I don't care what he says. I'm standing two feet away from the guy. He hollered at Hirschbeck. I know what he said."

The appeal was dropped. Alomar served his suspension, and the whole thing just went away. But, it was ugly.

In all, '96 was a good year for me. I had the chance to play nearly every day, show that I was capable of doing a lot of things, things I should have been doing earlier in my career. That was the most fun I had playing baseball. The knock on me was that I couldn't hit well. When I first came up, I worked with some managers who didn't think I could hit late in the game in pressure situations, against left-handed pitching, or just hit in the big leagues period, but I put together some decent numbers in '96. It's funny: when your manager doesn't have confidence in you, you lose confidence in you. If I'd played for a guy like Bobby Cox or Dallas Green or Cito Gaston when I first came up, I would've had a much better career. I should have believed in my ability more. When I did, I played well.

Not only did I get to play a bunch, but I caught Pat and did my part to help his game. He wound up winning the Cy. I also caught Juan Guzman. He had a good year in '96, having the lowest ERA in the league. Talk about beating the fire out of somebody. He was kind of like John Smoltz, a guy who threw hard breaking balls, a lot of them in the dirt. He threw more dirt balls than anybody I ever caught. A couple of years, he led the league in wild pitches. Nasty stuff. I remember catching Juan one game in Texas where I blocked a ton of pitches. With Guzman, it seemed like one after another after another. After the game, I ran into Pudge Rodriguez. He was doing the medicine ball, and I was outside to lift weights a little. He stopped me. He said, "Dude, I've never seen a catcher block balls like that in my life."

"Well, I've had a lot of practice with him. If you catch Juan, you'll get better at it," I said.

He laughed, but that was a hell of a compliment. Pudge was a great catcher. Won so many Gold Gloves.

It was nice to play every day. And, it was nice to do it for an organization that took care of their players so much. The team arranged for us to have cars to use for the season. They gave us other perks like phones, VCRs. Had a nice family lounge where wives and kids could watch games at the SkyDome. Were real good about bringing families along for road trips. Good clubhouse facility. Of all the teams I played for, the Blue Jays did the best job of treating their players like they were special. And, I really enjoyed my time in Toronto. Beautiful city. Cito was good to play for. I had some reservations about playing in Canada. Took a long time to go through customs every time we came back from a road trip. Fill out a bunch of paperwork. But, all in all, I loved playing in Toronto. Definitely a highlight of my career. And, being in Toronto gave me the opportunity to work with a guy like Pat. Great dude. Great pitcher. Also, during the '96 off-season, the Blue Jays made a big free agency move, which meant that I'd have the chance to work with one of the game's all-time best right-handed pitchers: Roger Clemens.

CHAPTER 11

ROGER CLEMENS

If there were a mold of a perfect catcher, he would have great hands. He would be quiet behind the plate and be able to catch the ball without a lot of movement and make some balls off the plate look like strikes. He would call a game well. He knows the hitters and the umpire behind him. He manages a pitcher through a game and figures out what the pitcher is throwing the best on a given day and shapes the pitch selection around that to get the most from a guy, be it the number one starter or a journeyman, and helps him get through six or seven innings. He solves problems. He's dead honest and gives you feedback on how you're pitching and what adjustments you need to make. He keeps the game moving at a good pace. Charlie's the mold. I worked with some other guys who did these things well. Rich Gedman had great hands. Darrin Fletcher and Brad Ausmus called games well too. Ausmus was real quiet behind the plate also. Jorge Posada was great behind the plate and could also get it done at the plate with hitting. Charlie was the complete package behind the plate. He stands out. He knew what he was doing. He had everything you wanted in a catcher. My son is a catcher, and I tell him to watch tapes of Charlie and Brad Ausmus to study how the position should be played.

—*Roger Clemens*

[*Note: Roger Clemens won the Cy Young Award seven times (1986, 1987, 1991, 1997, 1998, 2001, and 2004), more than any other pitcher in Major League history, as well as one Most Valuable Player Award (1986) during his twenty-four year career.[1] Charlie caught Clemens in 1997 when he won his fourth Cy Young Award. This year marked a new chapter for Clemens. It was his first season away from the Boston Red Sox, the team with whom he had spent the first thirteen years of his career. His split from the Red Sox was bitter, with Boston's general manager Dan Duquette asserting that Clemens's best years were behind him and Clemens stating, "The Red Sox have gone from a team that stood for tradition and loyalty to one that's strictly cold business."*[2] *During his last year in Boston, Clemens's record was 10-13 with a 3.63 earned run average, and 257 strikeouts.*[3] *He responded in Toronto with a 21-7 win-loss record, a 2.05 ERA, and 292 strikeouts, winning the pitching Triple Crown by leading the league in wins, ERA, and strikeouts.*[4] *He also led the league in complete games (nine), shutouts (three), and innings pitched (264).*[5] *He was thirty-four years old. Despite his outstanding individual numbers, the Blue Jays finished with a 76-86 record in last place in the American League Eastern Division, twenty-two games behind the first place Baltimore Orioles.*[6]

Charlie caught Clemens for the bulk of 1997, working with him in twenty-three games, twelve of which were wins.

When Clemens retired after 2007, his record was 354 wins (ninth most all-time), 184 losses, a 3.12 ERA, and 4,672 strikeouts (third most all-time)—Hall of Fame worthy numbers under any measure. Shortly thereafter, allegations surfaced that Clemens used performance-enhancing drugs. Although Clemens vehemently denied these allegations, including denying these charges while testifying before Congress, the accusations clouded his reputation and his achievements. In August 2010, Clemens was indicted, and he faced six federal criminal charges: three for making false statements, two for perjury, and one for obstruction of Congress.[7] *In June 2012, after five-and-a-half years of investigation and scrutiny, Clemens was vindicated, acquitted on all charges.*]

I n 1982, I was in college, playing ball at Wichita State. Early in the season, we faced the Texas Longhorns in a doubleheader. For the Longhorns, Calvin Schiraldi pitched one game. Roger Clemens pitched the other. I think Schiraldi pitched a no-hitter and Clemens threw a one-hitter, or maybe it was the other way around. At any rate, they beat us both games. Afterward, our coach, Gene Stephenson, was pissed off, stomping around. Said something like, "Hell, even *I* could hit those guys. They're nothing special. Their stuff's not that good." I remember shaking my head and saying to Brent Kemnitz, our pitching coach, "Man, if I have to face guys like that in the big leagues, I'll never make it. Those are the best two pitchers I've ever seen." Brent and I laugh about it now, but even then, Roger had awesome stuff. Great control. Outstanding arm. And, once he started playing pro ball, he learned to throw even harder. He studied power pitchers like Nolan Ryan, Tom Seaver, Sandy Koufax, Bob Gibson, and Don Drysdale. He figured out how they used their legs to generate more power. He emulated those guys and applied their approach to his game.

Roger was the dominant right-handed pitcher of his era. When I caught him, his stuff was fantastic. I first worked with him in spring training in '97, and I was bowled over by how electric his ball was. Sharp and crisp fastball. Threw it extremely hard with a velocity of ninety-five to ninety-eight miles per hour. He got on top of the ball and created a downward tilt to it. He also toyed around with a two-seamer fastball he called his "Racer X." It had a little extra movement, a little sink action to it. His regular fastball, though, was so tough to hit. It got there in a hurry. Moved so quickly that most guys couldn't even foul off a pitch. Most hitters would cheat. Start their swing early to make contact with the ball. Even then, they couldn't do much with it. On average, he might give up five hits in a game. Maybe two of them would be hit hard. That's how dominating his stuff was.

Even though his fastball was incredible, the pitch that really made the difference for him and extended his career was his split-finger fastball (a forkball is real similar). Just like it sounds, you throw a splitter by positioning your fingers wide apart. A split-finger slips out from the pitcher's hand and looks like a fastball but then it fades. If a guy throws ninety-five miles per hour, his splitter is usually eighty-eight or ninety miles per hour. Just a little slower. Difficult pitch to read. Nobody knows where it's going and it looks like it covers the strike zone and then it just drops. Guys wind up swinging at a pitch that's really a ball. When it's nasty, it moves even more, maybe to the left, maybe to the right. Other times, it's like a changeup or an off-speed pitch. Usually produces a lot of ground balls. Mechanically, it was the perfect pitch for Roger to throw, with the way he used his legs and got on top of the ball and created such a good downward trajectory to it. Mike Scott, the pitcher for the Astros in the '80s, showed him how to throw it. Roger worked on it some in spring training and side work. Threw it a little bit while he was in Boston. Really refined it and showcased it in Toronto. What I liked about the pitch was that he could throw it to left-handed and right-handed hitters with the same effectiveness. By changing the finger pressure and where he placed his thumb, he could make the ball go down and away against left-handers or just go straight down against right-handers. Lefties had to reach for the pitch, and they had a hard time hitting it. The bottom line is that he had two good pitches from one. That pitch was so good that he could rely on it and dominate a game even if he didn't have his best fastball. An equalizer. A devastating pitch that changed how he could approach hitters. There's no telling what kind of record he would've had if he had started throwing it earlier in his career. And, it was so good that I called for the split a lot. Maybe twenty times during a game. Sometimes back to back to back against aggressive hitters or to guys who wouldn't come off the fastball.

On top of all that, Roger had great control. Threw a bunch of strikes. Could place the ball anywhere he wanted: up, down, in, or out, places where it was difficult for a hitter to get good wood on the ball. Couple that with great velocity, and he was a tough, tough pitcher to hit. It's a rare combination to throw hard and have excellent control, but his control was so good he could throw a ball into a coffee can. Literally, Roger could get the ball to me within half of a baseball of where I set the target. Amazing. Because he had both speed and control, he could strike out a lot of guys. Nolan Ryan was the same type of pitcher. So was Bret Saberhagen. With such excellent control, that's another reason why Roger was able to have such a long career. He could hit his spots so precisely that he continued to be effective after he couldn't throw his fastball in the high nineties anymore.

As far as control and what guys can learn from Roger: some of it is God-given talent. Some of it is precise mechanics. When most pitchers land their front foot after they release the ball, that foot may move an inch or two this way or that way. Not Roger. He had refined his mechanics so much that, each time he landed, his foot was in the same spot. Over and over. The guy had an incredible work ethic, probably the hardest working guy I ever played with. He worked on his delivery so that it was consistent each time he threw a pitch.

Roger had a lot of strengths—he's one of the all-time greats ever to play the game. But, he wasn't perfect. Didn't have a good curveball. He wanted to throw it, but I never called for it. It was a high school quality curveball. He thought it was better than it really was. During warm-ups, he always slipped a hook in there. I'd shake my head and say, "Dude, why do you bother throwing that? I'm *never* calling for your curveball."

He said, "You'll call for it some day."

"Well, put it in your back pocket. And leave it there."

I never called for his curve. Never.

He had a weak changeup too. Didn't call for it much. But, with how powerful his other pitches were, it didn't matter that his curve and his changeup weren't as sharp as other guys'.

———————

Roger had a great season when I caught him. Won over twenty games. Threw a bunch of strikeouts. He was on top of his game, but one reason why he had such success was having Cito Gaston as a manager. Cito just let his players play. He didn't try to control things and how you prepared. He was a great guy to play for, probably the easiest manager I ever worked with. He pretty much left you alone as long as you played hard. He believed that a player's ability would shine through. His approach fit great with Roger. Roger was disciplined. Worked hard. Liked to do his own thing. Cito never interfered with how Roger wanted to prepare for a game or how Roger wanted to pitch. He let Roger be Roger. In '97, there was no reason to get in his way. He was dominating.

I enjoyed playing with Roger. He was like John Wayne on the mound. Intimidating. A big dude at like six-four, weighing 240 or 250, staring you down. He had that confidence that no one was going to beat him. Knew he was the best pitcher in the game. He cherished being that guy who'd be depended on. He wanted to pitch in the biggest game, with all of the lights on him, and show everybody how good he was. And, Roger played the game the way it's supposed to be played. Wasn't a headhunter. Wouldn't throw at a guy because Roger was getting his ass handed to him. But, if a guy deserved it—if a guy slid into second base with his spikes up and landed a cheap shot, or if the other team hit one of our guys—Roger wouldn't hesitate to retaliate. Protected his teammates. And, he's a good guy. He'll go out to little league games and give talks. Teach the kids pitching tips. If somebody asks him for a favor, he'll do it. Need him to be in a golf tournament? He's there. Need some baseballs signed for a few kids? Done. Most guys, they're not like that. Not as generous as he is. But, Roger wants people to see that he's a good dude. He was good to his teammates. Showed rookies the ropes. He would lead by example, a "Watch me, and I'll show you how to do things" approach. Take young guys under his wing. He would help out the clubhouse guys, the trainers. We called it the Clemens scholarship: he would take guys out to eat, and do things that most people wouldn't do. And, he'd do it first-class. That's how he did everything: the parties he threw, the way he traveled. When he pitched, it reminded me of a boxing match in between rounds, because between innings, Roger would have three guys working on him, rubbing him down to keep his arm loose. And, at the end of the year after he won the Cy Young Award, he gave me a custom-made rifle, a real nice piece of hardware. Had the stock inscribed: "From 21 to 22. Catch Ya Later." That's just how he did things: first-class.

Roger is a real likeable guy. Fun to be around. He's a Texan, has good roots. Family was important to him, and he was real involved with his kids. They were first and foremost to him. Our kids are around the same age. We'd bring them to the park early and spend time together hitting them ground balls, fly balls, throwing them batting practice. Any time a guy spends as much time with his family as Roger did, he has to be a halfway decent dude. And, we're alike in some ways. We're both straight shooters. He'd call a spade a spade. He'd call guys out if they weren't running hard or giving their best effort. And, he wasn't afraid to ask Cito a question that was on everybody's mind but that everybody else was reluctant to bring up. The deal was that the '97 season was kind of a mess. We had some distractions with the team not really playing well. We had several injuries. A lot of kids coming up from Triple A to play. Add to that talk in the papers that the team was going to be sold. That Cito was going to be fired. In the midst of all that, Cito kind of disappeared. Stayed away from the clubhouse and the team. Stayed in his office a bunch, and just kind of avoided dealing with players. Acted like he didn't want to be there any more. Guys were kind of like, "What's the deal? Is he here? Is he gone? Is he all in?" To clear the air, Cito had a meeting. Told guys not to be distracted, to play hard, don't worry about Cito's situation, that he'd take care of that. Then he said, "Any questions?" Roger stepped up and asked the question that everybody wanted to know.

"Hey, Cito. Do *you* still want to be here? Do you still want to manage? You act like you don't want to manage any more."

Maybe Cito's batteries were run down. Maybe he felt like people didn't give him the recognition that he deserved, winning two World Series in Toronto. Sometimes, as players and as managers, we feel like we're owed something. We're really not owed anything, though. All we're supposed to do is go out and do the best job we can every day. Maybe, after a few years away from the game, Cito figured that, you know what? Next time, I'll do things a little different. And, he came back with Toronto and did a hell of a job with a young group of guys four or five years later.

But, like I said, Roger didn't have any fear about asking the question that was on everybody's mind but that nobody wanted to ask. He would say what needed to be said.

With that, Roger could take it, too, if he wasn't doing things exactly the right way. The first day of spring training, we had a team meeting. Roger came in a few minutes late. I think he got tied up in an interview. When he came in, I said, in front of everybody, "Hey, dude. Everybody else is here but you. Next time, you better be on time. I'm here, you gotta be here." I told him in a way that was kind of joking but serious too that no one was better than anyone else on the team. I think Roger appreciated that. He would've said the same thing to me if I was new to Boston and showed up a few minutes late to a meeting. I think that's why we got along so well. He liked how I went about my work. I appreciated how he did his. Later, Pat Hentgen told me that, when Roger and he were running, Roger said of me, "Damn, that dude got all over me." Hentgen told him he better be on time; otherwise, I'd embarrass the shit out of him. It's true. Being late is one of my pet peeves. I was never late. Always early. Used to have nightmares about showing up late to practice.

And, I enjoyed Roger. At the beginning of the season, I think we'd just flown in to Toronto from spring training. We either just had our first practice at the Sky-Dome or were getting ready for it. I took Roger to the Lone Star Steakhouse, right by the SkyDome, for lunch. We sat down. Ordered. And, like five or six fans came up to our table. They wanted my autograph. The year before, I'd played pretty well for the Blue Jays. Developed a nice following. For some reason, the fans liked me in Toronto. But, across the table from me was one of the greatest right-handed pitchers of all time. None of these people recognized him. Nobody asked him for his autograph. The look on his face: hilarious. A back-up catcher and a Hall of Fame pitcher, and everybody's going to the back-up catcher for his autograph.

I gave Roger grief about it. I said, "Lookit, dude. You might have been a big deal in Boston, but you ain't shit here in Toronto."

He laughed.

I gave him hell, too, when he went to the Yankees. At first, he wore number twelve there. I guess he flipped his usual twenty-one and made it twelve. Then he switched to twenty-two. That was the number I wore in college and what I wore most of my professional career. I called and left him a voicemail: "It's about time you started wearing a real number."

From day one of spring training, you could tell that Roger had something to prove. He left Boston with him and the GM having a to-do about Roger not being in shape. Not working hard. That ate at Roger. He took the mound every start in '97 wanting to show Boston that they made a mistake by not re-signing him. Pride was a big motivator for him, and he wanted to pitch at the top of his game. Another drive for him was that he thrived on the limelight. He wanted the ball in those big games when it was lights, camera, and action. The bigger the game, the better he pitched. In most situations, I think he'd have a tough time pitching for a team not in a pennant race. But, even though we finished in last place and were below .500, I think he found motivation in every start: showing Boston what they missed out on. It's tough when a team doesn't want you anymore. Won't pay you what you think you're worth. Boston thought he was washed up—he was going to prove them wrong.

In April and May, Benito Santiago caught most of his games. Even though Roger's record was good, the two of them were having communication problems. They would have a game plan about what pitches they'd throw to certain hitters. But, during the game, Benny would call pitches the complete opposite of what they discussed. This upset most pitchers. Some of the other guys in Toronto like Pat Hentgen had a problem with this. Benny was a real talented guy. Not a very good listener, though. After a while, I think Roger went to Cito and said he couldn't work with this cat because Roger was trying to tell Benny where he wanted to go in a game but Benny wouldn't listen. Maybe he didn't. Roger never said anything about it to me. But, after the first part of the season, I pretty much caught all of Roger's starts.

It didn't take too long until I figured out the things that Roger liked. He never had to tell me, "Hey, you're moving too soon," or "Hey, I'd like it if you did this." I just picked up that he liked to pitch down and away. Liked to throw his split-finger for his first pitch and back to back early in the count. Liked for me to move my body to different parts of the plate for each pitch. If the pitch was going to be outside, he wanted me to set up on the outside of the plate. This was one of the ways that I did things a little differently than Santiago—Benny would just set up in the middle of the plate for every pitch. A big thing for me was to establish a good flow to the game. One way I did that was to get the ball back to Roger quickly and get into position and be ready to go for the next pitch. Roger and I both liked to work fast, so this was a natural fit. Once I was in position, he liked for me to remain as still as possible.

We clicked with pitch selection too. Before games, we reviewed lineups. The advance scouting reports. We both had experience. Knew the hitters. We would come up with our game plan in five or ten minutes. It wasn't rocket science—I said we should call pitches that played to his strengths and that made hitters uncomfortable. In all of these meetings, I ended with, "We're going to go with what you have working until they make us change. We'll go with our strengths and then adjust from there." We rarely had to regroup between innings. The cool thing was we thought alike, and we developed that pitcher-catcher rhythm. I'd put down the pitch I knew Roger wanted to throw, and Roger would know that's what I was going to put down, and he was like, "Man, this guy knows exactly what I'm thinking." He didn't have to think about anything. All he had to do was pitch. It's fun to get in that rhythm. It's the best thing about a baseball game. And, Roger liked the way I called a game. He knew where I was going when I called pitches. He'd shake me off maybe four or five times during a game. If I signaled for the same pitch again after he shook me off, he'd go with me. Reach back and give a good effort. Some guys, if you did that to them, they would kind of half-ass it because you're asking them to go in a direction they don't want to go or believe in. Or, you have to go out to the mound and explain why you want that pitch. Not with Roger.

On the mound, Roger was intense. Like a racehorse going 100 miles an hour. Locked in. If we were in a difficult situation and really needed to get an out, I'd challenge him. I would tell him, "We got to get this guy out. This is what we've got to do." Sometimes, he'd snap at me. Tell me no, we need to get around this guy and face the next one. We could be blunt and honest with each other. None of it ever carried over to the clubhouse or the next day, though. We forgot about it. And, sometimes, all I needed to do was get him to slow down. Give him a chance to get some oxygen because he was going full blast out there. He wasn't one of those guys you needed to get on to bring his attention back into the game. He was balls to the wall all the time.

With some catchers, when you're catching a guy like Roger Clemens, a legend who's racked up a lot of awards and recognition, there's a tendency to be a little hands-off. A little reluctant to be direct or offer suggestions for how to improve. Or, a little intimidated so the catcher doesn't say the things he would ordinarily say. I didn't get wrapped up in all that. My job was to keep the pitcher on track so he could perform well. So, even if I was dealing with a Hall of Fame-type guy like Roger Clemens, if I thought he had a shitty curveball, I'd tell him. Tell him not to throw it. I wouldn't give in to him and think, "Hell. That's Roger Clemens. He wants to throw a curveball, well, I'll sign for curveballs." I had to stick with what I knew made the pitcher most effective in a given situation. I wasn't helping anybody out by sugarcoating things or telling him only what he wanted to hear instead of what I knew was right. So, I didn't talk to guys like they were special or better than I was or better than anybody else on the team. And, I think Roger respected that. Liked that honesty. What you saw was what you got. And, I wanted to do all that I could so that we won. But, that's just how I played the game. Like one time, when Roger was pitching. He was throwing well, but his stuff wasn't electric. He needed to catch some breaks. We were a few innings into the game, and we had already committed one error. Roger made a good pitch, and the hitter tapped a ground ball to short or second base. It should've been a double play ball that got us out of the inning. The middle infielders tried to make it look fancy, though, and they booted the play. A couple of runs scored, and we got behind. Think we got one out instead of two. Anyway, right after that, I marched out to the infield. Roger said he saw me coming, and he figured I was going out there to chew the fat with him and tell him, hey, get focused; don't be distracted by the error. But, I walked right past Roger and went out to the second baseman and shortstop and told them, "Get the job done. It's not about flash and flair. Just get your work done right."

Even though we weren't in a playoff race, I caught some memorable games with Roger. His first game back at Fenway with Toronto was the most dominant performance I ever caught in my nineteen years of professional baseball. It should be replayed on the MLB Network over and over. It was an emotional game because he was coming back to the place where he had started his career and made his mark.

What was cool about the game was that it was a playoff atmosphere in the middle of the season. At the beginning of the game, the fans went crazy. They were booing. They hated Roger. Called him traitor and all kinds of stuff. They were all over him the minute he took the field or whenever he walked out in between innings to go to the mound. We walked in from the bullpen after warming up, and he said, "Hey, O'B. Walk in front of me."

"Why's that?"

"If somebody shoots at us, you'll get hit."

I laughed. I said, "Thanks a lot, bud. I'll walk beside and make sure they get a good shot at you."

He went out in the first inning. He was amped up. Overthrowing and trying to do too much. Gave up a couple of singles, then he hit Mo Vaughn, one of his best friends on Boston, with a fastball inside. Poor old Mo. He made a bunch of noise when Roger hit him. One run scored, but I told him to settle in. Relax.

"Watch where I sit," I said. "Get the ball to me."

After that first inning, Roger calmed down. And, then he just mowed through hitters. As he started pitching better and striking guys out, the fans started getting behind him. He pitched eight innings and punched out sixteen guys. When he went out for the eighth inning, Cito told him that it'd be his last inning. It was like Roger saved the best for last. He threw ten pitches. Not one of them was under ninety-seven miles per hour. And, in those ten pitches, he struck out their three best hitters, Nomar Garciaparra, John Valentin, and Mo Vaughn. I say ten pitches, but actually it was nine. During the game, the umpire called one of the pitches a ball, but if you watch it now on replay, you can see that the ball was really a strike. When Roger walked off the mound, the crowd went nuts. Now, they were cheering *for* him. Roger stared up to the booth where the GM, Dan Duquette, sat. Roger kind of gave a little hand wave to him. Intense. One of the coolest things I've ever seen. If you're looking for a dominant performance with all eyes on you, you couldn't ask for a better one than how Roger pitched that afternoon.

I also liked working with him because we could buckle down and make the game work when he didn't have his best stuff. He had an incredible season, but there were times when the ball just didn't do what it normally would. He had a couple of shitty games against Seattle. His fastball wasn't very good. His split-finger was nothing. Location was off. His breaking ball wasn't breaking. It's supposed to drop and go down and away, but it'd just twist in the middle part of the plate and not have any downward tilt to it. That's when pitches get hammered. But, part of the age and maturity process is figuring out something that works when you don't have your best stuff. It's just a different way to compete. I'd tell him, "Stay with me," and we'd adjust. We wouldn't pound dudes like normal. I knew it, he probably knew it, but I didn't announce to him that he didn't have his best shit and that I was doing my best to work with what he was giving me. He probably figured it out by the way I changed calling the game and that he'd have to *pitch*: really concentrate and be a little finer and paint the corners. Not overthrow. That he'd have to get on top of the ball a little more and create more of a downward tilt to it. Execute each pitch. Mature pitchers figure this out. They know they can't throw the ball 100 miles an hour any more, so they come up with a way to make quality pitches. With Roger, when he didn't have his sharpest stuff, I'd rely on his control to bail us out. Stay away from the inside part of the plate. And, before you knew it, we'd be into the third inning. Coming up with a way to make it work. What was shaping up to be a bad outing was turning into a quality start.

If Roger had a weakness to his game, it was his fielding. He wasn't an athletic pitcher like Greg Maddux or John Smoltz who you could count on for making a few fielding plays each game to get some outs. Roger worked extremely hard on his fielding. In fact, the first time I saw him with the Blue Jays, he was at a spring training practice. He was the first guy out there. Roger had somebody standing at first base, was tossing balls to the ground, practicing picking them up, and throwing to first base. I was the second guy there. I told him I'd help them out by hitting the ball to Roger, and then he could field the ball and throw it to first. Sometimes, during pitchers' fielding practice, I'd play first base while he took ground ball after ground ball. Once he caught the ball, he kind of hesitated before throwing it to a base. Couldn't throw it to first or second the way he could throw the ball to home plate. He knew this part of his game could be improved, so he worked on it. He didn't want to embarrass himself by making a bad play.

More so than any pitcher I caught, Roger liked knowing who was umpiring the game behind the plate. The umpires rotated from third to second to first to home plate, so you could tell who he was getting for his start. Roger knew their tendencies and what kind of strike zone each of them had. What kind of pitches he could throw. Which side of the plate they saw the best. I think he kept books on the umpires. He loved pitching when John Hirschbeck umped. All the pitchers loved Hirschbeck because he had a very consistent strike zone. It bugged Roger when the rotation was thrown off or if a guy had to leave an umpire crew and they called up a guy from Triple A to fill his place. I think that's how it was with most pitchers, but he was more open or vocal about saying that he wanted to know who was calling the game.

Roger did another thing that was different compared to most pitchers: he didn't spend a lot of time in the bullpen warming up. Most guys might throw fifty or sixty pitches to get loose. Roger would throw maybe fifteen or thirty pitches, which was unheard of. Wouldn't waste his bullets in the pen. I'll bet that these short warm-ups along with good mechanics (fundamentally, he was sound with strong legs that worked well with his top half, so he was able to get everything he could out of his body to pitch with high velocity without putting a lot of stress on his shoulder), and a strong work ethic (the guy was always going on these long distance runs around town), helped his endurance so he could throw 130 pitches a game and complete a lot of games. Helped extend his career. That and his split-finger.

He had rituals or routines. Before a game day, he liked to eat pasta to give him carbs to burn. Two days before he pitched, he tried to get a lot of sleep. He said the night before a game, he wouldn't sleep well at all. Didn't matter if it was a day game or a night game, a game in the middle of the season or a World Series game: he'd toss and turn, thinking about the hitters he was getting ready to face.

Before games, he visualized situations. He'd review the lineup and identify spots where he might get in a jam. Say it's two or three good hitters in a row. He might have runners on second and third with one out a couple of times during the game. Roger would play out these situations in his mind and think about how he would pitch to get out of them. That made it easier for him when, during the game, he found himself in that jam. It wasn't a surprise—he had anticipated it, and he knew how he'd handle it.

I know Roger has had a bunch of shit going on with all these allegations that he used steroids or performance-enhancing drugs. I'm glad he was found innocent and didn't go to jail. When I played with him, I never suspected that stuff for a minute. I spent a lot of time with him. I never saw anything remotely connected to steroids around the guy. I have a tough time believing he did them. He was so dominating without them, I don't know why he'd use them. Plus, his stepdad died young of a heart attack, forty-something years old. I know that really stuck with him and was always a concern of his. Family was important to him, and I don't think he'd do anything to risk his health and the time that he could spend with his kids. If you take steroids, you know it's going to affect you in some way. With his family history, it'd really surprise me if he would take that risk. And, I can't see that his body changed drastically from when I played with him in Toronto through the rest of his career. He always had a barrel chest. Big butt. Thick legs. With the way he worked out all the time, if he was taking steroids, I think you would see drastic body changes. I've been around guys who used steroids, and I can tell how the drugs change your body. Like José Canseco. We were coming up in the Oakland farm system at the same time. One year, he ended the season lean at like 190 pounds. Next year, he showed up at spring training weighing 240. He said something like, "I ate a lot over the winter." Even though it wasn't openly stated that he was doing steroids, you knew he had to be because of the way his body changed so rapidly and drastically. He was doing his cycles and lifting weights and getting big in a hurry. With Roger, if he were doing steroids, he would've become way bigger. He didn't. That right there tells you something. And, just his personality, I know he would've said something about it. To try it. That it made him better and would make me better. He never said a word, though.

And, the deal is: I don't think the guy would cheat. One time, I had a ball that was pretty scuffed up. With a scuffed ball, the pitcher can make the ball move violently another eight to twelve inches in one direction and really get an advantage over the hitter. I threw the ball out to him real quick before the umpire could toss it out of play. Roger threw it back to me. So, I carried it out to the mound. I was like, "Dude, this is a good ball. What are you doing?" He looked at it and gave it back to me. He said, "I don't need that." His stuff was so good that he didn't need to cheat. Seeing him have the chance to get an advantage and refuse it, I have a hard time thinking that he'd take steroids or do anything else that would give him an unfair advantage. He'd rely solely on his ability to win.

Some people might look to his win-loss records and compare '96 to '97 and argue that the reason why he went from ten wins to twenty-one wins was because of steroids. I disagree. Your win-loss record is more indicative of how your team is playing. Doesn't really account for whether a guy is pitching well or not. A guy might have no run support. He could pitch lights out and give up one or two runs, but if his team doesn't score any runs, he'll get the loss. The more important statistics to pay attention to are a pitcher's ERA and strikeouts. Look at that, and you can tell there's really no difference in Roger between those seasons: ERAs of 3.63 in '96 and 2.05 in '97; 257 strikeouts in '96 and 292 strikeouts in '97. Both years, he was pitching well. And, like I said, Roger thrived on the limelight and pitching in big games. If the last few teams he was playing on in Boston were so-so, maybe he didn't have the same kind of motivation he had playing on a good team in a pennant race. Plus, I think the difference between those two seasons is the development of his split-finger fastball. He threw it more in Toronto, and as the season went on, the pitch got better and better.

In 2012, I appeared in court and testified in Roger's trial. Said pretty much what I just did: the reason why Roger extended his career and was able to pitch until he was forty-five was because he developed a new pitch, the split-finger fastball. I didn't care for testifying. I thought I should do the right thing. Tell the court the truth of what I knew about Roger. But, when the government cross-examined me, it was frustrating. They asked the same questions three times, like whether Roger was a fierce competitor, did I agree that Roger was a fierce competitor, and didn't I say that Roger was one of the fiercest competitors I ever saw? Made it look like I was giving different answers, with comments like "Are you sure?" and "Remember you're under oath." I testified that I remembered seeing syringes of vitamin B12 shots, energy shots, lined up while I was in Toronto. The prosecuting attorney kept quizzing me on whether I remembered if the liquid were red or clear. They asked about the Blue Jays' medical team. I said they weren't very good, not near as good as the trainers I worked with in Atlanta, but that I got a number of shots from them for torn ligaments in my wrist and knee. They asked if I knew that Roger said he ate Vioxx like Skittles. I told them I ate Naprosyn, an anti-inflammatory, like Skittles. Then I corrected my testimony. Said I ate them like M&Ms because I don't care much for Skittles. The lawyer then reminded me that this trial involved serious criminal charges. I get that. Understood it then. But some of the questions they asked were ridiculous. One was about whether the clubhouse attendants contributed to the team. I answered that pressing the uniforms and making them look all neat didn't make a bit a difference as to how we played on the field.

"Are you sure, Mr. O'Brien?"

I answered, yes, I was sure. Nobody picking up a jock strap from the floor had any bearing on whether we won or lost. Clubhouse guys' work was for cosmetics only.

Anyway, I don't plan on spending any more time in courtrooms. But, testifying for him was the right thing to do. His lawyers asked me to testify. So, I did. Told them the truth of what I knew about Roger. I think his defense team went to some of his other former teammates and asked for their cooperation. Some guys refused. Don't know why. Don't know if it was intimidation or fear or what, but like I said, I did the right thing. Told the truth about what I knew about the guy. Period.

––––––––––––––

Roger was real driven. Wanted to post great numbers. All the Cy Young Awards and that kind of stuff were important to him. He wanted to be known as one of the best pitchers who ever took the mound. And, in my mind, he is one of the most dominant right-handed pitchers of all time. He deserves to be in the Hall of

Fame. It'd be an unfair punishment if he's not voted in because of all this steroid or human growth hormone scandal. But, you never know what the writers and voters will think even though he was exonerated at that trial. Keeping him out of the Hall of Fame would be the worst punishment you could give him, the thing that would bother him most. And, I understand why: he was one of the best to ever play the game. And, he knows it.

CHAPTER 12

CHRIS CARPENTER

Charlie was a guy who you learned from. He had strong character. A tough character. He didn't put up with any BS. If you treated the game and the clubhouse the right way, he respected you, no matter what age you were. That's what I take from him. How you respect the game. The guys and your teammates. How they've gotten there. If you do that, you get respect back. He was that guy who made sure that guys didn't screw around. If you didn't respect the game, he was going to let you know. I take this now into my game and into my clubhouse from the things he taught me about what it means to be a teammate and what it means to be a part of that locker room.

—*Chris Carpenter*

[*Note: The year 1997 was Chris Carpenter's first season in the Major Leagues. He spent two stints with the Blue Jays that year, with three starts in May before returning to the minor leagues and then being called up at the end of July for the remainder of the season. He pitched in fourteen games, and Charlie caught three of them, including Carpenter's first big league win (August 19, 1997, against the Chicago White Sox; the other two games were no decisions). He finished the year with three wins, seven losses, and a 5.09 earned run average.[1] He pitched six seasons with the Blue Jays and, in 2002, was named their Opening Day starter against Pedro Martinez and the Boston Red Sox at Fenway Park, the ballpark where Carpenter watched games as a child. That season, his shoulder bothered him and compromised his ability to pitch effectively. Doctors discovered that his labrum needed to be repaired—specifically, he needed surgery to tack the labrum to the bones in his shoulder. Instead of seeing how he responded to the procedure, the Blue Jays released Carpenter. Carpenter pled with the team to keep him on the roster so he could retain his health insurance, as his wife was pregnant with the couple's first child. He offered to sign for the league minimum as a way to preserve his health insurance, but the Blue Jays declined, advising him that it was doubtful that another Major League team would offer him a contract. Carpenter, however, generated plenty of interest as a free agent. At baseball's winter meetings, he received six big league contract offers. After Carpenter received these offers, the Blue Jays returned to the table, wanting to sign him to a Major League contract. He quickly refused the offer. He liked the idea of joining the St. Louis Cardinals and reuniting with former Blue Jays teammates, pitcher Woody Williams and catcher Mike Matheny. He signed as a free agent with St. Louis, missed the entire 2003 season, and suffered a setback when his shoulder rejected one of the tacks holding his labrum in place. He required another surgery to repair scar tissue around the tack. After the surgery and feeling an immediate improvement in his range of motion, Carpenter knew he would pitch again.*

Not only did Carpenter pitch again, but he also returned as one of the game's best pitchers.[2] He anchored the St. Louis Cardinals' staff and won the Cy Young Award in 2005 with a 21-5 record, 2.83 ERA, four shutouts, and 213 strikeouts.[3] The excellence continued when, in 2011, he helped the Cardinals surge into the playoffs and ultimately win a World Series championship with his 10-2 record and 2.73 ERA during the second half of the season.[4]

Carpenter pitched for fifteen seasons, winning 144 games, losing 94, striking out 1,697, and posting a career 3.76 ERA.[5]]

I worked with some guys at their peak. Guys like Greg Maddux, Pat Hentgen, Roger Clemens. They had been in the league for a while. Perfected their craft. And, they were so good at what they did that the writers recognized them as the best pitcher in their league. Those are incredible experiences. Working with those guys and doing the little things to help them out, playing a small role in their success: I'm proud of that. But, another cool thing was to work with a young guy, somebody new and unproven, to look at him on the mound, see the kind of stuff he was throwing, and know that, once he harnessed his talent and adrenaline, spent a season or two in the big leagues and learned how to get guys out at that level, he'd be one of the game's top pitchers. That's what it was like working with Chris Carpenter. Watching the kid, you knew you were seeing something special. It was just a matter of time for him to figure a few things out and pull it all together.

Carp had everything going for him. He's a big guy. Like six-foot-six. With that kind of frame, you have an advantage. Gives you extra leverage. With longer legs and arms, you can reach out farther when you release the ball. Seems that size makes pitchers throw downhill better. Just makes it that much more difficult for guys to hit you. And, he threw hard. Had great control. Great arm. Threw some great pitches. Our pitching coach, Mel Queen, showed Carp how to throw a changeup using the circle change grip. He threw it well. Used it in a lot of situations—to right-handers, to left-handers, back-to-back. Got him through a lot of games. His curveball was sharp, too. A lot of break. And, he threw a ninety-five to ninety-seven mile per hour fastball. The way he released the ball, the ball came out nice and easy. And, even as a twenty-two-year-old kid, he had that drive. That focus and determination that he'd do whatever it took to win games.

His intensity stands out. When he was young, he was real high strung before he pitched. Couldn't eat. Really wouldn't talk to anybody. If anything, he was angry around people. The first game I caught him, I went out to the mound to talk to him. He was so hyped. First inning, and his hat was soaked. Sweat dripping off the brim. And, he was breathing so hard that he could barely talk to me.

I said, "Damn, dude. You're going to have to lighten up. You can't make it through a year like this. Your heart's gonna blow up."

He kind of nodded.

I said, "You need to slow down. Breathe. You need so much oxygen in your body to perform."

That should show you that Carp wasn't a guy who needed a kick in the ass. He needed somebody to pull the reins in. Slow him down. Get him to pace himself so that he could finish the race. Because, he was going to give you everything he had. And, if he didn't have his best game, he was going to search for something that would work.

Carp reminds me of a story Jay Howell told me. Jay was our closer when I first came up to the big leagues in Oakland. I didn't play a lot, pretty much just warmed up guys, including Jay, in the bullpen. Jay was one of those guys who needed all confidence, no criticism. While he was throwing, he'd ask, "How's it coming?" and I had to say, "Outstanding. Really sharp," even if it wasn't his best. One of those guys that needed to be built up. Sometimes, though, I had to mess with him. I couldn't help it. That's just how I am. I'd answer, "How's it coming? It's coming out of your hand, man." Then he'd look at me all befuddled. So, usually, I just answered, "Coming out hot."

Jay's first big league game was pitching for the Cincinnati Reds on the road against the Dodgers at Dodger Stadium. He got the call in the bullpen that he was coming in. So, he sprints to the mound and meets his catcher, Johnny Bench. Bench says, "What do you throw, kid?"

Jay's still breathing hard from his run, so he pants, "I've got a fastball, curve, and slider. My curve's better than my slider."

"Okay." They figure out the signs, and Bench goes back to the plate. Jay's out there on the mound. His first hitter is Steve Garvey. Then it all floods in: he's making his big league debut. He just talked to Johnny Bench. He's getting ready to pitch to Steve Garvey. The adrenaline kicks in, and it's pumping so hard, he can't really see. Can't really hear. But, he can't just stand out there and do nothing, so he winds up and pitches. Throws the ball as hard as he can.

He hits Steve Garvey right square in the helmet.

Remember, he's playing the Dodgers at Dodger Stadium, so the crowd starts booing him. Garvey winds up lying on the ground, and Jay's like, oh shit, what've I done? He goes toward home plate to check on him. Make sure he's okay. But, the Dodgers' manager Tommy Lasorda comes out there too to check on Garvey. Then Lasorda starts ripping into Jay.

"You piece of shit. You're just a Triple A pitcher. You don't belong here. You don't know how to pitch. Get out of here, you piece of shit."

Lasorda's right in Jay's face. So close that Jay can feel Lasorda's spit. Jay's like, hell, I didn't know what to do. I'm fresh in from Triple A. Nervous as shit, can't even catch my breath. I threw, and the ball just got away from me.

They helped Garvey off the field, and Jay didn't even remember walking back to the mound. He just took a deep breath and tried to calm down. The next batter was Ron Cey. Jay got him to ground out, and he got the next two guys out too. He goes back to the dugout, and he's so jacked up, his legs are shaking. Then George Foster, the Reds outfielder, stops and talks to him.

"That's great, kid," Foster says in his high-pitched voice. Jay's legs won't quit shaking, but George is there patting him on the back saying, "They've thrown at our hitters all season long, and we don't do anything about it. We need to throw at them more. Great job."

Welcome to the big leagues. It's overwhelming and exciting. But, part of being a young player is figuring out how to keep an even keel. Just go out there. Do your job. And, don't get too high when things are good or too low when things are shitty. It takes time to figure this out, but you have to do it.

For a rookie pitcher, Toronto was an ideal setting for Carp. He had guys like Hentgen and Clem to learn from. Woody Williams. Guys who knew what it took to compete at a high level for a long time. Those dudes had him on scholarship the whole season. They took care of him. Covered his cab rides to the park. I doubt he paid for many meals that year. Maybe that's something he passed on to younger players as a veteran. But, when I talk about Hentgen and Clemens taking care of Carp, they did a lot more than pick up the tab. They took him under their wings. Showed him how to be a professional. The importance of exercising, taking care of your body. In between starts, Clemens would take him running. Work out with him. Showed him the time and commitment it takes to prepare your body to pitch nine innings so you're not out there, looking over your shoulder to the bullpen in the fifth, ready to get out of the game. Clem was the hardest working pitcher I've ever seen, and it'd only help somebody to watch him and how he went about being ready to play. And, Roger and Pat helped Carp develop the mental toughness you need to pitch at the highest level. Part of that was by showing him the importance of his bullpen session in between starts. How, during those ten minutes, you need to visualize the hitters of the next team you're facing and concentrate on making your pitches. Side days are just as much about practicing your physical mechanics as they are about getting mentally ready to pitch. During a game, you'll have times when you have to concentrate on making your pitches. If you can figure out how to develop this concentration during practice so it's that much easier to do in game situations, that's critical. And, they taught him about warming up. How to pitch to hitters. How to deal with travel, figure out when it's a good time to get to the park. The importance of paying attention to the games when you're not pitching and not screwing around and gazing around at the stands. The right way to interact with the press. Representing your organization that's giving you a chance to be a Major League Baseball player so that you're a good reflection of it on and off the field. Staying away from all of the temptations that are out there. Hentgen and Clemens: neither one of those guys were party guys. Both of them were hardworking dudes, great mentors for a young guy to model himself after. Chris couldn't have asked for two better people to learn from. And, I think Carp will tell you that. I know one time he told Hentgen that he learned more about how to pitch from Pat than he did from anybody else. Hentgen was real big on making the most of his starts, of putting everything he had out on the field. Making that day important and not taking anything for granted. Because, if you don't take it seriously, somebody's going to come up from behind you and take that opportunity from you. There's a line of guys behind you, just waiting for their chance to pitch in the big leagues. Watch Carp as a veteran, and you could tell that he treated each start like it might've been the last time he got the ball. Left it all out there.

As a young player, Carp was real receptive to receiving advice. Everybody's advice, really. Eyes and ears were wide open. You could tell that he wanted to be the best that he could be. All he had to do was figure out a few little things, figure out that he needed to slow down and pace himself. Keep his breathing even. Learn how to pitch more under control, and the sky was going to be the limit for him.

I like to think that I helped him as a rookie, too. I caught him only a few times—Benny Santiago worked with him mostly. I'd catch Carp on a day game after a night game to give Benny a break or something. Even though we didn't work together a bunch, I did a couple of things for him. One was that I treated him the same as everybody else. Some guys were real big on keeping rookies in their place, making them earn your respect. Not me. You put on a Major League uniform, you have my respect. I know what it takes to get there. So, I never gave any shit to rookies. Never called a guy "Rook." I saw that sort of thing when I was coming up. Hated it. Swore I'd never do it. I treated rookie pitchers the same as I treated the veterans. Demanded just as much from that tenth or eleventh guy on the staff as I did from Pat or Roger. Carp never had to prove himself or go through any of that shit with me.

The other thing is that it helps to have a veteran catcher working with rookie pitchers. That way, the catcher is a buffer or even an advocate for the pitcher with umpires. Kind of like how some of the older players tried to keep rookies in their place, some umpires would make rookies earn their respect. Test them. Make them run a little bit of a gauntlet. Make them get more of the plate than some of the veteran guys for them to call strikes. And, the umpires tended to give more calls to the veteran hitters than they would to rookie pitchers. Because I'd been around the game for a long time by then and knew the umpires, I could work with them and say, "Dude, he's always around the plate." Or, "Man, that was a good pitch there. Let's go. We've gotta have those pitches." Make the focus more about good pitches than about the fact that the guy pitching has been in the big leagues for only a month. Younger catchers may be a little more tentative. A lot of times, young catchers won't say shit to umpires. But, a veteran guy can help cut through some of the proving yourself bullshit. Get the umpires focused on making the right calls instead of showing a kid on the mound who's in charge. Everybody's seen the *Bull Durham* story. A lot of it is true. An older catcher can help a young pitcher. With umpires. With hitters. Different situations.

I worked with Carp only a few times. But, I was lucky enough to catch his first big league win. Saved the ball for him. Took him out to eat after the game. We beat the White Sox at Chicago, first game of a doubleheader. He threw six innings. Gave up some hits, but not too many runs. Threw a lot of strikes. One inning, he faced their three best hitters. Frank Thomas led off and singled, but then Albert Belle hit a ground ball to short. We turned a double play. Robin Ventura flew out to right, and we were out of the inning in like six pitches. Carp got the job done, and the bullpen stepped in and finished the game for us.

Carp's record wasn't great in '97. You look at box scores and think, "Geez, this guy just doesn't have it." He'd pitch a few innings and give up eight or nine hits. Part of that is deceiving. A guy can give up nine hits, but maybe only two of them are good hits. Two balls that are hit hard. If Carp was overthrowing and trying to do too much and winding up elevating his pitches, a guy could make contact. Lot of jam shots. A lot of balls off the end of the bat, and it dorks in for a hit. Or, maybe it's a five- or six-hopper dribbling through the infield. When the ball's up and you make contact, it'll drop in for a hit a lot of times. When the ball's down, you're likely to get an out if the hitter makes contact. Carp ran in to some of that where he wasn't keeping the ball down enough. And, when he first came up, he had some bad luck. It wasn't a question of batters ripping him. He was pitching well. He just wasn't catching any breaks. Like I said, it takes time to adjust to the big leagues. It's rare for a young guy to understand immediately how to get guys out at a big league level. Takes a while to figure out. Get your feet wet.

One of the things that I think Carp and all young players have to work through is finding himself as a player. When you're a young player, coaches try to put their stamp on you. They want some piece of you, knowing that there's a possibility you'll be a big league player. So, they tell you to do this, don't do that. Part of that is to help players develop. Part of it is self-promotion, though. That way, if a coach taught a pitcher a great changeup, down the road, he can say, "See that guy? See that great changeup? That's because of me." Take credit for it. Help him keep his job or get another one. Because of that, you hear a lot of different messages with coaches trying to mold you this way or that. When really, it should be, "I made a couple of suggestions to the guy, and he went running with it." But, players have to listen. You can always learn something. Some of these lessons can be helpful. Filter through them, and at the same time, remain headstrong and committed to what got you to that level in the first place. But, when you start scuffling, that's when it seems like you start listening to everybody. Maybe this guy knows. Maybe that guy knows. You get in a rut, everyone in the world is trying to figure it out. Tell you what you should be doing. And, you're looking for all the help you can get. Before you know it, you're far away from what got you there in the first place. That's the thing to watch out for. Instead of just going back to the drawing board and saying, "Hey, I'll figure this out. I'm going to do what I do best and go for it."

To get through this, a young player can look to veteran players, guys who've gone through the same thing. Listen to them. Soak in what they have to say. Figure out if it's something that'll work well for you. If it does, keep it. If it doesn't, get rid of it. It's kind of like listening to your dad. You pay attention to what he says. You may not always do what he says, but you respect and value his opinion.

Watching Carp pitch as a veteran, you could see that he settled in. Was comfortable in himself, his strengths. He'd throw his game, rely on his strengths, and take ownership of the fact that the "W" or the "L" followed his name. It wasn't the pitching coach's game. The manager's game. The catcher's game. It was his. He'd run it. And, he'd win or lose it the way he wanted to, the way he thought was right. This is all a part of developing and finding out who you are as a player. Saying, "Hey, this is what I do" and doing it. Figuring out when to throw a breaking pitch for a strike and when to keep it out of the strike zone. Fine-tuning his control so he didn't throw as many wild pitches. Having a good feel of what pitch to throw at the right time. That was Carp. He used his fastball well. Moved on such a good downward plane that I would've gone more down and away with it. But, he liked to pitch inside. Had a good balance mixing in his breaking ball at the right times. Sometimes, he'd come up with a cutter. When I caught him, he didn't throw a cutter. It's funny: when I worked with him, he had a great changeup. But, after his shoulder surgery in '02, he lost it. I thought he'd work on it in spring training and try to bring it back, but he never found it. The bottom line, though, is that he did a great job of understanding his strengths on a given day and going with them.

I'd get a kick out of seeing him get fired up on the mound. Hollering at batters. Staring them down after he got them out. He didn't do that sort of thing as a rookie. You can get in a lot of trouble doing that as a young guy in the league. Back then, he was more tentative. Didn't want to make anybody mad. But, as a veteran, he was probably less concerned with pissing guys off. I think that change is part of finding out who you are. Being comfortable with how you're doing things. If that intensity fuels him, I say go for it. I always liked working with guys who pitched on the edge. I called it pitching with an attitude. Carp definitely pitched with an attitude. In the 2011 playoffs he struck out a batter, and you could read his lips telling the batter to sit the fuck down. I think some of that bravado may come from some of the guys he worked with early in his career: Hentgen and Clemens. Those guys were prime examples of intimidating dudes. Guys who stared at you, and their whole message with their expressions, how their bodies moved, how they pitched to guys was, "I'm going to kick your ass." No question he pitched with a lot of emotion. How you create that intensity—that's just one of those things that makes those Cy Young guys so special. There's something inside them. It's part of their makeup. You either have it or you don't.

After getting smoked in the face with back-to-back foul tips and seeing stars because of it, I knew that catcher's masks could be improved. Offer better protection. So, one of the things I worked on while I was in Toronto was developing a new catcher's mask. It looks like a goalie's mask in hockey.

Growing up, I was a big hockey fan. My mom's family was from up north, and they were hockey fans. Seems like my Uncle Joe was always taking my brothers and sisters and me to the Tulsa Convention Center to watch the minor league Tulsa Oilers play. I was a huge Tony Esposito fan. Chicago Blackhawks. Great goalie. I guess because of all that, I played hockey. Goalie. Really liked wearing the equipment and being the last line of defense between the other team and scoring. It's a lot like catching with all of the gear and trying to stop a puck the same way a catcher blocks a ball. And, goalie was a good position for me because I wasn't the best skater in the world.

Toronto's spring training camp was near Tampa. One time, Corey Schwab, the goalie for the Tampa Bay Lightning, came by and hung out with us. He and I started talking. I told him how I played goalie when I was a kid. How much I enjoyed hockey. How I watched it whenever I had the chance. We hit it off, and he said I should come by and watch some games. I took him up on the idea, and he invited me into the locker room.

While I was in there, I picked up the goalie's mask. Put it on. It was lighter than a catcher's mask. Didn't have as much padding. But, I was amazed by how well you could see out of it. How the visibility was so much better compared to a catcher's mask. And, I started thinking how cool a catcher's mask would be if it offered that increased visibility but with some extra padding. Catchers get hit with baseballs a lot more than goalies get hit with pucks. You need that extra protection.

After the game, I kept thinking about combining parts of the goalie's mask with the catcher's mask because, when I first came up in the big leagues, catchers' masks were heavy. That weight absorbed the energy if you were hit with a foul tip. But, the more I played, the lighter the masks became. Started making them with graphite. With those lighter-weight masks, it got to the point where, like I said, if you were hit in the mask with a ball, you were seeing stars. I'll guarantee you: you had a lot more guys with concussions once baseball moved to those lighter masks. You take a beating with some of them.

Finally, I thought, well, hell. I need to try this. I was tired of what I was using. And, I had an idea to make something a little different. I figured now was the right time to pursue it. And, I thought it would be cool to add some color and some unusual designs to it. I always liked having colored catching gear. Colored cleats. Just something a little different from everybody else.

In May '96, I talked with a Toronto sports reporter, Bruce Barker, about my idea. He put me in touch with a guy named Eric Niskanen. Eric worked for Van Velden Masks, a company that makes goalie masks. We met for lunch. Our wives joined us. We sat down, and I told him, "Look, I don't want any glue out of this. I just want something that will protect me better. If you make me what I'm looking for, I'll wear it."

Eric was like, "Glue?"

I call money glue.

Anyway, we talked. Told him what I had in mind about adding some hockey elements to the catcher's mask. Combining a helmet with a protective face mask in one piece instead of a mask that you strap on to a helmet. Doing this, the mask would be more open around the face than a traditional catcher's mask and create better visibility. Showed him how the goalie's mask has a chin cup. Instead of that, I wanted a catcher's mask face pad, but at the same time, offer protection around the jaw line that traditional catchers' masks don't have. I wanted the mask to be curved and smooth, with no part of it sticking out. This way, the ball would just deflect off the mask. I wasn't looking for something heavy, but I wanted more protection than what I had with the usual mask strapped to a helmet.

Eric understood what I was telling him. I left town for a road trip. When I came back, he had a prototype waiting for me. The big change that Eric and his group had to work on was making the mask cage so that a ball couldn't go through that opening. They had to make some other tweaks, too. Goalie masks are designed to stay on your head. But, with a catcher's mask, you need to be able to flip it off easily and quickly to catch foul balls. Eric made that design adjustment. He also made a couple of other changes like making the screws holding the mask to the helmet not visible. The thinking was, that way, if a ball hit the cage, the screws wouldn't snap out. He did the same thing with hiding the buckles. On a goalie's mask, the buckles are up front. We couldn't have that for a catcher's mask because, if a ball hit it, the buckle would break. Eric beefed up the protection of the back plate of the mask too with some extra padding in case you get hit with a bat. We had a back and forth where I would explain what I wanted, what changes needed to be made. Eric would go back and make adjustments. Then I'd test the new version. Put it on and stand in front of a pitching machine and get hit with balls in the face. See how it worked.

Using the mask in a game wasn't as simple as I fine-tuned it so I liked it, then strapped it on and went out and played. Major League Baseball had to get involved and approve it. In fact, Major League Baseball heard that I was wanting to wear a hockey helmet instead of a catcher's mask. They told me they'd fine me $10,000 if I wore it in a game without getting their approval first.

Dealing with Major League Baseball was a lengthy process. Frustrating too. They seemed to create roadblocks for no real reason. First, they said that Eric and Van Velden couldn't design or distribute equipment used in baseball games unless they became a licensee of Major League Baseball or found a licensee willing to sponsor them and take the equipment under its wing. When I heard that, I called Mizuno. Really liked using their gloves, one of their smaller models like what Bob Boone wore—fit kind of high on your fingers. I met with Mizuno. Showed them the mask that Eric and I worked on. Told them I wanted to use it and asked if they'd be interested in working with us as a licensee.

They laughed.

They said, yeah, the mask looks cool and all, but no one will ever buy it. No one's ever going to use it. Thanks, but no thanks.

"We'll see," I said.

The next group I called was All-Star Sporting Goods. Talked with Stan Jurga. Stan is one of the most down-to-earth, genuinely good guys I've met. Stan has always been helpful, designing chest protectors and shin guards for me, giving me catcher's gloves. When I was with Milwaukee, Stan made me this bright yellow chest protector with blue stripes, just how I wanted it. When I wore it, they said I looked like Big Bird. I didn't care. It had a little flair.

I told Stan about the mask, how I thought it could help me by improving visibility and offering better protection from baseballs. His company was a licensee to make and distribute catching gear. Would he be interested in helping us out?

Stan's reaction was the complete opposite from Mizuno's. He loved the idea.

"This is exactly what we need," Stan said. He took the idea and ran with it. He worked out a deal with Eric and Van Velden and figured out how to mass-produce the masks. He worked with Eric to reshape the shell and make the masks a little less bulky. He improved the ventilation so the mask wouldn't get so hot. Stan also said we should streamline the jawline some so that it was easier for the catcher to turn from side to side or move his head up or down.

Some folks have a vision. They can see something that's not there yet, the possibilities. How you can create something cool and different and worthwhile. Others completely miss it. But, the thing about Stan is that he realized you always need to look for and appreciate new ideas. Catcher's masks hadn't changed much in the last one hundred years. Hell, baseball equipment, period, hadn't changed much in the last one hundred years, with the exception of players wearing batting helmets instead of hats. With the hockey-style mask, he saw an opportunity. I wanted to use the mask just for me, but Stan saw how this could be used on a much wider scale. He had a vision, and he made the most of it.

With All-Star as our licensee, Eric Niskanen went back to Major League Baseball to get approval to use the mask. More roadblocks. They said we hadn't demonstrated that it was safe to use, that it would protect catchers. Eric followed up and asked for their safety standards. Said he would make whatever changes he needed to satisfy their standards. The crazy thing was that we found out that Major League Baseball didn't have safety standards or a testing protocol for any of its equipment before I introduced the mask. If they did, they never shared the standards with us. After Eric kept pressing for standards but never getting them, he decided to conduct some safety tests himself. He invited a couple of guys from baseball's Rules Committee to visit Toronto and see how well the hockey-style mask performed, compared to the traditional helmet and mask I'd been wearing. They agreed to attend. Eric showed what would happen if a one hundred mile per hour fastball hit the hockey-style mask. Passed with flying colors. Deflected right off. Then he showed the same fastball hitting the helmet I wore and strapped a traditional catcher's mask to. The helmet shattered. The hockey-style mask absorbed the ball better, like one hundred pounds of force, and reduced the catcher's chances of getting a concussion by two or three times, compared to the old-style catcher's mask.

With our test results, we proved that the hockey-style mask was safer than what catchers were using at that time. Major League Baseball's response: make some design changes. Make the mask look more like a traditional catcher's mask. Where I didn't want wires from the mask sticking out so that balls would deflect better, Major League Baseball liked the wires flared out. They liked bringing the wire cage all the way down the jawline. Why? Because these things made the mask look more like a regular catcher's mask. At that point, it wasn't a question of safety or protection. They were worried about tradition. Looks. They were saying that this isn't right for baseball, that baseball's not hockey. So, they made us open the mask up more. Take some of the weight off. Moved it out some so it didn't sit as closely on your face. That's fine. We did that. But, in doing these things, the mask lost some of its safety levels. It was still better than the old-style mask, but the version we originally presented could withstand more pounding from baseballs than the version they finally approved. The bottom line: the hockey-style mask gave the catcher better visibility and better protection. That's why I liked it. Why I wouldn't drop it when Major League Baseball kept throwing up these roadblocks and kept dragging its feet before finally saying I could use the new mask in a game. I think they thought I'd just go away. I didn't drop it, though. Took nearly an entire season to get them to approve the mask. Finally wore it in a game for the first time on September 13, 1996. We played the Yankees. Erik Hanson pitched for us. Andy Pettitte started for New York.

It's funny: in one game, I used the original mask that Major League Baseball told me I wasn't allowed to use. It had a wild-looking Blue Jay painted on it. I really liked it. Thought it looked a lot cooler than the helmet Major League Baseball finally approved with its plain Blue Jays logo, and they told me that the mask had to be pretty vanilla with a team's logo on it, period. You couldn't personalize the masks like goalies do in hockey. The original mask really jazzed up the Toronto logo. But, it was the last game of the season. I wore the original mask. The Commissioner's office contacted me. Said they were investigating me for wearing this mask that they didn't approve. Said they might fine me. I told them that the mask they approved was broken, that somebody stepped on it in the clubhouse. I didn't have any backups. Didn't have time to fix it. I said, "There's no way I was going to wear that old piece of shit I used to wear. If you want to fine me for being safe, go ahead."

I never heard another word about their investigation.

Several guys have used the hockey-style mask. Told me they liked it a lot. Mike Matheny. Brad Ausmus. Today, Buster Posey wears it. My boys are catchers, one in the Dodger minor league system and the younger one in college, and they wear it. *Popular Mechanics* ran a story about the new mask. Took a picture of me behind the plate with the mask. My brother John is in the batter's box, hitting. My brother Tom used to umpire, so he put on his umpiring gear. He's behind me, calling balls and strikes. It's pretty cool. And, you can watch a baseball game at any level now, from little leagues to college to minor leagues to the big leagues, and you'll see the hockey-style mask. You'll see it a lot, actually. Most little leagues and public schools require catchers to use the hockey-style mask because it's so much safer. Some umpires wear it. I still think it's a good idea. Improves safety, and that's the whole point of the protective equipment players wear on the field. I know it helped me. I don't know how many concussions I had with the old-style mask. Ten? Fourteen? All I know is, after the ball smashes into the mask going one hundred miles an hour, I'd see stars. Ears ringing. Wanting to vomit. All the concussion symptoms you hear about. But, with the hockey mask, I wore it for four seasons, and I never once felt that. Still got hit with baseballs, but it was a one hundred percent improvement as far as I'm concerned.

Watching Carp pitch as a veteran was fun. I point to the 2011 playoff game, Carp against Roy Halladay, Game Five, the last game of the National League Division Series. Carp and Doc were teammates in Toronto. They're still good friends. Take fishing trips every off-season. This game was their first time to face each other. And, it's a great teaching tool. If I were coaching, I'd use that game as an "Art of Pitching" example. A blueprint of how to pitch in the big leagues. A great matchup of the two best pitchers in the league. Halladay won two Cy Youngs. Had no-hitter type stuff nearly every time he went out on the mound. You had two guys who knew how to pitch, throwing at the top of their games. They changed speeds. Pitched to their strengths. Worked batters. Kept the ball in different locations. Knew who to walk. Those guys disrupted hitters' timing to a tee. If they got into trouble, they had that next level they could go to and get out of a jam. Doc did it—had the bases loaded, but he got out of the inning without giving up any runs. Carp pitched beautifully, too. Threw a complete game and gave up only three hits, I think. Kept the ball down and away so the Phillies hit a bunch of ground balls for outs. That's probably the best game he's pitched, and the dude's been in a lot of big games, won some World Series games. Just an epic game. Hated to see either guy lose because they both looked so good out there. And, it was a tight game. The Cardinals won 1-0. Scratched out a run in the first inning and that was it. You couldn't ask for a better game to watch. The crowd was so into it. Electric atmosphere. Games like that don't come around too often. It was special to watch, and I'm not surprised at all that Carp was involved in one of those games for the ages, a pitching duel that will be remembered and replayed for a long time.

CHAPTER 13

JACK MCDOWELL

Charlie is a good dude. He was a great teammate. It's just his personality overall. It's laid-back yet intense, which is cool, you know? There are guys who are intense, and they come off and rub people the wrong way. But, when you carry your intensity in a way and still have a personality with it, and still be able to project that intensity without rubbing people the wrong way, that's what Charlie had. He had a good way with people.

—*Jack McDowell*

[*Note: After completing his two-year contract with Toronto in 1997, Charlie became a free agent. He considered his options—the Anaheim Angels and the San Francisco Giants in particular expressed interest in him. Ultimately, he decided to sign with the Chicago White Sox, a Midwestern team closer to his Oklahoma home and with a core of players like Frank Thomas, Robin Ventura, and Albert Belle that he thought would make the club competitive. Until injuring his thumb, Charlie played solidly for Chicago in 1998, working with a young pitching staff and hitting a career high .262. Near the trading deadline, the White Sox dealt him to Anaheim, who was leading the American League Western Division by one game.[1] While he was excited to be in a playoff race, injuries hampered Charlie's time with his new team. He appeared in only five games with the Angels in 1998.*

During his tenure with Anaheim, Charlie caught Jack McDowell, the 1993 American League Cy Young Award winner. In 1993, McDowell's win-loss record was 22-10, and his earned run average was 3.37.[2] He threw 256 ⅔ innings and led the league in wins and shutouts (four). At his peak, he was known for his fastball and forkball, endurance (from 1991 through 1993, he pitched more than 250 innings each season), and intimidating presence on the mound.[3] However, when he joined the Angels, McDowell was injured, compromising his ability to pitch. In 1998, he appeared in fourteen games, pitching only seventy-six innings. He attempted to return from arm injuries in 1999, but in four games, his record was 0-4 with an ERA of 8.05. On August 9, 1999, the

Angels released McDowell, and he retired after twelve seasons with a win-loss record of
127-87, a 3.85 ERA, and 1,311 strikeouts.
  Charlie caught McDowell in two games, one in 1998 and another in 1999.]

Every athlete has to face leaving the game, knowing that it's time to walk away because your body can't do what it used to no matter how hard you train or push yourself. When I played with Jack, both of us were in this situation. He was coming back from two surgeries (one on his elbow in '97 and another on his shoulder after '98). My health was spotty too. I had a broken thumb when I was traded from the White Sox to the Angels in July. The thumb was still healing when I broke my knuckle. I was hitting against Rolando Arrojo of the Tampa Bay Devil Rays. He threw a pitch, and the ball smoked my middle finger's knuckle against the bat. Exploded the joint. I looked at my hand, and the knuckle stuck out into my palm. I tried pushing it back into place. You could hear the bones crack and grind. That ended my season. The next year, I spent time on the disabled list for a partial tear of the plantar fascia ligament in my right foot. At thirty-eight or thirty-nine years old, my body broke down more than it did when I was in my twenties or early thirties.

Jack's injuries affected how he pitched. His arm just wasn't the same as it was in the early nineties when he was dominating. In his prime, Jack threw hard. Had a nasty fastball that topped out in the lower to mid-nineties. When I caught him, he was throwing in the mid-eighties. It was a nice, straight fastball, but it had definitely lost some velocity. Had a good curveball, but he hurt throwing it. During his heyday, his bread and butter was his forkball. His brother taught him how to throw the pitch when Jack was in high school, a sophomore playing shortstop and pitching. Because he played in the infield so much, Jack's throwing motion was real short-armed. With that motion, he couldn't get much break on the ball when he tried to pitch. But, with the forkball, Jack found a way to get some topspin on the ball. Could really make it move. He refined the pitch so that, at one point, it was one of the best forkballs in the big leagues. By the time I worked with him, though, he hurt throwing it too. When he was healthy, he had the luxury of looking to his forkball if his hook wasn't working for him or vice versa, but he didn't have these options pitching with a blown-out arm.

Because he wasn't the same pitcher he was five years before when his stuff was freakish, I adjusted. You normally have a game plan and a thought process for pitch sequence based on the fact that the pitcher throws one or two pitches real well. But, if these pitches aren't available because a guy isn't healthy, you improvise. With

Jack, I didn't call as many pitches inside. Didn't ask him to throw as many forks or hooks because they physically hurt him. Instead, I called for more fastballs and changeups and pitches on the outside part of the plate, things that Jack could still do well. Jack had a good changeup. Good control. So, I relied on these strengths. It all goes back to the point I made about Bobby Cox: put your guys in a position where they will succeed. Don't ask them to do things they can't do. And, Jack had varying degrees of success. Against Baltimore, the first game I caught with him, he didn't get into a rhythm. Couldn't get the ball over the plate. One pitch he couldn't even throw. I can't remember if it was his forkball or his slider. But, he physically wasn't able to throw the pitch, so I didn't call for it. That game, I tried to help him get by. Help him to hit his spots. Hope the hitter doesn't hit it or, if he does, he hits the ball to somebody. Really, I paid attention to each pitch. If he threw one that looked pretty good, maybe we'd stick with that or try to build on it. Sometimes it worked. Sometimes it didn't. Jack was very frustrated with his performance and the fact that he wasn't pitching the way that he was once capable of. When that happens, it's challenging. Becomes a mind game when you've done something well for so long and then you're unable to compete at the same level. It wears on you.

The second game we played was much better. He gave up a couple of runs. Pitched into the seventh inning. Threw a lot more strikes than balls. Had a good feel for throwing the right pitch at the right time.

Even though he was pitching on fumes, Jack competed like hell. Like that game against Baltimore: he couldn't throw one of his better off-speed pitches, but he still went out there. Pitched with very few bullets, but did the best he could with what he had. A lot of cats wouldn't go out there like that. You couldn't stop Jack, though. He was intense. Pitched like he was pissed. Like he had a chip on his shoulder and he had to prove that he was the best guy on the field. I loved this edginess. He called himself a psycho on the mound with how he could get fired up at hitters or umpires. Definitely an emotional guy out there. To his credit, he tried to channel that intensity toward getting the batter out. Off the field, he had a rock-and-roll band, and he carried that rock-and-roll attitude with him when he played baseball. He'd get fired up if somebody took a big swing, hacking and falling down. Jack would be watching from the bench and say, "Shit. I'm gonna bust his ass for that." Skinny dude, and he was always talking about busting somebody's ass. And, he would do whatever he needed to do to beat you. If he needed to stomp on a base runner's foot, he'd do it. He gave everything he had, and the team fed off his attitude. You could tell that his arm wasn't the same that it once was, but he was trying like hell to pitch, doing a ton of work on the side—having ultrasound treatments on his arm, icing it, giving it cold saunas, anything to rehab it into shape. Everybody was pulling for him because he was such a good dude. And, even though his shit was short, he still had that attitude that all the great pitchers have: he didn't care who he was facing, he was going to go out there and beat you. He wasn't going to back down and throw the batter the pitch that the batter wanted. Jack was going to throw *his* game. Throw his best stuff and make the batter beat him. That competitiveness was his biggest strength when I caught him. That fire, that attitude: those things make me wish I could have caught him earlier in his career when his arm was good and he was pitching so well for the White Sox.

That said, Jack may have been too intense. He'd get pissed off at himself. That could make him lose focus on what he needed to be doing. I'd talk to him and try to keep him calm and give him a direction. "This is what we're going to do," and I'd lay out the road map of the next three pitches he needed to throw.

Because we played so little together, I can't really say that Jack and I established a routine or a rapport. It's tough when a catcher is traded in the middle of the season because he doesn't have spring training to learn what the staff likes, what a pitcher's strengths and weaknesses are. Instead, you're learning this during the game. A guy may tell you, "I like this, I don't like that." To really understand what he does well, though, what his limitations are, you need to catch him. Like most things, this takes time. Spring training is great for catching a guy four or five times and figuring out what creates a flow with him. You don't get this if you're traded midseason. It's a challenge to pick this up on the fly in game situations.

Jack was vocal about what he liked to do. How he wanted to handle certain situations. He was a smart guy. Articulate. Opinionated. Knew what he threw. Knew what he did best. Had no problem telling you this. Because of Jack's experience, our manager, Terry Collins, didn't get in his way. TC was smart enough to recognize that Jack was well-respected and knew how to get his work done. So, TC left him alone. Generally, he let guys do their own thing and prepare how they wanted to.

Even though Jack had real strong opinions about pitch selection, he listened to my suggestions. Part of that was knowing that I had been in the big leagues a long time. I knew the hitters. I knew which pitches to call. And, if Jack shook me off, I immediately signed for a Plan B pitch. Didn't waste a lot of time figuring out what the next alternative was. Jack liked that I could automatically go to that pitch he wanted to throw and not disrupt his rhythm to get there.

The first part of '98, I played on the White Sox. Some of those guys were around when Jack pitched for them and won the Cy. Robin Ventura said that Jack was a hell of a pitcher. That the team loved playing behind him when he pitched. He worked fast. Threw a lot of forkballs, which meant a lot of ground balls to the infielders. Making your infielders work: they love playing behind a guy like that.

Real quick about my time playing in Chicago: I enjoyed it. Was able to play with some great dudes. Frank Thomas could smoke a ball. Robin Ventura was a great guy. Hell of a hitter. Good third baseman. Did a great job keeping the team loose. That year, Albert Belle played this song over and over in the clubhouse, "Let Me Clear My Throat." I'd give him shit about it. I'd say, "Bert. Come on, dude. We've got to hear this shit again?" Ventura, though, did a great DJ Kool impression of hacking and sputtering and clearing his throat. Cracked everybody up with it.

I really liked playing with Albert Belle. He kind of reminded me of Eddie Murray: a guy with a surly reputation who's supposed to be this real aloof asshole, but that was the farthest thing from the truth. Great dude. Great teammate. Played hard and busted his ass every day. Played the game the right way. Went hard into second base. Never hit a fly ball but then just walked to first base like a lot of those superstar guys will do. Intelligent hitter. He was keen on picking up pitches and figuring out what pitches were coming. Had a completely different personality from what you saw with the media or in the interview room. He didn't like the media. Didn't trust them. But, around his teammates, I thought he was great. He was very quiet. Unassuming. Didn't demand attention or the spotlight. Just a guy who showed up every day, ready to work hard and ready to give everything he had. And, an incredible power hitter. I'd have him on my team any time.

When I was traded to the Angels, I was fired up. I was joining a team in a playoff race. The times I was traded, I looked at it positively: I was going to a team that wanted me. And, when I went to New York and then later to Anaheim, I was traded from clubs that weren't going anywhere to teams in pennant races. Most guys, that's what you play for: the chance to win it all. And, the Angels were a hell of a team. Were in first place when I got there. I was looking forward to working with Chuck Finley again—we'd played winter ball together years before. The club assembled the nucleus of talented guys who went on to win the Series a few years later. Darin Erstad. Tim Salmon. Young guys like Troy Glaus who could hit some bombs and play incredible defense at third base. Veteran guys like Jack who'd been through everything—slumps, hot streaks. Guys who are good examples to younger players in how they carry themselves through different situations. It's not so much what they tell the young guys but what they show them by example. Stability.

Professionalism. We also had some good pitchers like Jack and Finley, in Ken Hill and Tim Belcher. Great team.

Seems like as soon as I joined them, though, I got hurt. I was on the DL for about a month. I went home. Looking back, I should've stayed around the team. It takes a while to fit in to a new situation. Because of that, I should have rehabbed there instead of back in Tulsa. And, once I got back home, I was like, "Man, it's nice to be here." Be there for the kids' first day in school. Open house. Football practice. Volleyball games. All those things that you miss when your family is half a country away from you and life goes on without you. That was great, but professionally, my desire and focus to rehab wasn't as intense as it should have been.

One of the guys I liked working with in Anaheim was Marcel Lachemann, the pitching coach in '98. He was a fatherly, soft-spoken guy. Easy to talk to. He taught in real simple and folksy terms. He was very knowledgeable. Had been in the game for a long time. Been around a lot of good people. He was one of the better pitching coaches I worked with. Everybody loves Latch. He wouldn't force-feed decisions down guys' throats. He would approach things more by offering suggestions: "You might want to think about doing . . ." was his way of helping the pitcher figure out what was wrong and then coming up with a solution on his own. This worked real well for Latch and the pitchers he worked with.

We had a different pitching coach in '99, Dick Pole. His approach was more direct. More of a force feeder, telling the pitcher how he should handle certain situations. "This is what you need to do" was Dick's way of doing things. He's had a lot of success, and he's like Latch in that he's been in a lot of different places and worked with some good people through the years and learned a lot. Latch's approach, though, of telling enough information to a guy to let him figure out a problem on his own, was better received by players than Dick's style. But, how well this teaching or coaching style worked depended on the player being taught, too. Some guys responded better to Dick than they did to Latch. Like I said, Greg Maddux attributed a lot of his success to Dick and what he learned from him coming up in the minor leagues and his first few years with the Cubs. For me, Latch's style works better.

––––––––––––––––

It's too bad that Jack had the arm troubles he had. I don't know if it's because of his body type—taller and skinnier—that he just wasn't built to throw a baseball for a long time. He didn't have the big, thick legs and big butt like a lot of the power dudes have. He had a great arm. Was a great competitor. Came from a great college program, Stanford. Maybe that's part of why he was such an astute observer of the game. He really praised Stanford for molding pitchers to be complete players, to make them concentrate on holding runners on and fielding bunts. More than just knowing which pitch to throw. Every day, pitchers did something to compete defensively. They had bunting drills where their coach, Mark Marquess, put the team's fastest runner on second base. Marquess would lay down a bunt. Pitchers would have to field the ball and throw the runner out at third. This while the whole team is standing on the foul lines, ragging on the pitcher and getting all over him. High competition. Jack said it prepared guys for game situations so they could execute the same play when the pressure was on. They were used to it because the pressure was on in practice.

Like I said, Jack was into music. Had a band, Stickfigure. That name was great. Perfectly described his build. He'd take his guitar with him on the road. Played in his room, I guess. Most guys bring their golf clubs, not guitars. He liked that rock and roll shit. I liked contemporary soul stuff. Different ends of the spectrum. But, Jack could tell you about the music clubs across the country in the different Major League cities. Liked to go to CBGB's and Brownies in New York. First Avenue in Minneapolis. Whenever he was in Minneapolis, he'd eat lunch at this place about a block away from First Avenue, the Loon Café. One time, he was eating there, and he started talking music with the staff, and someone said, "Hey, come on down and meet Karl." Karl Mueller was the bass player for Soul Asylum, an alternative band. He worked as a cook at the Loon Café for his day job, I guess. Jack met him and thought it was the coolest thing.

Jack was just a real down-to-earth dude. Didn't think he was better than anybody. If you asked him about moments that stand out in his career, he'd tell you a story about giving up a dinger to Kirby Puckett. He'd tell you that story because it was a cool baseball moment and he experienced it, not because he was a superstar who performed brilliantly in that moment. Ask him about winning the Cy Young, and he'd be low-key and self-deprecating about it. Kind of like, "Wow. Randy Johnson came in second in the voting to me? The guy had nineteen wins and 300 punch-outs, and they give the award to me? That doesn't make a whole lot of sense." Ask guys what they did to celebrate winning the Cy, and some of them bought cars or went on trips. Jack was like, "I don't even remember. Probably went out and had a couple of beers. Same thing I do every night."

There's no telling what Jack might've accomplished if he'd been pitched fifteen healthy years. At his peak, he was one of the game's more dominant pitchers, no question. Even with a blown-out arm, he was a hell of a competitor. I'm convinced that if Jack had been healthy in '98 and pitched like he had in the early nineties, the Angels would've made the playoffs. We had the talent to win. Jack would have been the difference maker. With his going out there and leaving everything that he had on the field, the other pitchers would have fed off that attitude. He would've lifted the staff. But, like I said, our time together was the end of the road for both of us. The Angels released me the first part of August 1999. They let Jack go a few days later.

CONCLUSION

Well, I showed up late to spring training, so I had some catching up to do. [T]hey wanted me to pitch. I believe it was a Double A game, and they said, "Do you mind if this kid catches you?" and I said, "No. I've watched him catch. I like the way he moves." We went down, and he warmed me up, and we just seemed to hit it. It was as though we had been working together for a long time. I know that was more to his credit than to mine, but we had a good game. I remember he came over to me. "What do you want to do?" I said, "Well, basically, I like to go hard ahead and soft behind." I said, "I'm not going to shake you off. If you call a pitch, I'm going to add. I will wipe my glove on my jersey, and I will add. So, I will never shake you off." And, so, after five or six hitters, it was almost like he was reading my mind. And, I think that is a gift that a lot of catchers don't have. Let's face it: a lot of catchers were moved to that position from another position, but Charlie, to me, was a guy who was born to be a catcher. You know, on our club right now, we have Craig Kimbrel, and I swear when he was born, his dad looked at him and said, "Closer." Well, I think it was kind of the same with Charlie. From the first time I met him, he seemed like a guy who was born to be a catcher. He received the ball with almost pillow-like hands. He knew how to throw. But, I think he had that innate sense of what a pitcher was trying to do, and how can we use that to get the hitter. And, I do remember talking to him afterward, telling him how much I enjoyed working with him and how much I appreciated it. And, I know that they said that Jackie Moore, the manager, said, "Do you want to work some more minor league games?" I said, "I'd love to, and I'd like to have Charlie O'Brien catch me." And, I said, "This kid can catch. I'm telling you: the kid can catch, and all the minor league games I have this spring, I'd love to have him as my catcher."

—Don Sutton

n 1999, the Anaheim Angels released me. I'd battled some injuries, but I'd come back. Felt healthy. Thought I could still play. When they told me it was over, I wasn't ready to leave the game yet. I wanted to go out on my terms. There were certain things I wanted to accomplish. Personal goals. Play until I was forty. Play three decades in the big leagues. I wanted to walk out and retire on my own instead of somebody saying, "Hey, we're letting you go," and you can't get another job. A pride thing more than anything. So, I signed a deal to play with the Montreal Expos in 2000. Going in to spring training, I figured that would be my last year in the big leagues. I figured right.

At first, things were going well. Had a good spring. Hitting-wise and catching-wise, I felt good about how I was playing. But, in spring training, I tore my plantar fascia ligament again. I had hit a home run and was running around first base when I tore it. That set me back. If I hadn't have gotten hurt, I think I would've made it through the season. But, the injury held me back. Kept me in Jupiter, Florida, for extended spring training. That made it really hard to play. Tough to stay motivated to get well and then to start playing again. But, I pressed on. The Expos sent me to Double A in Harrisburg, Pennsylvania, for a rehab assignment. I played well enough for them to call me up to the big leagues. And, I played a few games with the Expos.

To be honest, Montreal was a nightmare. There was such a language barrier where most folks spoke French. It was the last year the club was in Montreal. They were in the process of selling the team. There was all sorts of talk about moving the team because attendance was so bad. We played in Olympic Stadium. Huge place. Sometimes, it felt like there were only one hundred people in the Stadium. The team wouldn't spend any money. Didn't try to keep their good players because they couldn't afford them once they became eligible for arbitration. It was just miserable. Hard place to stay motivated.

Ultimately, Montreal decided to go in a different direction. Let me go. The manager, Felipe Alou, called me in to his office. I think the general manager, Omar Minaya, was with him.

Felipe said, "Hey, Charlie, we're bringing up a pitcher. We're going to let you go. Do you want to be the bullpen coach?"

That's the conversation. Fifteen years in the big leagues. Caught thirteen Cy Young Award winners. Played in and won a World Series. Got some big hits. Taught guys how to pitch. Blocked balls. Called the right pitches to get guys through tough situations. And, it all ends like that: "We're going to let you go."

Baseball's impersonal. Baseball cares only about the player, not the person. Kind of like how I received my World Series ring from the Braves. I had signed as a free agent with Toronto after the World Series, so I wasn't with the Braves when they presented World Series rings. So, I got my ring from a UPS delivery man. Out of sight, out of mind. Not a word about how I contributed to the team and helped us win a championship . . . sign the clipboard, please. A cold way of doing business.

And, it's hard, leaving the game. Some guys, the minute their skills start to slip, they hang it up. Others hang on and play a few years even though they're not the same player they were during their prime. Sometimes, you get the luxury of deciding when to leave. You can call your close teammates together and tell them that you've made your decision and that there's no talking you out of it: you're retiring and moving on. Other times, your manager tells you that the team is going in a different direction and letting you go, and it's embarrassing. Somebody telling you that you're not good enough any more. You kind of want to slink out of the clubhouse and not have anybody notice you leave.

I said, "I don't know. I'm going to go home and think about it for a little while."

"We'd love to have you stay in coaching."

I didn't want to be a bullpen coach. Not then. My wife, Traci, had just gotten into town with the kids. Literally, it was their first or second day in Montreal. We'd found an apartment. Just gone to the grocery store that morning to stock the refrigerator. I'd brought my sons Chris and Cameron with me into the clubhouse. Chris was eleven. Camo was seven. They were playing video games with Vlad Guerrero when I stepped out of Felipe's office.

I said, "Boys, we gotta get out of here."

"Where are we going?"

"We gotta go home."

"Why aren't we staying here?"

I said, "They're letting me go."

They didn't understand. It didn't make any sense. They had just gotten there.

"They just told me they didn't want me anymore." That's a hard thing to tell your kids.

So, we loaded up. Headed home. Went back to Oklahoma and started working at my ranch full-time with my dad. It's around a thousand acres. South of Tulsa fifty miles and west of Beggs. Now, instead of going out to the mound and telling the pitcher, "Okay, here's what we're going to do. First pitch. . . ." I'll mend a fence. Plant crops. Guide a hunt for trophy bucks. Something different every day. I like it. And I like the tranquility out there. The only noise you'll hear is the wind coming through the hickories.

I stay involved in baseball. Watch my sons play. As I mentioned earlier, Chris is in the Dodgers minor league system. He catches. Playing in Chattanooga this summer, so I've seen a few of his games. Saw him make a throw from home to second with a release that was so fast I was like, "Damn. That's like some of the shit I used to do." My youngest, Cameron, is a catcher too. He's playing college ball at West Virginia. It's good he's in the Big 12. That means Traci and I can watch him play when they're on the road to Kansas or some of the Texas schools. And, it's an easy trip to drive over to Stillwater or down to Norman to watch him play.

I volunteer at my old high school, Bishop Kelley, and work with the kids playing baseball. Some pay attention and listen to you. Others think they've already figured it out. That's fine. I just try to pass the baton along, share what I know about the best game there is, the game I love.

ACKNOWLEDGMENTS

The thirteen Cy Young Award-winning pitchers were all gracious and helpful. All agreed to share their recollections of working with Charlie, and we included these stories and insights throughout the book. Bobby Cox, Greg McMichael, Don Sutton, Jeff Torborg, and David Wells also shared their memories of working with Charlie. Eric Niskanen and Stan Jurga recalled the process to develop and obtain approval for the hockey-style catcher's mask. To all: thank you.

Teams' media departments and alumni associations assisted us in contacting some of Charlie's former teammates. We thank Dina Blevins (Kansas City Royals), Leni Depoister (Chicago White Sox), Jeff Evans (Seattle Mariners), David Holtzman (Kansas City Royals), Jay Horwitz (New York Mets), and Adrienne Midgley (Atlanta Braves) for their help.

The Jefferson County (Alabama) Library System provided excellent research resources.

We received encouragement and advice as we wrote this book and worked to find it a publishing home. We thank Seale "Brother" Ballenger, Paul Brown, Wayne Coffey, Rob Dromerhauser, Bob Gillespie, Tom Hopke, Kirsten Schofield, George Singleton, and Cuz Strickland for their insight.

We thank Thom Lemmons and Texas A&M University Press for their excitement and support of this book.

We thank our families, Traci O'Brien, Alisa Deao, Andi Bunch, Chris O'Brien, Cameron O'Brien, Shawn Wedge, Jack Wedge, Sloan Wedge, Sophie Wedge, and Sadie Wedge, for their patience and support while writing this book.

NOTES

CHAPTER 1. PETE VUCKOVICH (1987)

1. www.baseball-reference.com/players/v/vuckope01.shtml.
2. Tom Flaherty. "Hill Ace Vuckovich 'Locked in a Bubble,'" *The Sporting News* (Aug. 16, 1982).
3. "Notebook: AL East Brewers," *The Sporting News* (Aug. 11, 1986).
4. www.baseball-reference.com/players/o/o'brich01.shtml.
5. Tom Flaherty. "Facing the Inevitable," *The Sporting News* (Mar. 23, 1987).
6. www.baseball-reference.com/players/v/vuckope01.shtml.

CHAPTER 2. DAVID CONE (1990-92)

1. www.baseball-reference.com/players/c/coneda01.shtml.
2. Jack Curry. "It's Almost Too Amazin'! Cone Argues While 2 Runs Score," *New York Times* (May 1, 1990).
3. John Ed Bradley. "Baseball '93," *Sports Illustrated* vol. 78, no. 13 (Apr. 5, 1993).
4. Ibid.
5. Ibid.
6. Joe Sexton. "Cone Breaks Off Negotiations on Multiyear Pact," *New York Times* (Feb. 5, 1992).
7. http://www.baseball-reference.com/players/c/coneda01.shtml.
8. Ibid.

CHAPTER 3. FRANK VIOLA (1990-91)

1. www.baseball-reference.com/teams/NYM/1990.shtml.
2. Joe Sexton. "Another Early Evening for Viola," *New York Times* (Aug. 24, 1991); Joe Sexton. "Viola Makes His Pitch, and the Braves Hammer It," *New York Times* (Sept. 8, 1991).
3. Joe Sexton. "A Suggestion for Viola," *New York Times* (Sept. 19, 1991); Murray Chass. "Baseball: A Change of Place for Viola: It's Boston," *New York Times* (Dec. 20, 1991).
4. www.baseball-reference.com/players/gl.cgi?id=violafr01&t=p&year=1996.

CHAPTER 4. DWIGHT GOODEN (1990–92)

1. http://www.baseball-reference.com/players/g/goodedw01.shtml.
2. Wayne Coffey. "Twenty-five Years after His Phenomenal Rookie Season, Dwight Gooden Takes Aim at His Demons," *New York Daily News* (Nov. 14, 2009).
3. http://www.baseball-reference.com/players/gl.cgi?id=goodedw01&t=p &year=1990.
4. Tom Verducci. "The Hero Trap," *Sports Illustrated* (July 11, 1994, 88).
5. http://www.baseball-reference.com/players/g/goodedw01.shtml.

CHAPTER 5. BRET SABERHAGEN (1992–93)

1. Mike Sielski. "There's No Accounting for This," *Wall Street Journal* (July 1, 2010).
2. http://www.baseball-reference.com/leagues/NL/1993.shtml.
3. Bob Klapisch, and John Harper. *The Worst Team Money Could Buy: The Collapse of the New York Mets* (New York: Random House, 1993).
4. www.baseball-reference.com/players/s/saberbr01.shtml.
5. Ibid.
6. Ibid.
7. Ibid.

CHAPTER 6. JOHN SMOLTZ (1994)

1. http://www.baseball-reference.com/players/o/o'brich01.shtml.
2. http://www.baseball-reference.com/postseason/Playoffs_pitching.shtml.
3. Evan Grant. "Braves' Staff Was the Stuff of Legends," *Baseball Digest* (Aug. 2008, 77).
4. "Pitchers' 20/40 Club," *Baseball Digest* (Sept. 2008, 88).
5. http://www.baseball-reference.com/players/s/smoltj001.shtml.
6. Ibid.
7. Ibid.
8. Evan Grant. "Braves' Staff Was the Stuff of Legends," *Baseball Digest* (Aug. 2008, 77).

CHAPTER 7. STEVE BEDROSIAN (1994–95)

1. http://www.baseball-reference.com/players/b/bedrost01.shtml.
2. "Baseball; Mark for Bedrosian with Save No. 12," *New York Times* (June 30, 1987).
3. http://www.baseball-reference.com/players/b/bedrost01.shtml.

CHAPTER 8. GREG MADDUX (1994–95)

1. http://espn.go.com/mlb/player/bio/_/id/1800/greg-maddux.
2. http://www.baseball-reference.com/players/m/maddugr01.shtml.
3. Ibid.
4. Ibid.
5. http://espn.go.com/mlb/player/bio/_/id/1800/greg-maddux.
6. Ibid.
7. http://www.baseball-reference.com/awards/mvp_cya.shtml.
8. Ibid.
9. http://www.baseball-reference.com/bullpen/Greg_Maddux.
10. Ibid.
11. www.baseball-reference.com/players/m/maddugr01.shtml.
12. Ibid.
13. Ibid.

CHAPTER 9. TOM GLAVINE (1994–95)

1. http://www.baseball-reference.com/players/gl.cgi?id=glavit002&t=p
   &year=0&post=1.
2. Michael Knisley. "High Class Hurlers," *The Sporting News* (Nov. 6 1995).
3. http://www.baseball-reference.com/players/g/glavit002.shtml.

CHAPTER 10. PAT HENTGEN (1996–97)

1. http://www.baseball-reference.com/players/h/hentgpa01.shtml.
2. "Hentgen Extends Jays' Streak," *Toronto Globe & Mail* (Aug. 24, 1996, A14).
3. "May 22," *Washington Times* (May 22, 1997, 4).
4. "Toronto Pitcher Hentgen Retiring," *UPI NewsTrack* (July 24, 2004).
5. http://www.baseball-reference.com/players/h/hentgpa01.shtml.

CHAPTER 11. ROGER CLEMENS (1997)

1. http://www.baseball-reference.com/players/c/clemer002.shtml.
2. Mark Starr. "The Rocket's Red Glare," *Newsweek* (July 7, 1997).
3. http://www.baseball-reference.com/players/c/clemer002.shtml.
4. Ibid.
5. Ibid.
6. Gary Gillette, and Pete Palmer, eds. *The ESPN Baseball Encyclopedia,* 4th ed. (2007).
7. Michael S. Schmidt. "Clemens Lied about Doping, Indictment Charges," *New York Times* (Aug. 19, 2010).

CHAPTER 12. CHRIS CARPENTER (1997)

1. http://www.baseball-reference.com/players/c/carpech01.shtml.

2. Stan McNeal. "Looking out for No. 1: The Playoff Picture Is Fuzzy, but This Is Clear: Chris Carpenter Will Be the Most Important Player in the Postseason and the Reason the Cardinals Win it All." *The Sporting News* (Oct. 7, 2005).

3. Ibid.

4. Tyler Kepner. "Cardinals Plan to Lean on Ace Who Got Them in," *New York Times* (Oct. 1, 2011, D3).

5. http://www.baseball-reference.com/players/c/carpech01.shtml.

CHAPTER 13. JACK MCDOWELL (1998–99)

1. http://www.baseball-reference.com/teams/ANA/1998-schedule-scores.shtml.

2. http://www.baseball-reference.com/players/m/mcdowja01.shtml.

3. Franz Lidz. "Jack of Two Trades," *Sports Illustrated* vol. 75, no. 5 (July 29, 1991).

INDEX